DIGITAL TELEVISION PRODUCTION

A handbook

Jeremy Orlebar

A member of the Hodder Headline Group
LONDON
Distributed in the United States of America by
Oxford University Press Inc., New York

First published in Great Britain in 2002
by Arnold, a member of the Hodder Headline Group,
338 Euston Road, London NW1 3BH

http://www.arnoldpublishers.com

Distributed in the United States of America by
Oxford University Press Inc.,
198 Madison Avenue, New York, NY 10016

British Library Cataloguing in Publication Data
A catalogue record for this book is available from the British Library

Library of Congress Cataloging-in-Publication Data
A catalog record for this book is available from the Library of Congress

ISBN 0 340 76322 1 (HB)
ISBN 0 340 76323 X (PB)

2 3 4 5 6 7 8 9 10

Production Editor: Wendy Rooke
Production Controller: Martin Kerans
Cover Design: Terry Griffiths

Typeset in 10.5 on 14 pt Gill Sans by Cambrian Typesetters, Frimley, Surrey
Printed and bound in India

What do you think about this book? Or any other Arnold title?
Please send your comments to feedback.arnold@hodder.co.uk

This book is dedicated to Amanda and Tessa for their love and support.

Contents

Acknowledgements

Thanks to Melissa, James, Simon, Sarah, Fiona, Claire, Todd, Mark, Ollie, Ursula, Amy the juggler and Mark Thomas, as well as to Amanda, Andy, Sam, Sophie, Kate, Billy, Nadia and Katie, and to all the other students who kindly agreed to appear in the photographs. Thanks also to Mike Turner and Godfrey Johnson for professional advice. The author would like to thank Ravensbourne College of Design and Communication and Farnborough College of Technology for permission to photograph students.

Introduction

From initial tentative ideas to full-scale dramas and magazine programmes, this book covers the complete television production process and gives you the tools to be part of the digital revolution.

If you own, or have access to, a camcorder and computer editing equipment, then this is the book to help you get the most out of your camera and your editing software.

If you are on a media course at a college or university, this book will be an invaluable companion to your practical television studies. It concentrates on showing you how to realize your ideas and turn them into desirable, broadcast-standard productions using low-cost digital equipment.

In this book you will find:

♦ a full explanation of the practical aspects of television preproduction in Part One;
♦ an easily followed practical guide to the techniques of television production in Part Two;
♦ a full explanation of the postproduction process in Part Three;
♦ related theoretical knowledge underpinning the television production process, in all three parts;
♦ many practical examples;
♦ lists of production essentials, handy tips and useful advice, throughout.

What digital can do for you

The digital revolution has democratized television production. Anyone with exciting ideas and modest video equipment can make programmes of interest to broadcasters, digital channel companies and web-site producers. Affordable shooting and editing equipment offers anyone the opportunity to create high-quality video drama, factual programming, corporate or promotional videos. As higher-quality Internet services become more available, 'streamed' video will become a must-have component of any web site worth visiting.

The buzzwords are 'broadband' and 'convergence'.

Broadband applies to the Internet. It involves updating the modem in your computer and the telephone line for much faster access to the Internet and web content. The connection is more reliable and there is easier access to multimedia content. With reference to video, broadband means that better, higher-quality moving images will be able to be accessed quickly and easily via the Internet. With broadband it is possible to view on a computer monitor a movie with high-quality, full-frame picture definition.

Convergence describes the coming-together of computer-generated graphics, interactive pictures and sound and conventional television techniques. This leads to interactive television, which has many possible and as yet unexplored uses. One particular use is in the TV coverage of a football match, where the viewer can choose any particular camera angle from the selection offered by the broadcaster, rather than rely on the director's choice.

Your digital TV set linked to a broadband telephone or cable system becomes a two-way communication command module. It allows you to play interactive games, e-mail, use digital graphics communications as well as view the large number of broadcast digital television channels. There is, of course, a cost in subscribing to all this additional digital material.

Convergence is gaining a growing audience because it offers the chance for graphic designers, artists and architects to work with filmmakers and video artists. Once you are in the digital domain, there are many ways of expressing your creativity. All sorts of alliances are being forged, bringing with them many new opportunities for film and television programme-makers.

The Light Surgeons, a group of UK filmmakers, graphic designers and DJs, entertain and surprise audiences with their live digital audio-visual show. The Light Surgeons mix images from video, computer graphics and digital photography with music, in the same way that DJs mix dance music.

There are digital film festivals springing up all over the globe actively seeking new and distinctive, digitally created video material. Then there is the 'fanfilm' scene. Independent filmmakers using digital equipment make films for the Internet based on popular series and characters such as *Star Wars* and the *X Files*. These films take copyright characters and put them in their own stories, which fall into a murky legal area between parody and fan fiction – both legal in US law. But they are popular and the big players are taking note.

The official web site for *Star Trek* movies has agreed to partner the *Star Trek* fan-film network to feature fan-made films. Good news for Trekkies. Some fans think there could be over 50 *Star Trek* fan films on the Internet by 2002.

What this book can do for you

This book gives you all the practical and theoretical tools you need to realize your ideas into broadcast-standard video productions. It helps you understand the possibilities of the digital video camera, and the process of low-cost

Box 0.1 Using a digital camera

production and video editing. It leads you to explore ideas and develop video concepts that could interest broadcasters and new media providers.

In the digital world, acquisition of video material is easier than ever, but good television programmes and films with exciting ideas are as difficult to achieve as they ever were. Equipment has changed, but the basis of quality programme making remains the same: a good story and high-quality production skills and techniques.

Preproduction

1
An idea

Making television programmes is not rocket science. You need to have an idea and lots of energy to turn that idea into a visual reality, and then immortalize it on tape. Working with modern digital kit means that you do not need a big team of people, or a lot of money, to make your own movie or television programme. But you need to know how to get the best out of that digital camera and how to make something someone else will want to watch.

The hugely successful feature film *The Blair Witch Project* was reportedly made for £18,000. That sounds too much for an average 'home' budget, but by Hollywood or broadcast television standards it is less than tea money. You can make films or programmes for a great deal less than that without compromising your story or production values. The award winning European film *Festen* was made with a camera costing less than £500.

Very low-budget feature films shot on freely available digital cameras and edited on a home computer are regularly shown at film festivals. *One Life Stand*, shown at the 2000 Edinburgh Film Festival, was written, shot and edited on digital video by the director May Miles Thomas. Made on a 'staggeringly low budget', it elicited considerable praise from the *Guardian*: 'this is a very fine film indeed.' Documentary films, or factual TV programmes, can be expensive on research time, but in many ways the digital camera is a boon to documentary filmmakers. You can have very long takes and the kit is extremely portable, while the quality of sound and vision can be excellent. So how do you do it? First of all you need an idea.

Your idea

Who you are, what you are interested in, and what you watch on television or in the cinema are the essential building blocks for a good television programme idea. It is best to start with something simple. Before making a feature film I suggest that everyone starts by thinking through a three-minute film story.

Your first three-minute film story idea can come from something you are interested in or know about. Perhaps there is something new that excites you. Many people started playing golf on their local pitch and putt course, or learnt to juggle or sail board after trying it out on holiday. Before immersing yourself in a new sport or activity, find out more about it by making a three-minute film. You might be fascinated by the new craze for microscooters (or steam trains, or hill walking or salsa dancing). Do some basic research on the Internet. You will be amazed at how much access you get to clubs, associations and so on, just by saying you want to make a short video. Follow up your initial interest with practical research. Talk to people.

Now you can shoot a three-minute film to persuade other people that microscooters, or steam trains, or hill walking or juggling is just for them. Longer than three minutes and nobody will watch; shorter and you will not do it justice. Box 1.1 shows an example of an idea that could make an interesting three-minute film.

Finding an idea

It is not always easy to find a suitable idea even for a three-minute story. Most successful programme items that work well in a television magazine programme, or that make highly watchable, longer factual programmes, stem from simple ideas. There is nothing totally new in television but lots of ideas come round again in different form.

Look at *Who Wants to be a Millionaire?* It is just another quiz show not a million miles from *Mastermind* but with that added suspense ingredient.

Be inventive, but not derivative. Build on what you know works but try not to copy what is already on television.

Let's keep to factual ideas for the moment.

- ♦ Asking how something works could lead to a *Tomorrow's World* type item.
- ♦ Talking to a group of 10 year olds on Brighton seafront might give you an idea for what they would like to see on television about Brighton.
- ♦ Asking clubbers to explain what they like about 'garage' music might lead to a music item on current trends in dance music.
- ♦ Searching newspapers, magazines and in particular the specialist press could lead you to one of those unusual or 'off-the-wall' stories that make good television.
- ♦ Checking fanzines and the specialist music press could uncover an interesting music item.

Box 1.1 Microscooter fever

You may not be able to rollerblade, but anyone can use one of the new aluminium microscooters. They are very popular with young people – why? What can you do on a microscooter? Will the craze last, like skateboarding?

Asking these sorts of questions will get you into the mode of story-telling for television. Find some young people on their scooters and interview them. Don't just spray your camera around and shoot everything in sight. Plan it; find a real enthusiast and tell the story from their point of view. Find out more about it. There may even be a world champion living in your area. Get inside the mind of a microscooter maniac. You will need to shoot a variety of shots that will go together to make a visually entertaining story.

Ideas wall

Most production offices have an ideas wall. If you are still trying to find a suitable idea, try using those small coloured sticky office notepads on a blank wall.

1 Write down the name of six favourite places you actually know or would like to know, using one note page per place. Stick them all up on the wall in a line under each other. Some will be accessible like the local beach or even the Lake District; others may be harder to get to like Rome.

2 Write down the names of six people who interest you. Be as specific as you can – for example Alastair: stand-up comedian, Helen: bass guitarist – or just use names of people you know. Put them on the wall.

3 Write the name of six specific activities that interest you on another six bits of paper and put them up on the wall opposite the places – for example, shopping, bungee jumping, clubbing or even drinking Bacardi Breezers.

4 Think laterally. What will create the unexpected or the most unusual?

5 Now move your bits of paper around to make a meaningful line of three: location, activity and person. You might get –

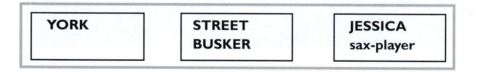

| YORK | STREET BUSKER | JESSICA sax-player |

This may seem not particularly unexpected or unusual, but think what you could do with it.

♦ It could be a three-minute story about the secret life of a street busker in York: what does he or she do when not performing? Combine this with pictures of the performance and you almost certainly have a good story.

♦ Try it another way: how much could my saxophone-playing friend Jessica make in a day as a street busker in York? Compare this to guitarist John in a different city. Not only have you got two locations but you also have the stimulus of a competition.

♦ The film could be about the trials and tribulation of getting to be a street performer – rehearsal, choosing what music to play, whether to play on your own or with someone else, and the worries about permissions and will anybody like you.

Box 1.2 Your idea checklist

♦ You have explored a number of options and you now have a good idea.
♦ You have done some basic research into this idea.
♦ You are convinced you can make a viable television item/ programme out of your idea.
♦ You are ready to continue the preproduction process.

In other words, mix the ingredients up with what is possible and whom you know. You should now have the germ of an idea for your first three-minute story. So do it.

Good luck.

2
Treatment

There are three main stages in turning your idea into a television programme: preproduction, production and postproduction.

FROM IDEA TO SCREEN

The television production process

PREPRODUCTION

              PRODUCTION

                            POSTPRODUCTION

Idea to screen

Your idea is the first element in the preproduction process. Transforming your idea into a viable television programme is what you do in preproduction. When everything is ready you can start filming. This is production. After you have shot everything, you go into postproduction to edit the pictures and remix the sound to make a finished film or programme.

Preproduction

Before you begin filming, you need to get everything together so that you are totally on top of your show before you start spending a lot of time and money shooting. This is the preproduction process. You have already started preproduction by getting your idea into shape.

If your idea is for a factual programme, then during preproduction you will create a number of important documents. If you are creating a drama, then you will find more information in Part Two, where creating a film drama is covered in more detail.

☞ For details of creating a film drama, from script to screen, see Chapters 26–31.

This is what you need to make a factual programme (much of this work is best done in preproduction, but some things like commentary script will be in rough outline only at this stage):

- a treatment;
- a list of contributors with telephone numbers and addresses;
- outline script for pieces to camera and intended voiceovers;
- a schedule for the whole production;
- an overall budget;
- a crewlist;
- a postproduction schedule;
- technical requirements;
- locations with risk assessments;
- copyright sorted out;
- permissions signed;
- a storyboard for visual sequences;
- finance available.

Treatment

A treatment is the professional way to offer a broadcaster your idea. By writing a treatment you really have to visualize exactly what your story is going to look like and how it is going to be fashioned for your audience. I always ask anyone who comes to me with an idea to do a treatment, even for a three-minute film. It is amazing how a treatment crystallizes the idea and tunes up the storytelling process, because you have to go through every sequence of the film in your mind.

A standard treatment is no more than one page long, and has essential information grouped under headings. When you have fully thought out your idea and researched it thoroughly, you can do a fuller multi-page version called a proposal. But you should always do a treatment first, as executive producers and people handling budgets will ask for one.

A standard one-page treatment includes the following information in this order.

- *Programme title.* A good title often gives a pointer as to what your programme is about.
- *Producer and/or director.* Include the name of the person in charge of the production.

☞ For a full description of production roles, see Chapter 6.

♦ *Duration.* Select a recognized TV duration – for example, 10 minutes, 15 minutes or 30 minutes.

♦ *Audience.* It is important to define your audience as clearly as possible – for example, an 18–35 adult audience, a young teenage audience up to 16, or a family audience. It is helpful to suggest a possible transmission slot – for example, late night on BBC2, or daytime on a popular lifestyle digital channel.

♦ *Résumé.* A résumé is a short version of the structure and content of the whole programme. It is the most important part of the treatment. Be concise and cover the essential storyline, outlining the most compelling, original and televisual aspects of your programme.

♦ *Suggested elements*

  ● Set out the exciting, audience-grabbing aspects to your show in terms of content, style and people.
  ● Include the names of characters who have agreed to feature in the programme. *Be realistic. Madonna will not be available unless you have special access.* But lesser luminaries may well be interested in taking part if the subject matter is something that really interests them.
  ● Say what the show looks like in terms of televisual style.
  ● Say where it will be filmed.
  ● Say whom you have in mind to be your presenter (be realistic).
  ● Say what aspects of the programme are unusual or special.

♦ *Shooting days.* Say how many days shooting this production will need. You must get this right. The budget will depend largely on this detail, especially on a single-camera low-budget shoot.

Treatment budget

At this stage your budget is an estimate of what you are likely to spend. If you are going to offer this to a broadcaster with the idea that the broadcaster might fund your idea, then make sure the budget is not too high. Broadcasters are, of course, very aware of how much television production costs, but they are also very keen to get good-quality material at a knockdown price.

Resist making your production look too cheap. That will not fool anyone. It may bind you into producing something for much less than the real cost. It could end up costing you an arm and a leg, if you have to fund the difference out of your own pocket to achieve a decent standard of production conforming to the broadcaster's standards.

Prepare your estimated actual costs under these headings:

♦ *Tape.* You will need DV tapes for shooting, and postproduction. Also VHS tapes for viewing and sending to contributors.

♦ *Transport.* Getting actors, crew and participants to and from locations can be expensive. Work out whether it is best to hire a van or people carrier. Remember to include preproduction costs for finding locations.

♦ *Accommodation.* There is not always a handy auntie living in your preferred location – estimate on a B&B basis.

♦ *Editing time.* How long will it take you to edit? Basically you can off-line edit about 5–7 minutes a day. Allow time for digitizing the rushes. If you are doing it on your PC, then build in any extra costs for digital storage etc. For full details on postproduction, see Part Three.

♦ *Subsistence.* You and your crew need to live when on location, and believe me you get very hungry when filming. Build in a daily cost of two meals per day for each crew and participant. Sandwiches are not enough!

♦ *Special equipment.* If you are doing something special and think you need to hire a camera crane or, heaven forbid, a helicopter, then this must be costed in at this stage.

> ☞ For details on production equipment, see Chapter 24.

♦ *Crewing.* You may have to pay a daily rate for specialist crew members such as a camera operator, or make-up.

> ☞ For full crewing costs, see Chapter 5.

♦ *Copyright.* If you are using recorded music (on any format tape or CD) or want to buy in visual archive material, you must include this in the budget. Music can be expensive, and it is vital that you check the copyright details.

> ☞ For all you need to know about copyright, see Chapter 37.

Budgeting tip

Under normal conditions an experienced production team can shoot 5–8 minutes of edited material – drama or documentary – in an average day. If you are just starting out, or you have limited filming experience, then you should be able to shoot about three minutes of edited material in a day.

Treatment example

Mark Smith, a cameraman, had the idea to film a day in the life of the River Thames from the point of view of the professionals who work on the river such as the harbour service and river police. Mark lived near the Thames and had always been interested in the way the river was used and thought it would make a good programme possible for cable TV. He also had access and characters – both essential for this sort of fly-on-the-wall documentary.

He has done some research, and has found a lively character who is an ex-river worker and has stories to tell. He has secured access to the Harbour Service and their boats. He now has to create a programme story out of these elements. His treatment is shown in Box 2.1.

This is a typical very low-budget production using Mark's own camera and a friend to work as a sound recordist. He will edit at home on his PC using Adobe Premiere. You can see from his budget estimate (Box 2.2) how inexpensive a factual programme can be.

Box 2.1 Cable TV treatment example

PROGRAMME TITLE	*The Working River*
DIRECTOR and CAMERAMAN	Mark Smith (include address & tel. no.)
DURATION	15 mins approx. Suitable to be shown on a cable network in the south-east of England.
AUDIENCE	Wide demographic audience anticipated. The documentary will aim to attract viewers of *Airport*, *Horizon* and *Dispatches*. Focusing on 25–40 year olds, male and female, including those who may work on the river or have a passion for waterways and what they have to offer.
FORMAT	DV

RÉSUMÉ
When people think of the River Thames, they regard it with low esteem and can only imagine images of murky water and the Thames flood

Box 2.1 *continued*

barrier. However, this could not be further from the truth. The River Thames is a vibrant river, which attracts tourists, as well as partygoers and the endless characters who work on the Thames.

The jobs on the river are extremely varied in their roles, from the River Police and the divers to the driftwood boat operators and pier masters. All of these gel together to form a 'working river'. It is these types of jobs on the Thames that help to make it one of the most famous rivers in the world. The River Thames is controlled from the Thames estuary to Teddington lock; like air traffic control, there is a control centre that monitors all movement within the Thames, monitoring super cruise ferries to tug boats. Both the Harbour Service and River Police work in conjunction with each other to help with this control as well as providing an emergency service. Although the Thames has been modernized in this way, it still keeps a sense of tradition, including the Waterman's Apprenticeship ceremony, which takes place at Waterman's Hall and has not changed for hundreds of years.

SUGGESTED ELEMENTS

♦ Filming the Port of London Harbour Launch Service; a fly-on-the wall approach to a typical day's work, including filming an emergency call-out of the Harbour Service.

♦ Focus on the lives of the River Police, explaining how their job differs from the Harbour Service, and film a river 'incident'.

♦ The River Thames operations control room: interview with operations officer whilst on the job, as well as discussion of past incidents in which the operations room played a major role.

♦ PLA Diving Department: interviews with divers, what they pick up from the river; filming a typical day of a diver.

♦ Follow an evening on a party pleasure boat, including filming the night's party, with possible interview of captain about his/her job.

♦ Greenside dock is one of the largest private cruise moorings for boats along the Thames; interviews with dock master, including the many 'upper-class' characters who moor their luxury boats within the dock.

♦ Along the Thames there are a variety of small piers. These are usually manned by older characters who used to work either at sea or on the River Thames. One character, Tom, will give an insight into the river and how it has changed over the years.

Box 2.1 *continued*

♦ Filming of an apprentice on the river following the various obstacles he/she has to tackle when training to become a waterman. Include visit to the historical and ornate Waterman's Hall and filming the apprenticeship ceremony.

SHOOTING DAYS   7–10 shooting days

BUDGET   £350 (see budget breakdown)

Box 2.2 Treatment budget estimate

The Working River

Production expenditure forecast

Expenses

Tapes, DVCAM: 4 × 60 mins	£100.00
Transport/fuel costs	£80.00
Food costs	£35.00
Technical resources: hire, camera filters	£20.00
Copyright material: music	£100.00
Miscellaneous costs	£15.00
Total cost	£350.00

3
Creating a programme

Your treatment puts flesh and bones onto your idea, but you still have to deliver real people in real locations to create your factual programme.

Three elements are essential to make this happen on the screen: story, characters, access. These are necessary elements for any documentary about anything that you are likely to see on television except possibly wildlife, and even then you can substitute animals for characters.

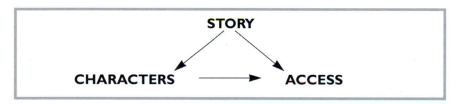

Story

You already have a good idea, but is it a good 'story'?

A story in television terms is the retelling for the camera of an interesting event or events. It must have a beginning, a middle and an end. This has to be accomplished within the time frame of the programme, whether it is 10 minutes or 110 minutes. Viewers have short attention spans and need to feel that they are watching a programme that is going somewhere, and has some substance to it. It is vital that your idea is told as a story that will have a strong beginning, involve the viewer, and reach a satisfying conclusion.

A good story

'Dog bites man' is a story, but not one that will interest anyone. 'Man bites dog' is a much better story. It is unusual and immediately arouses the interest of the viewer – why on earth would someone do that?

To make the story really stand up the dog should probably be of the furry friend variety, and not just any old mutt, and definitely should not have suffered in this encounter. So this could be a story of the 'skateboarding duck' variety. It is an amusing and unusual encounter between animal and man.

The character who has done the biting must be interesting, and the production must have access to that character. He must be able to talk about it and be interviewed.

To make a good television item out of this story you also need the two other elements – characters and access.

Characters

Television is about people. Factual programming needs characters on the screen that are engaging and watchable. The best characters will give you breadth, action and even humour.

One director I know came up with an exciting idea to film a docusoap about life in a famous flower market. In his treatment he showed that there were many stories to tell based on the way the market changed from day to day, and season to season. His idea was a good one, but it was only saleable as a television programme because he had identified several key interesting and distinctly charismatic characters. The stories created by these sympathetic market traders made fascinating television.

Watch any docusoap on television to see how important the characters are, and to see how they are worked into a storyline by the production team. Story and characters often go hand in hand.

How do you know if your main documentary characters are going to be a

Fig. 3.1 This still is taken from a documentary about fashion designers. Which character had the best story to tell?

hit with the audience? This is not easy, but there are some things you can do to make sure they are not a total flop, and a waste of your filming time.

Ask yourself these questions when deciding on your characters.

♦ Can he or she be natural in front of the camera?
♦ Does this person really capture my attention both to look at and to listen to?
♦ Would I like to see this person in my living room at home with my family?
♦ What sort of audience would this person appeal to?
♦ Can this person do the job I need him or her to do for this programme?

If you are still in doubt, then the rule of thumb is: can I work with this character?

If the answer is yes to all or most of these questions then you should go ahead and book that person for your programme. If not, then you need to look for someone else.

Access

This is where I have known many documentaries to fall down. Many people come up with a great idea and an exciting sounding story, but then you find out that the characters live in Peru. Fine. Have they agreed to be filmed? Er, not yet. The film will not work unless you can get to them and they agree; and possibly the foreign country agrees to let you do that sort of film on its territory.

To tell your story and to film your characters you have to have access to them. This means they all have to agree to take part in your programme, and preferably sign a release form, before filming begins. Some people say yes initially, but then back down at the last moment. To keep this drop-out rate to a minimum, keep your characters 'warm'. That usually means ringing them up often, reassuring them and telling them what is going on.

You need access not only to the people, but also to the locations that will give authenticity to your story and your chosen characters. You must make sure you have permission to be there before you start filming. This is where the recce comes in.

☞ For details of the recce, see Chapter 7.

You will also need Contributor's Release forms and Location Permission forms. Make sure your contributors agree to take part and sign a form *before* you start filming.

☞ For templates of a Contributor's Release form and a Location Permission form that can be used or adapted for most situations, see Chapter 22.

4

Factual research

All television programmes need research. Television research is largely about people. It is either looking for information about people, or it is about getting hold of people. You have actively to seek out those interesting characters for your documentary. You may meet some of them in the course of your daily life, or even in the pub. Then comes the difficult bit of getting hold of them again, and persuading them to take part in your programme. A lot of people research is carried out on the phone.

How to get whom you want

Getting hold of people can be difficult. You have to find them, phone them and persuade them to take part in your show. It is a good idea to practise doing this on a student show.

One of the first jobs on a factual programme anywhere in television is as a researcher for programme contributors. You will have to contact potential contributors and persuade them to appear on the programme. Start practising your telephone manner now.

Telephone techniques

♦ Don't be fobbed off by the receptionist. Ask to speak to the manager or person in charge.
♦ If they are not there ask:
    ● When will they will be in?
    ● Have they got a mobile phone number?
    ● Is there someone else I can talk to?
    ● Can I leave a message (as a last resort)?

Useful opening gambits

♦ 'Hello, I wonder if you can help me I have just started work in television I am very interested in your —— [club, stadium, company] and would like to make a short (promotional) film that you could use about your work . . .'

♦ 'Hello, I am studying to work in television production. Your company has such a good reputation in this area I wondered if you would mind if I could come and interview you about . . .'

♦ 'Hello my name is —— from —— television production company. I am making a programme about —— for a local TV cable channel. I hear you are an expert. I wonder if you would be kind enough to let me interview you/film on your premises/make a film about you . . .'

Some useful answers

♦ 'No it will never be broadcast or shown to an audience without your permission.'

♦ 'The film is purely for my personal use and will not be shown outside the production team.'

♦ 'I can understand your reluctance, but I will be delighted to show you the finished film, and you may want a VHS copy to show to your clients.' (Don't promise something you cannot deliver).

If they seem reluctant to agree

♦ 'We can film at any time to suit you'.

♦ 'I am sure that you are very busy, but we are extremely quick and efficient'.

♦ 'We are only a very small crew/team with just a small digital camera . . . and we won't cause any disturbance.'

♦ 'Perhaps I could meet you to talk about the possibility of filming . . .'

Some don'ts

♦ Never agree to give someone a tape until after you have completed, and maybe broadcast, the item.

♦ Never promise an interviewee or guest the possibility of having any influence whatsoever on the editorial process, or of seeing a rough cut of the programme.

If things seem hopeless

♦ Try playing on their emotions, or their vanity.

♦ 'I am sure you have a daughter/son who is trying to get experience in a profession, and it's very hard if no one will help us.'

♦ 'I am sure you would be very effective on television.'

♦ 'It would be a pity to miss this opportunity to put forward your point of view.'

Getting people on your side

♦ It's very important that you get on your side as many people as possible in any organization.

♦ In a small organization try and get the receptionist/person who answers the phone on your side; ask them whether he or she can help you.

♦ It is worth asking if you can see your possible guest face to face: 'perhaps I can come and see you and we can talk about how we might do the filming.'

♦ If all else fails ask: 'Do you know anyone else who can help me?'

Where to find people

♦ If you are given a topic to research begin by going to the people and associations who should be able to help.

♦ Charities are often pleased to offer someone for interview or provide free information.

♦ If you are making a film about a topic – for example, go-karting or fishing – there is almost certainly a National Association who will be able to help you. They should be able to give you a name of someone locally.

♦ Try Yellow Pages.

♦ Town Halls nearly always have an information office. Try early in the morning – about 9.00 a.m.; they are sometimes less busy then.

♦ Use the telephone directories in a library, or online. Directory Enquires (192) is very useful if you have a name, but there is a charge for the service.

♦ Local papers can be helpful if they think you are a regular reader. Mention an article, or the name of a journalist, and ask for further information.

♦ If you want to film in a certain place – for example, a greyhound stadium – and the first one you try will not agree, then ask them to suggest one that might agree.

♦ Don't hang up without a further number to call.

♦ The best source of information about anything is now the Internet. Build up your own list of search engines and useful sites.

Telephone tip
Whatever you do, don't give up.

Your research book

The key to successful research is always to write everything down. The information may not seem relevant at the time, but you will be amazed at the number of times you are struggling to remember whom you spoke to just last week, unless you make a note of everyone you contact – you will need it.

I put everything down in a large A4 hardback book. I start a new page or half page for each day with the day's date at the top. For everyone I phone I write:

♦ full name;
♦ telephone numbers;
♦ e-mail address;
♦ the subject or reason for phoning;.
♦ brief notes about their answer: agreed to take part/bad talker/hesitant/ can't make it until after 22 March.

You may be working on several things at once. It is extremely easy to forget why you telephoned someone, what he or she said and even what his or her name is.

Working as a researcher in broadcasting

You will need all these skills and a lot of energy and determination to work on a broadcast programme. If you do get the opportunity to work for a broadcast company as a researcher, the programme editor or producer will almost certainly want to see and check your research notes every week. Make your notes legible.

TV researching can be a competitive business. Make sure your research book is kept with you at all times. Keep a photocopy of important pages. Some researchers use a Psion type of electronic organizer alongside their book. This is a good way of backing up your data. Or you can use an MP3 or minidisc recorder – useful for recording information on location and for recording research interviews. See Box 4.1 for the sort of information a programme editor will look for in a personal research book.

Who makes a good researcher?

When Carlton Television UK advertised for researchers they described the perfect researcher:

Box 4.1 A4 personal research book

5 August
Programme on British Film

Day 1 research

Possible Interviews	Tel. no.	mobile	e-mail
Lord Puttnam			
Tim Roth			
Ken Russell			
Ridley Scott			
Elizabeth Hurley			

Notes

Contact Bfi	Tel.	web site

Check articles on Guy Ritchie
Find out who directed Bridget Jones

To do
♦ Look up web sites on British film in the 21st century
♦ Find out more about lottery funding

'You must be brilliant with ideas, have superb organization skills with great attention to detail, but most of all you must be good with people.'

You can do it: you know you can.

Researchers get the blame

The role of researchers, and research on television programmes, is often under scrutiny from politicians, broadcasters and newspapers. Michael Grade has spoken publicly about his belief that TV researchers are not trained well enough to cope with the pressures of competitive TV scheduling (for example, the large number of talk shows that need guests, and are competing against each other). This has led to the occasional bogus guest being invited to take part in a talk show.

Broadcasters no longer offer training in research techniques. You will be expected to be trained before you take up a job. So where do you get the training? You really have to train yourself, and try to gain experience during

---

Box 4.2 Being a good researcher checklist

♦ Make sure you are aware and alert to the possibility that someone might not be whom they seem.

♦ Always check all details to ensure you are not conned by a bogus guest, or ensnared by unscrupulous companies or individuals out to make a fast buck.

♦ If you are in any doubt about a possible guest's credentials, check with a senior professional.

♦ Develop the attributes of a good researcher – perseverance, care with checking facts, lateral thinking, stamina and good luck.

---

a work placement with a broadcaster. And remember everything in the checklist in Box 4.2.

Useful web sites

Web sites come and go but most of these will be around for a long time.

Background to people in the news

♦ Try newspapers on the Internet.

♦ The *Daily Telegraph* archive service is free: www.telegraph.co.uk

♦ The *Guardian* site is well designed (and good for jobs): www.guardian.co.uk

♦ The *Mirror* site has good pictures: www.mirror.co.uk

Online news

♦ Best is the BBC: www.news.bbc.co.uk

♦ Or e-mail BBC news: newsonline@bbc.co.uk

♦ In the USA: www.abcnews.com

Sport

♦ For cricket: www.cricketunlimited.co.uk

♦ For football: www.news.bbc.co.uk/hi/english/sport

♦ Or: www.skysports.co.uk/skysports/football

Government

♦ Try: www.number-10.gov.uk/public/interact

♦ For official documents, and Hansard: www.the-stationery-office.com

♦ For the USA, e-mail: president@whitehouse.gov

Famous people
- Try Yahoo People search
- Or ask Jeeves 'How can I find someone?': www.askjeeves.com
- Try google.com

More and more of the rich and famous have their own web sites
- Demi Moore: Demim@aol.com
- Madonna: madonna@wbr.com

Academic research
- Put yourself on a university register
- Try: www.angelfire.com

Films
- For movie titles: www.imdb.com
- For filmographies, try the UK site: www.uk.imdb.com
- For nation-wide listings: www.filmunlimited.co.uk
- For the hippest movie news: www.aint-it-cool-news.com
- For scripts, including *Titanic* and the *Alien* series: www.script-o-rama.com/index.shtml

Media jobs
- The *Guardian* site is best: www.jobsunlimited.co.uk
- Also try Recruit Media: www.recruitmedia.co.uk
- Or try: www.mandy.com

Build up your CV
- For advice on CVs, covering letters, aptitude tests, and so on: www.aboutwork.com

5
The programme budget

One of the aims of this book is to give you the tools to set you free to make your own productions using digital kit. However, everything costs something. You will always need to think about a budget. If you are thinking of sending your video drama to a festival, or you want to show it to a potential broadcaster, then you will need to do a proper budget.

Budgets depend on many different variables, not least on who is supplying the finance for your production. The most important aspect of preparing a budget is to make sure you have costed everything, and then to make sure that you can deliver within that budget. There is never any excuse for going over budget. It means either that you prepared an unrealistic budget in the first place, or that you (the producer) let things go out of control during production.

The budget for a television programme is dependent on these costs:

♦ resources – videotape and equipment;
♦ people and their time – crew and production;
♦ subsistence – food;
♦ travel and accommodation;
♦ insurance – public liability insurance, kit insurance;
♦ office and communications – computer, fax, phone and mobile;
♦ talent – presenters and/or actors;
♦ props, costume and make-up;
♦ copyright and programme rights;
♦ special equipment;
♦ sundries.

Before drawing up a full budget for your television production you also need to know who the programme is being made for.

♦ Is it a production for a mainstream broadcasting organization?
♦ Is it a production for an Internet company looking for broadband material?
♦ Is it a personal project that you hope might be bought by a cable or satellite broadcaster? Many cable and satellite channels will gladly broadcast low-budget productions, but they may not pay for them.

♦ Is it a production you want to make to the highest possible standards but with low cost in the hope of submitting it to a film or video festival?

The level of finance will vary for each scenario. A good idea and a bad budget nearly always mean a bad programme, and you get a hole in your pocket. As soon as you press the record button on your camera, costs will incur, even if you have borrowed all the kit.

Mini budget production

Box 5.1 shows the things that you will need to budget for on a small production. Actual costs will depend on how much kit you can beg or borrow, and how much you can do on your own, or with a very small team. This is the sort of budget Mark was looking at for his production of the *Working River*.

> ☞ Mark's Working River production is discussed in Chapter 2.

A word about kit

♦ It is possible to 'blag' kit – that is, persuade a company that you and your production is so exciting and you are so brim full of talent that they will lend you a camera kit for nothing. It does happen, and it is worth asking, but you must have a worthwhile project to offer.

♦ You may be able to borrow kit from a college or a friend.

♦ In most cases you should add the cost of insurance. If you are working with actors or members of the public, then you should add the cost of public liability insurance.

> ☞ For details of public liability insurance and other production forms, see Chapter 22; and for production equipment, see Chapter 24.

Box 5.1 Mini budget production

♦ DV tapes
♦ transport
♦ subsistence
♦ insurance
♦ music or other copyright
♦ telephone: a mobile is essential
♦ computer: e-mail and internet access
♦ kit – camera and sound

Fig. 5.1 DV camcorder kit

Maxi budget production

Here are some guidelines for a 60-minute drama shot on location for broadcasting on a digital channel. It will be produced by an independent company and will not be as well financed as a drama for a terrestrial broadcaster, but this is a professional production.

Office and communications

The first expenditure will be on an office base from where you can run your production. This could be home, or a rented office or a canal barge (cheaper than an office and with a better view – and it can move).

Never underestimate the cost of mobile phones and office telephone calls, and Internet access.

Pay roll

You will need to have core staff on your pay roll. It could be any or all of these: producer, director, production manager, production assistant, first AD, second AD, actors or presenter, make-up artist, production designer, graphic designer, props buyer, costume designer, runner. Many will be freelance, but core production staff will need to be contracted for the duration of the production.

Script and copyright

A good script is absolutely essential; a good scriptwriter will be an expensive up-front cost, but well worth it, as it will save time in the long run.

Kit

To hire technical equipment or a large camera crane is very expensive. Shop around for special deals and weekly rates. Hire companies outside London often offer more competitive rates.

Crew

This should include camera, sound, lights, grip and assistants.

Cast

If you really want Kate Winslet, reach for someone else's chequebook and provide a script to die for.

Transport

This should include van hire, the cost of recces, rail fares, production hire cars and petrol.

Location trailers

You need to allow for caravans for artists, make-up, wardrobe and location catering.

Accommodation

Overnight accommodation for crew and cast on location dramas can be very expensive. You will probably get an overall 'deal' at a hotel, but you are still housing a large team.

Per diem

The Production Company will need to pay a *per diem* – a daily amount to cover coffee, lunch, supper and refreshments.

Props and set

It can cost mega bucks to create a sci-fi set or smash a lot of cars. Use locations where possible, or make the set yourself.

Make-up

You will need a make-up artist and an assistant, especially if there are any special hair styles or wigs required.

Costume

You will probably need a costume designer to hire or buy suitable costumes for the actors, and assistants to help with changes of costume, ironing and fitting.

Music

Specially composed music is worth considering for any production. It can cost less than paying copyright on commercial discs.

Miscellaneous

This will cover all the things you have forgotten. It is worth allowing 10 per cent of the total.

Contingency

Many productions carry more than the recommended 10 per cent of the entire budget as contingency to cover illness and anything not going according to schedule. Bad weather can eat up a contingency budget and insuring for bad weather is very expensive.

Press and publicity

Include a budget for location stills and other publicity material that can only be gathered during filming. The cost of hiring a professional viewing theatre for your press launch may have to come out of the programme budget.

Postproduction

You will need to budget for off-line and online editing. If you need to create special effects or recreate a period look with colourizing effects, then allow extra time and finance for the hire of high-end computer graphics equipment (for example, Quantel's Editbox) and an operator.

Episodic effects are getting more cost effective, but they take a lot of time and you certainly need to plan and budget for them.

You might want to create energy beams or time warps for your sci-fi drama. Perfectly possible, but you cannot do it on location. Ask an expert in a facilities house for a budget for the special effects you need. In fact, you may be surprised at how affordable a few seconds of effects can be.

Shooting days

When working out any budget for a television production, there is one thing you must get right: the number of shooting days. This is the most costly area and one most likely to escalate. The rule of thumb for a professional crew is that you should be able to shoot five minutes of *edited* drama per long day.

Working with a very small crew and digital kit you may be able to shoot up to ten minutes of edited drama a day. Television series in the USA often work on ten minutes a day. Do not expect to do more. At the beginning you

Fig. 5.2 Two-person camera crew

will be hard pushed to do five minutes, unless you have rehearsed the actors beforehand and it is all set in one location. You will find that the more you do the quicker and more efficient you all get.

Working with just you and one other, and a DV kit, it is possible to do up to ten minutes of factual programming a day. It will largely depend on travel and the availability of contributors.

This is an overview of the sort of costs you will incur on a high-quality drama. It is possible to make good drama for a lot less with fewer people and less resources. Basically, production professionals, talent and special equipment will be your most expensive items.

6

Production roles

Television production is largely about cooperation and teamwork. One of the joys of television production is that you can work creatively in a team. It does not need to be a big team, but it is always good to have someone to spark ideas off, or just to chat through ways of doing things.

You can do a lot on your own with your own digital kit, but for larger productions and especially drama you need to work in a team and as a team. On a production intended for broadcasting, or made with an independent company, the roles will look like this.

☞ For more detail of specific roles in drama production, see Chapter 27.

Producer

People often ask me what exactly does a producer do? Well, the answer is virtually everything, but he or she must learn to delegate as much of the work as possible. The producer has the ultimate responsibility for getting the production completed and on the air.

It is the producer who takes the blame or enjoys the fame. Enjoy it! The producer is the organizational and administrative head of the production who:

♦ must act not as a dictator but as a team leader and captain of the production ship;
♦ usually initiates the programme idea;
♦ selects programme concepts, production personnel, and controls the budget;
♦ is responsible for getting the programme on the air;
♦ is always looking for new ideas or new ways of doing things;
♦ is involved in raising money for the project;
♦ works closely with the director and production manager.

The producer's other responsibilities include: schedule, personnel, compliance and copyright, keeping under budget, making sure things actually happen when they are supposed to happen, talking to everybody – and accepting the BAFTA.

Fig. 6.1 TV production is all about teamwork

Director

The director is responsible for staging the production and directing performers and camera crew. The director casts the actors; works with the production manager on the shooting schedule; decides the final visual and audio treatment; does the storyboard; supervises all the editing; with the producer chooses music and digital FX, and is responsible for the overall look of the production. It is the director who makes sure the production looks like a million dollars and sounds like it.

Assistant producer

On factual programmes the assistant producer is often the researcher and location director of short inserts. The assistant producer can be the researcher/director on a small production, and can be studio director for factual programmes.

First AD

On a drama, the nearest to an assistant producer is the important post of the first AD – the first assistant director – who does much of the day-to-day organizational work on the shoot. The first AD can line up shots, set up locations, supervise rehearsals and be in charge of the actors. On a large drama, the first AD is helped by a second AD and a third AD, who is usually responsible for extras. On small dramas the first AD will be in charge of keeping order on the set.

Production manager

The production manager works with, and is answerable to, the producer. The production manager is in charge of resources and responsible for delivering the show on budget. Responsibilities include managing locations, crew and technical facilities, getting everybody to where they are meant to be on location, sorting out accommodation and all the other important details to do with servicing the shoot, hiring freelance crew, drawing up the shooting schedule and sometimes raising money for the production with the producer. Budget is the production manager's main responsibility, but he or she liases often and at all times with the producer and director.

Production assistant

The production assistant works closely with the producer and the director in the preparation of the script and the paperwork for all aspects of the production. A production assistant must be able to work effectively on his or her own and be a formidable communicator.

For a drama, the production assistant is in charge of the script from rewrites to the final postproduction script; he or she logs all takes and handles continuity.

On smaller factual programmes, the production assistant does all the paperwork and works as a production manager, booking hotels, cars and so on. He or she handles release forms and permissions.

Researchers

Broadcasters and new media production companies require researchers and production assistants to make short films or items from inception to transmission. You may be taken on as a researcher, but you must be able to think up, budget, research, shoot and off-line edit a story entirely on your own. This is multiskilling.

You will need to keep the producer informed of what you are doing and how it is going at all stages. Do not shoot anything without a treatment, sometimes a storyboard and always an approved budget – for a cable channel this will be basic. Have a file of stories ready to talk about at interviews on themes relevant to the channel or programme you hope to work for.

The crew

There are other people you will meet on a professional shoot.

♦ *Lighting cameraperson or DOP* (Director of Photography). The DOP is the supervising cameraperson who works with the director to achieve the 'look' of the film. He or she will have a camera operator working under him or her, and a team of qualified electricians (sparks) who set up and operate lights.

- ◆ *Gaffer.* The chief electrician is known as the gaffer. The feature-film term for the electrician who is second in command is the best boy.
- ◆ *Sound recordist.* The sound recordist supervises the recording of the location sound; he or she sometimes works with a sound assistant and a boom operator.
- ◆ *Camera assistant.* On video shoots, the camera assistant carries the tripod, sets up the camera, makes sure batteries are charged, loads tape and sets the time code. On a shoot using film stock, he or she checks the gate and loads film magazines.
- ◆ *Grip.* A grip is part of the camera crew and usually sets up the dolly and lays track.

> ☞ There is more detail about using a dolly and setting up a tracking shot in Chapter 30.

- ◆ *Runner.* A runner works to the production manager and 'runs' for anything anybody wants. Many professionals say this is the best way to start learning the business. I say that it is a good job after university or college as long as they pay you, and do not expect you to do it forever! It is certainly great for getting valuable work experience and seeing what really goes on on a big, or small, production.

People to be nice to at all times

- ◆ *Executive producer.* You may never see the execrive producer, but he or she holds the purse strings, and in broadcasting probably commissioned the production you are working on.
- ◆ *Associate producer.* For television drama productions the associate producer is very important in preproduction. He or she will have devised the budget with the production manager, and has overall control of it. The associate producer will be in regular contact with the director and producer during shooting, and is often influential in getting things done, not least by liasing with the executive producer.
- ◆ *Art director.* The art director is probably seen only on large TV dramas, movies and commercials, but is the creative force behind the visual concepts beloved of high-budget car and jeans commercials. For that stunning period look to a film, or a futuristic set, choose a good art director.

What would you do?

To secure a job on a professional factual production you should have production and reseach skills, and be able to operate a variety of equipment to a basic level.

♦ You will be able to use a small digital camera.

♦ You will be able to operate a rifle-type microphone (for example, Sennheiser MK H416P48) and a sound mixer.

♦ You will understand and be able to set up basic lighting equipment such as a redhead unit, or a small HMI or a blonde.

☞ Further details on lighting equipment can be found in Chapters 15 and 18.

♦ You will be able to use non-linear digital editing equipment such as AVID or Adobe Premier.

☞ Full details on postproduction can be found in Part Three.

♦ You should be able to direct a two-person camera crew – camera and sound for an interview.

♦ Even though you may not be working on a drama, many factual programmes use actors for short sequences. You will know protocols for dealing with actors, and be able to direct two or three actors in a straightforward single camera sequence.

☞ For a full explanation of shooting drama, see Chapters 29 and 30.

7

The recce

Recce comes from the French word *reconnaissance*, meaning a survey or discovery. It has come to mean finding locations suitable for filming.

Doing a recce

To make quality programming you must do a recce on every location, no matter how small or insignificant the location might seem.

♦ Always take notes.
♦ Use a minidisc or MP3 recorder to 'voice' notes or interviews giving information.
♦ Take pictures.

Taking pictures

♦ A Polaroid camera is popular.
♦ I prefer an APS or 35mm camera. Many high-street shops offer one-hour processing, and the pictures are better. The APS film system gives

Fig. 7.1 This lake looks beautiful in winter. Is it still suitable as a summer location?

you an 'easyfinder' page with all the pictures on a strip, and dates each
picture on the back or front – very useful.

♦ You can buy a 'throwaway' camera. These are available in all sorts of
unlikely places, such as open-all-hours stores or tourist attractions.

♦ Digital still cameras have the advantage that you can download images
into a computer, incorporate them into your text and/or print the
pictures on the computer printer. Small health warning – the special
paper and cartridges you will need to print a lot of photographs can be
expensive compared to high-street processing.

Exterior locations

♦ *The sun.* Check where the sun will shine on your location. In case you
are a little wobbly on the points of the compass, ask someone.
Remember: east – sun rising; south – sun at midday; west – sun setting.
If you are near a church, the altar is always in the end of the church
pointing east. If your script demands a sunset shot, then use the recce
to make sure you can get it at the time of year when you will be filming. Beware of any shadows that buildings may cast, especially in the
afternoon. They could plunge the quiet corner chosen for your long
romantic scene into semi-darkness before you finish it. Be aware of the
sun's movements.

♦ *Sound.* Stand quietly for a few moments and listen intently for ambient
sound. Hopefully that buzzing you can hear is the birds and bees and

Fig. 7.2 Venice: no traffic, but is it still a quiet location?

not aircraft taking off, or powerboat racing in the next valley. If it is, you need to check the source and maybe alter your location.

Interior locations

♦ *Sound interior.* Clap your hands and see how long the echo lasts – too long and you could have difficulties recording location sound. Also check for ambient noise. Roads can be very noisy at certain times of the day.

♦ *Power.* Check the exact location of 13 amp power sockets. You will almost certainly need a power source when you are filming inside a building. Your digital camera may have a long-lasting battery, but if you are using lights they need power. Camera batteries tend to run down more quickly than you think, so it is a good idea to put a spare battery (batteries) on to charge at the location.

♦ *Permission.* Try to get location release forms signed on the recce. You may not be able to manage this, but you can always ring the appropriate person later. You cannot expect to turn up somewhere and get instant permission to film. Often the person who can authorize the use of a location for filming has to be contacted separately. But this should always be done before filming begins.

♦ *Difficult locations.* Anything near or on land owned by the Ministry of Defence is particularly difficult, but not necessarily impossible. Filming royalty requires special permission from Buckingham Palace. Filming on the premises of multinational companies can be tricky, as they often have to refer to head office.

♦ *Street locations.* If you are using a small camcorder for factual productions, you can normally film in any street, providing that you do not block a public thoroughfare or cause an obstruction. Using film lights, or filming staged action (such as a chase sequence), requires police permission to use a public thoroughfare.

♦ *Parking.* Make sure that there is adequate parking for production vehicles and the crew for the whole day. This may need to be negotiated, as it could be expensive. A lighting or equipment van, or a generator, may need to get very close to the set where you are filming. If this is not possible, you may have to find a location where it is possible.

♦ *Drama.* If you are directing actors, then it is better to inform the local police. This is essential if mock firearms are part of action that takes place in a street. For a big scene, it is possible to get a road closed to traffic for part of the day. You need permission from everyone –

certainly the town council and local police. Check it out on the recce and ask to film in the quietest part of the day/week, which is often early Sunday morning.

The recce is an important and vital part of any production. It can also be a lot of fun. Get the recce right and it is more likely that your production will be a pleasure than a disappointment.

8
Health and safety

Health and safety are very important on any production. They cannot be ignored because they are the law. Under the 1974 Health and Safety at Work Act (UK) everyone in a place of work has the responsibility for his or her own safety, and for that of his or her colleagues, and even the public, if they are affected by the work going on.

Responsibility for health and safety

The producer is ultimately responsible at all times for the health and safety of the crew and the contributors, on location or in the studio. If the producer is not able to be on location, responsibility must be delegated to a named individual – usually the production manager.

If you work for the BBC or the ITV, or for most major broadcasters in the USA, you will have to pass a stringent health and safety course, achieving over 80 per cent, before you can go on a location shoot.

Risk assessment

One aspect you must look into before starting any production is Hazard Risk Assessment. What does this mean?

Once locations have been selected for your shoot, the next job is to check the health and safety aspects of each location. This might seem unnecessary if you are just doing an interview, but each location must be assessed for its potential to cause injury to anyone on your production.

For example, that location in a room in a high-rise office block is almost certainly safe, but what about that shot you want from the roof of the building? Is that a location where your camera operator can work safely? What about the wind factor, and safe access to the roof? You will need to check these things out before you can film from the roof.

Hazard Risk Assessment means that the producer of any location production must assess the chances of any accident happening on location. The risk must be assessed before any filming takes place. Then action must be taken to reduce any perceived risk.

How do you do this?

The Hazard Risk Assessment for a location shoot should be practical, systematic and concentrate on making sure all relevant risks are assessed.

Hazard Risk Assessment form

A production Hazard Risk Assessment form must be filled in and signed before filming begins. Box 8.1 shows a typical Hazard Risk Assessment form. For any production, you will need to identify the possible hazards for each activity involved. A hazard is something that could result in injury or harm.

You should consider the obvious hazards first.

- *Animals.* Hazards from animals include bites, infection or poison. Always have a trained handler on the set.
- *Cables.* Make sure cables do not cross public walkways unless covered with a ramped board. It is often better to put cables up high out of the way of people.
- *Dangerous environments.* Dangerous environments include waterways, derelict buildings, roofs and farming locations.
- *Electricity.* There is always a potential danger when using electricity. It could be fire and/or electric shock. Always use a contact breaker on all cables.
- *Night filming.* There is the potential for a number of hazardous situations if you are filming at night – for example, security.
- *Special visual effects.* Special effects such as explosives and fireworks must be supervised by a trained person.
- *Stunts.* There are two sorts of stunts: those done by professionals and minor stunts by presenters or contributors. Very accurate risk assessment is needed; seek professional advice if in doubt. A car chase is a stunt.
- *Working at heights.* Working at heights is defined as working over 6 feet from the ground. There are hazards working from a ladder or a scaffold tower. Train your crew on working safely with a ladder.
- *Working in public areas.* Check for safe access for you, your crew and the public, if you are working in a public area.

But remember that each production will vary, so you need to add further items to the example form shown here.

Box 8.1 Hazard Risk Assessment form					
Activity	If there is a hazard ✔	Severity	Likelihood	Risk factor	Action
Access					
Animals					
Audiences					
Confined spaces					
Crowds/rallies demonstrations					
Diving					
Electricity					
Fire/flammable materials					
Flying					
Hazardous substances					
Heat/cold/extreme weather					
Industrial machinery					
Lasers/stroboscopes					
Night filming					
Noise – very loud					
Radiation – X-rays					
Scaffolds					
Special visual effects					
Special needs					
Stunts					
Vehicles – on and off road					
Waterways					
Weapons					
Working at heights					
Working overseas					
Add extra items if necessary.					

Box 8.2 Assessing the severity of an accident	
Severity	**Type of injury**
Very Severe	Long-term disability or death
Severe	Major injury
Moderate	Deep flesh wound or degree of disability
Slight	Minor cuts and bruises
Negligible	No visible sign of injury or pain

How to fill in the Hazard Risk Assessment form

When you fill in the Hazard Risk Assessment form you have to assess the risk to the health and safety of personnel while they are working on your production. So you have to assess the likelihood of an accident happening while personnel are carrying out the activities associated with making your television programme.

You need to go through the following procedure for each activity.

♦ Identify any *hazards*. All hazards should be listed on the Hazard Risk Assessment form (see Box 8.1 for an example).

♦ Assess the *severity* of the risks. The severity of accidents is assessed on a scale from very severe to negligible (see Box 8.2, which shows how to assess the severity of an accident).

♦ Assess the *likelihood* that harm will be done. The likelihood of an accident happening is assessed on a scale from very unlikely to very likely (see Box 8.3, which shows how to assess the likelihood of an accident happening).

♦ Work out the *risk factor*. The risk factor is assessed in terms of a scale that goes from negligible to very severe (see Box 8.4, which shows the Risk Factor table).

Box 8.3 Assessing the likelihood of an accident	
Likelihood	**Situation**
Very unlikely	There is no known history of an accident happening in this situation.
Unlikely	An accident could happen but is unlikely unless there is an unusual sequence of events or failures.
Possible	It could happen in unusual circumstances.
Very likely	It happens often.

Box 8.4 Risk Factor table

Severity of hazard	Likelihood of accident			
	Very unlikely	**Unlikely**	**Possible**	**Very likely**
Very Severe	Moderate	Severe	Severe	Very Severe
Severe	Low	Moderate	Severe	Very Severe
Moderate	Low	Low	Moderate	Severe
Slight	Negligible	Low	Low	Moderate
Negligible	Negligible	Negligible	Low	Moderate

♦ Arrange for the necessary *action* to be taken. Once you have identified the hazards involved, you should then take action to reduce any identified risks (Box 8.5 indicates the type of action that will be required for the different risk factors).

Let us assume, as an example, that you want to take a high angle shot from a scaffold tower.

♦ *Identify any hazards.* Using a scaffold tower to take a high angle shot is classified as 'working at heights', and there are hazards associated with this.

♦ *Assess the severity of the risks.* How many people could be hurt and how badly? In theory someone could fall off the tower and break their neck – potentially a very serious risk.

Box 8.5 Action required for different risk factors

♦ *Very severe.* Someone from the production team must be in charge of all aspects of this activity and take immediate steps to reduce the risk, usually by employing professionals.

♦ *Severe.* Someone from the production team must be in charge of all aspects of this activity and report back on how this activity can be achieved safely.

♦ *Moderate.* Someone from the production team must be in charge of this activity and carry out standard checks and procedures before the activity can take place.

♦ *Low.* There is a risk, but the procedures are in place to minimize it.

♦ *Negligible.* The level of risk is acceptable.

Box 8.6 Completed section of Hazard Risk Assessment form

Activity	If there is a hazard ✔	Severity	Likelihood	Risk factor	Action
Scaffold	✔	Very severe	Very unlikely	Moderate	Production manager to check scaffold

♦ *Assess the likelihood that harm will be done.* If the scaffold tower is legally certified (known as a scaff. cert.) before use, and is erected by trained personnel, then the risk of the scaffold breaking is low, and the likelihood of an accident is very low. Of course, the camera operator must still take considerable care while working on the scaffold.

♦ *Work out the risk factor.* In this case, there is the potential for a very severe accident but, because precautions have been taken, and the likelihood is very unlikely, the risk factor is moderate.

♦ *Arrange for the necessary action to be taken.* In this instance, the production manager must be instructed to check the scaffold.

Box 8.6 shows how to complete the relevant section of the Hazard Risk Assessment form for this particular activity.

Once you have filled in the Hazard Risk Assessment form, you should be aware of all the possible problems. You should then take action to reduce all identified risks. A safe production is a happy one.

9

The schedule

You have done your research and you have been on some successful recces. You are now ready to do a schedule for your production. A filming schedule is a chronological list of what has to be filmed and when.

There are immensely complicated schedules for large factual shoots that involve a lot of travel, or there are straightforward schedules for small-scale productions. The trick is to keep the schedule as clear and simple as possible.

The Working River schedule

This is a straightforward schedule for a short shoot. Box 9.1 shows the schedule that Mark Smith created for his 15-minute factual programme *The Working River*, which was broadcast on a cable channel.

☞ Mark Smith's *Working River* programme is discussed in Chapter 2.

In his budget he allowed for eight days' shooting. This is extravagant by conventional TV standards, but this was his first production. Also he was saving by shooting on DV with no crew costs, so he could afford to go to a number of different locations.

Some details remained provisional until nearer the actual day of the shoot, but well in advance he was able to draw up a broad schedule for each day. This has to be done if you need to book your crew. Mark was the director and cameraman, and he was taking a multiskilled sound recordist. Having completed the schedule, he was then able to book his sound recordist.

As Mark would be editing the programme at home, he was not too worried about creating a postproduction schedule. If you need to book editing with an editor, then you should create a schedule to cover post-production. Nearer the day he could draw up a call sheet, giving more precise details, such as where to meet and directions on how to reach the locations.

Box 9.1 Shooting schedule for *The Working River*

Shooting date	Location	Time	Confirmation or provisional
2 March	Port of London Authority, Gravesend Harbour Crew 'D' Contact . . . Tel. 020 . . .	Call 11.00 Wrap 18.00	Confirmation
3 March	The London Eye Embankment Waterloo	Call 10.00 Wrap 14.00	Confirmation
8 March	Age Exchange Reminiscence Centre 11 Blackheath Village London SE3 Tel. 020 . . .	Call 10.30 Wrap 17.00	Confirmation
15 March	Albany Theatre Douglas Way Deptford London SE8 4AG Tel 020 . . .	To be confirmed Hoping for a.m.	Provisional
17 March	Port of London Authority, Gravesend Harbour Crew 'D' Contact . . . Tel. 020 . . .	To be confirmed Probably late p.m.	Confirmation
20 March	Port of London Authority Charing Cross pier Embankment Contact . . . Tel. 020 . . .	To be confirmed	Provisional
25 March	Port of London Authority Middle Reach Putney Bridge Middle district crew	Call 12.00 Wrap 18.00	Confirmation
31 March	Princess Pocahontas Pleasure Cruise Embankment Pier London	Call 18.00 Wrap midnight or later	Confirmation

> ☞ Postproduction is discussed in Part Three.

Most productions have two schedules. The overall *Critical Path schedule* (see Box 9.2) depends on the duration of your production, and to a certain extent on the budget. Then each day of shooting has a separate *daily schedule*, which can be incorporated into the call sheet.

> ☞ For an example of a call sheet, see Chapter 20.

For a low-budget 'home' production like *The Working River*, where the initial research has been done and a treatment agreed, then a shooting schedule is all that is required. There is no immediate pressure on time, and the editing will be done to get the programme on the air at the date of transmission.

The Night Bus schedule

The Night Bus was a 20-minute documentary for a late-night terrestrial channel, in widescreen, shot entirely on a London night bus. There was no commentary, only the sync. sounds, the words of travellers and location music – for example, from the harmonica-playing bus conductor. This was an atmospheric documentary. The people, the drivers, the sights, the changing scenarios of the different times of night, and the humour all told the story of this underbelly of city life.

The production for this documentary was over an eight-week period. Filming was on DV, with a small team and a tight budget.

Box 9.2 shows a Critical Path schedule. This is the sort of schedule you do right at the beginning of the production. It shows the order in which things have to be done and the deadlines by which they have to be completed. Use it as a template for your production. This schedule is realistic for a small team of two or three, but they might have to work weekends in the last week or so to get everything done.

A Critical Path schedule shows which actions have to be completed by the end of the weeks indicated; if they are not completed, then it will not be possible to go on to the next phase. When you are filling in a schedule, start by working backwards from the end of the last week – here week 8.

There are a few important dates that have to be booked early, depending on what sort of production this is going to be. For broadcast quality, you need to schedule an *online edit* and *sound dub*. These are going to be very costly aspects of your production and need to be booked in advance at a facilities house. In this schedule a private viewing for contributors and their

Box 9.2 Critical Path schedule for *The Night Bus*

	Action	Week 1	Week 2	Week 3	Week 4	Week 5	Week 6	Week 7	Week 8
Preproduction	Treatment	Fri.							
	Schedule		Wed.						
	Budget		Thurs.						
	Content research			Wed.					
	Recce			Wed.					
	Permissions			Deadline					
	Storyboard								
	Book kit								
	Permissions								
Production	Call sheets				Mon.				
	Film schedule			Fri.					
	Filming days				Thurs.–Sun.				
	View/log rushes					Tues.–Thurs.			
	Thank you letters								

Box 9.2 *continued*

	Action	Week 1	Week 2	Week 3	Week 4	Week 5	Week 6	Week 7	Week 8
Postproduction	Paper edit					Mon.–Tues			
	Digitize rushes					Wed.			
	Off-line edit						Mon.–Fri.		
	Write/record commentary							Mon.–Tues.	
	Create titles/credits				Engage graphic designer			Deadline titles	
	Online edit							Fri.	
	Sound dub								Mon.
	Private viewing								Tues.
	Press pack								Thurs.
	Public viewing								Thurs.

families, and work on publicity, are factored in. The broadcaster may help with this, but you still have to do most of the preparation yourself.

☞ For a discussion of an online edit and sound dub, see Chapter 36.

You can add to the schedule any other relevant aspects of the production – for example, you might need to include script development, casting a presenter and read-through time.

10
Storyboard

The important part of a storyboard is the story. It is a way of telling your film story visually, rather like a cartoon strip. The pictures may be pasted onto card and even laminated to withstand constant viewing.

Essentially a storyboard tells the story of your film in small pictures. You do not have to be a good artist. The importance of a storyboard is to see the juxtaposition of shots to tell your story – how each scene or sequence is to be filmed and edited to make your story effective on the screen. Pin men and one-dimensional drawings are quite acceptable.

A storyboard must show:
♦ the position of people in each shot;
♦ the shot size;
♦ any important background element which is essential for the scene;
♦ the important action.

For a drama production the storyboard is created by the director so that all the crew can see exactly how each shot will be framed and how the story holds together. It shows how each shot should look, and how it links with the next shot.

Factual programmes can also benefit from a storyboard, first to show how the factual story will be presented on screen and secondly to show how key sequences will be shot. For example, if your programme is about the future of supersonic flight, then you might want your presenter to stand in front of Concorde, or a bluescreen in order to put a still of Concorde in later. Either way, the framing and sequence of shots are affected by where your reporter stands. This can be worked out most effectively by doing a storyboard.

☞ For an explanation of bluescreen, see Chapter 14.

Storyboard example

Box 10.1 shows an example of the first part of a storyboard for a short drama set on a desert island. Even though it is only a few minutes long, this

Box 10.1 Storyboard example, showing a sequence for a drama

1.	2.	3.	4.
Arial LS of island establishing shot.	Wide shot.	Establishing shot (alternative).	MS/LS of John sitting on beach.
5.	6.	7.	8.
BCU of eyes wide open, spotted something.	MS of John taking a closer look.	WS as he starts running towards sea.	BCU of his feet running in sand.

Box 10.1 continued

9.	10.	11.	Dissolve from shot 11 to shot 13.
WS of him at water's edge.	MS of John using binoculars to check what he has seen.	WS of him as he realizes what he has seen at sea. Starts running towards sea.	Dissolve from him running into the sea to a MS of him with a big grin, sitting on the beach.
		13.	
		MS of him sitting back on the beach with a smile on his face.	

section of the drama has to be carefully storyboarded, to set the right mood and to get the sequence of shots in the right order. The storyboard has to show how the director will handle the castaway's dilemma: there is the possibility of rescue, but also the possibility that the castaway may have to stay on the island forever.

☞ For a full explanation of shot sizes, see Box 14.1.

☞ For an explanation of abbreviations for shot sizes, see Box 14.1.

11
Becoming an interviewer

A television interview is a way of enabling people to give information, facts, views, comments and opinions for your production. It will help your production, and your career, if you become good at interviewing people. This chapter will help you develop interview skills, and suggest ways of setting up successful interviews. It is a good idea to work on interviewing before you actually do it on camera, which is why it comes under preproduction.

The role of the television interviewer

The television interview does not work in the same way as a magazine or newspaper interview, where the personality of the magazine interviewer is important. The magazine reader usually wants to know how the interviewer got on with the subject, and what sort of relationship they had, and what the interviewer thought about the subject. In television the interviewer seeks to avoid the limelight.

Of course, television programmes can be built entirely around the one-to-one celebrity interview. Here the personality of the interviewer is important. Many entertainment programmes rely on contributors interviewed by well-known presenters.

There is, however, no need to employ an expensive presenter in order to make an interesting and watchable interview-based programme, either for broadcasting or as a corporate video. In fact, it is often better for the person who has done the research and the recce to do the actual interview.

 Interview alert
Some people are very boring when they are interviewed. You must find this out during the recce and maybe say no to filming the interview.

A television interview for a factual programme will usually avoid having the interviewer in shot. This puts more emphasis on the contributor. Many factual programmes rely on contributors who have been carefully interviewed to drive the programme.

Do your own interviews

The researcher, director or producer who remains off screen often conducts interviews. It is best to record the questions on tape, so that you can hear them and know what was asked when it comes to editing. Where a programme has a presenter, then the presenter should ask the questions and be in shot. Otherwise it is better for the interviewer to remain out of shot.

☞ For interviewing with a presenter, see Chapter 16.

If you are going to produce, direct or research successful factual programmes, you need to develop a good interview technique. This does not mean that you have to be Jeremy Paxman. On the contrary.

A good interviewing technique means developing a manner and way of talking to people that brings out the best of them, and delivers a high-quality interview for the production. People who are not used to appearing on television can find taking part in an interview a nerve-wracking experience. You do not want to put someone through the experience and then not use the interview.

How to be a good interviewer

To get a good interview, you need to develop a sensitive interviewing technique, but you also need to have good organizational skills, to make sure that the interview takes place as planned.

Organizational skills

Start with the recce. You will almost certainly get a better interview if you can talk to your potential contributor face to face before filming. If that is not possible, then fully brief him or her on the phone beforehand, and satisfy yourself that this will be a worthwhile interview for your production. The programme budgets for digital channels will not run to unused interviews.

♦ Explain where you want the interview to take place and why.
♦ Get the release form signed by the contributor.
♦ Write and confirm the time and date of the interview and the location. I have turned up on too many locations for interviews set up by

someone else to be told by a potential contributor that the interview cannot take place because there was no written confirmation.

♦ Telephone the day before to confirm that everything is all right with the contributor, and that you will definitely be filming the next day. It can be very frustrating, but contributors are in the habit of developing mysterious allergies and illnesses the day before filming. Always telephone to reassure contributors.

Interview techniques

♦ Develop a relaxed approach to interviewees. A stressed contributor = a bad interview.
♦ Write down your questions.
♦ Talk through the subject matter of your interview fully with the contributor before the actual interview.
♦ You are there to help the *contributor* look and sound good on camera. This will, in fact, be to your advantage, because, if your contributor performs well, then your production will benefit.
♦ Go over the sort of questions you are going to ask. Be precise and say you will start by asking this question, and then you will continue with that question.
♦ Mention that you may pick up points for further clarification during the interview. Then the contributor will not be surprised if you politely interrupt or ask a supplementary question.
♦ Give your contributor all the help and encouragement he or she will need to respond to your questions in an informal way, with the aim of getting clear, uncluttered answers and good programme material.
♦ Be a good listener.
♦ Never be rude, even if you are interviewing a serial killer.

☞ Shooting interviews is fully covered in Chapter 14.

Interviewing: post-research checklist

From your point of view it is a waste of time and money to go to the trouble of interviewing someone whom you will not use. After you have researched and found a potential contributor, use the checklist in Box 11.1 to check you have found someone with the necessary criteria.

Box 11.1 Post-research checklist

Will the potential contributor:
- make a valuable contribution to the production?
- be suitable to appear on television (this usually means that his or her visual appearance will not distract from what he or she is saying)?
- be lively and interesting?
- be willing to take part in your production and to sign the release form before you start filming?
- be willing to appear for a very small fee?
- have something new and worthwhile to say that will enhance your story?
- be available when you are available?

Completing preproduction

There is no absolute line between the end of preproduction and the beginning of production. The two flow smoothly into one another, but by now your preproduction should be virtually complete.

It will make your production run more smoothly if you have completed these elements of the production process.

- ◆ You will have written a treatment.
- ◆ You will have developed your idea into a workable programme idea with a story, possible characters and access to your characters and suitable locations.
- ◆ You will have researched and found some major contributors.
- ◆ You will have created a realistic programme budget.
- ◆ You will have got a production team together.
- ◆ You will have done a recce on some locations.
- ◆ You will have checked health and safety considerations on your locations, and prepared Hazard Risk Assessment forms.
- ◆ You will have created a Critical Path schedule.
- ◆ You will have created a storyboard, if appropriate.
- ◆ You will have tuned up your interview skills.

You are ready to move into full-scale production.

Production

PART TWO

Production

12
Factual programme production

Production is the process of shooting your television programme or film. It involves realizing all that hard work you did in preproduction.

Production values depend on many factors and most of them are to do with money. This book sets out to help the filmmaker with a tight budget. The aim is to get the best possible production values using a single camcorder and the best affordable sound kit. But you should aim to build a production team to realize a worthwhile idea.

The production team

In preproduction we looked at all the possible roles on a television production. I always think better results are obtained working in a group rather than entirely on your own. It is a difficult job doing even an interview on your own. You have to set up the camera, ask the questions, change the shot size and do the sound with only two hands. You also have no one to discuss things with, or chew over how things are going, or whether you have just filmed a good interview or a terrible one.

However, modern television budgets dictate that programmes should be made with as few people as possible. A professional crew may be only two people. Typically on a low-budget factual programme there will be:

- ◆ a cameraperson who operates the camera, checks the sound, and does the lighting;
- ◆ a director/producer who does the research, asks the questions, and holds the mic.

☞ For a drama production team, see Chapter 27.

This works in my experience, but it is the minimum team possible to shoot a factual programme. Many independent productions have just two people. Between them they may be fully experienced and multiskilled, and can handle the whole show.

Increasing the team by just one person, a production assistant/researcher to help with everything in the office and on location, is a very good idea. You could occasionally employ a sparks – electrician – to handle a difficult lighting set-up and sort out any electrical problems. For any tricky sound situations like recording music you may need a sound recordist who knows what he or she is doing. I would also add someone to do the editing, unless you want to do that yourself.

Modern productions are very flexible, but an ideal team for a factual production might look like this:

♦ *director/producer*, who instigated the programme and had the original idea;

♦ *cameraperson/assistant producer*, who looks after all the technical requirements of the production, including sound and lights;

♦ *production assistant/researcher*, who does a lot of setting up and original research, and hoovers up all the rest of the work – particularly the copious paperwork that any made-for-the-public television production will generate. This person may also act as the sound recordist on an interview;

♦ *sound recordist*, who may not work full time on this production but can be called in for special sound recordings;

♦ *video editor*, who may be the producer or any other permanent member of the team, or may be an experienced editor called in just to do the editing for this show.

If you are just starting up, then it is almost certainly better not to work on your own, but to have a small dedicated team to spread the workload, and get different perspectives on what is happening.

Your final team may be large, or just two of you, but you will still want to tell your story to the highest possible production standards. You may want to set your film in noisy and very noisy places, and in some dark and dingy places. You will want to shoot beautiful pictures in wonderful locations, or you might want to depict the gritty reality of a subject living in poverty.

You will need some creative production techniques, and where better to start than with the basis of nearly all factual productions – the interview.

13
Preparing for interviews

Interviews are at the heart of almost every factual programme. Get the interviews right, and the programme will be interesting, informative and entertaining. That means being very well prepared for each interview.

Preparation is much more than selecting the best people to appear on your show. You need to do careful research, and then ask the right questions in the right way in order to coax a good performance from your contributors.

You may be talking to someone who has never been interviewed before on television. You want that person to tell his or her story in a coherent, natural way. As an interviewer, you will always have to be creative to obtain a really good performance from a contributor.

You will set up the interview during your research. You may already have honed your interviewing style, but there are still key techniques that you need to employ on the actual day of recording to help things run smoothly and get the best possible interview. You do not want to embarrass yourself and your production by having to go back and do the interview again, because you forgot a vital question, or there was no sound on the tape – it happens. So concentrate on the key techniques and then see Box 13.1 for a vital checklist.

☞ For detailed advice on how to improve your interviewing skills, see Chapter 11.

Key interview techniques
Preparation
♦ Find out as much as possible about your contributor.
♦ Prepare your questions in advance.
♦ Sort out the exact locations where your interview will take place at the recce (see Fig. 13.1) – it is amazing how many directors do not do this. Then they wonder why their interview looks so boring.
♦ Prepare what you are going to say and do on the day to relax and reassure your interviewee that this is much better than going to the dentist – very much better.
♦ Think about what pictures you are likely to need as cutaways.

> **Box 13.1** Interviewer's checklist
>
> ♦ Fully research each contributor.
> ♦ Ask open questions.
> ♦ You will use only a small part of the interview, so you need whole sentences for answers.
> ♦ Be a good listener.
> ♦ Recce the location for the interview, and try and make it reflect the mood and content of the interview.
> ♦ Put your contributor at ease.
> ♦ Keep eye contact.
> ♦ Encourage your contributor to appear to talk naturally, as if the camera was not there.

Fig. 13.1 Interview in Frascati, Italy: use such a beautiful location to the full

☞ For a discussion of cutaways, see Chapter 14.

Ask open questions

You will usually want to cut out your questions and just use the answers. Those answers need to be as comprehensive as possible. Some producers I know say that for most programmes the interviewer should ask no more than three or four carefully chosen 'open' questions.

If you ask a Second World War veteran RAF pilot 'Did you fly Spitfires in the war?', you will get the answer 'Yes I did' or 'No I didn't' – not very useful

for your exciting programme on the origins of the Spitfire aircraft. But if you
ask an 'open' question, then you will definitely get a more useful answer.

An open question is any question that elicits more than a yes-or-no answer.
A question that begins with one of the six W words is an open question:

- **W**ho
- **W**hat
- **W**hen
- **W**here
- **W**hy
- ho**W**

You could prepare your questions to the Second World War veteran pilot
along these lines:

- '*When* did you first fly a Spitfire?'
- '*Where* were you based?'
- '*Why* did you choose to fly fighters and not bombers?
- '*What* was it like flying a Spitfire?'
- '*What* were the advantages when you were fighting enemy aircraft?'
- '*How* did you prepare yourself for a scramble?'
- 'When you look back, *what* is your most enduring memory of that time?'

Open questions allow for longer, more interesting answers. Some answers
may overlap. This is fine, as it gives you more options at the editing stage.

Answer in sentences

To help you edit together the answers, without using intrusive questions, you
want your contributor to give you answers in whole sentences. To achieve
this, you usually have to tell the contributor how you want the answers to
be structured. One way to do this is to say 'Would you mind starting your
answer by including the question', and then give an example.

So the Spitfire pilot might be encouraged to begin his answer to the question 'What was it like flying Spitfires?' with

- 'Flying Spitfires was like . . .', or
- 'I found flying Spitfires . . .', or
- 'Flying Spitfires was rather like driving a Formula One car today. It was
  technically demanding . . .', or:
- 'I found flying Spitfires was technically demanding because it was rather
  like . . .'.

Before the interview starts you may have to help your interviewee compose
the beginning of answers in this way. Don't be worried about doing this. It will
give your interviewee more time to think what he or she really wants to say.

Interview alert

It is always best to tell people what you are going to ask them, unless you are working for a news programme. You may not want to use the exact words you are going to use, but you should outline the topic of each question.

Some experienced interviewees, especially politicians and top people in industry, will insist that you stick to the agreed questions, and just will not answer that difficult question you slip in. If you ever interview royalty, the Palace will insist on the questions being sent in beforehand and absolutely no deviation. Be warned.

Listening

You will never make a good interviewer unless you become a good listener. Only by listening carefully to what the contributor is saying will you be able to formulate a follow-up question that carries the story forward.

♦ Yes, do have prepared questions, but be ready to adapt and move the story forward by asking supplementary questions, which arise out of the interview.

♦ It will help you concentrate on listening to the answers if you look at the contributor all the time, and nod or smile occasionally. But don't overdo the nodding; it can put people off.

♦ The important thing is to let the contributor know that you are listening intently and like what you are hearing. Basically you do not want him or her to stop talking.

♦ Write notes of only one or two words on your pad, as looking down may affect the concentration of the contributor.

♦ If you are not happy about an answer, instead of asking the contributor to do something again, just ask the question in a slightly different way.

♦ Explain what has happened to the contributor if you have to stop for any technical reason. It is usually the battery that gives out, but it could be that an aircraft goes over and you have to do the question again because of the noise.

Eye contact

Contributors are often unsure that what they are saying is of value for a television programme. When interviewing, keep your eyes very firmly on the contributor and concentrate hard on listening to the answers. Your contributor gauges the value of what he or she is saying by looking at you and judging your response. If you look bored or start filling in your expenses form, the interview will die and so could your production.

Encourage the contributor that the answers are really interesting, and valuable, by nodding and smiling. Maintain eye contact at all times. Try only to glance at your notes. Do not grunt or laugh, or keep saying yes or no.

It is important to leave a long moment of silence after the contributor has stopped speaking. This helps in the editing, and may encourage the contributor to continue talking without you asking another question.

The trick is to convince your contributor that he or she is being of considerable interest to you, and then it will seem that the camera is not really there.

Sensitive interview scenario

Television interviews can often be on sensitive issues. With any interview it is important to follow the key interview techniques, but with sensitive issues you need to be more careful how you phrase the questions and how you follow up the answers. You are involved in making a 15-minute video about the high rate of teenage pregnancies in the UK. The Prime Minister has commented that parenthood for under 16s can lead to 'shattered lives and blighted futures'. The programme is aimed at teenage parents and will offer help and advice. It is essentially sympathetic, but needs to raise all the issues. You have been asked to find and interview teenage mothers and fathers to be.

Production notes

The contributors for this programme will probably be unused to television and may be quite shy about appearing. You will have to obtain permission from their parents if they are under 18 years old. Getting hold of contributors on issues like this is never easy. You may have to do a lot of persuasion to convince everyone that you are working on a video project that may be beneficial to them.

Reassure your interviewees that you are making the programme in their interest. You will not destroy their reputation; you just want to hear their story.

Questions

You will need to formulate your questions carefully. Some teenage parents will be very happy to be expecting a baby and will tell their story in an easy and relaxed way. Others may be unsure of what the future holds. They may have very little support. This could turn to anger or fear if you ask an insensitive question. Not only would this be intrusive and unhelpful, it would scupper the whole interview. You probably went to a lot of trouble to get an interview of this sort. Make sure you do not throw away this opportunity. Prepare well and be sympathetic to the needs and personality of your contributor.

Question order

The order in which you ask questions is important too. In the above scenario, it will be prudent not to ask as your first question 'How did you get pregnant?' This will be a sensitive issue, as it is unlikely to have been a planned conception. Much better to ask 'How do you feel about being a mother?'

Or you could take a sideways approach for your first question: 'Where were you when you first heard that you were pregnant?' This puts the emphasis on a place and time rather than on the actual business of being a prospective mother or father.

14
Shooting interviews

This is the culmination of all your research and hard work during preproduction. You have persuaded exciting people to take part in your programme, and you are now going to interview them on camera.

There are good and bad ways of doing most things and shooting interviews is no different. Sometimes the not-so-standard ways may work in the context of a programme, but you need to know the classic interview techniques and then you can experiment.

Setting up

♦ *Contributor*. Sit or stand the contributor in the location where you want to do the interview. Sitting is more relaxing. The interviewer/director should run over questions while the camera is being set up.

♦ *Tripod*. Interviews always look better filmed with the camera mounted on a tripod rather than hand-held. Set up the camera on the tripod in the chosen location. Make sure the camera is level, not looking down or up at the contributor.

♦ *Eyeline*. Set up the interviewer's chair as close as possible to the tripod and the camera lens. Make sure the interviewer's eyeline is at exactly the same height as the camera lens, and at the eyeline of the contributor.

♦ *White balance*. Always do a white balance in the exact location of the interview.

☞ For an explanation of white balance, see Chapter 24.

♦ *Test the mic*. Always do a sound check to make sure the mic. works. Either use a personal mic. – try and hide it out of shot behind a lapel – or use a rifle mic.

♦ *Focus*. Focus on the *eyes*, not on the nose or mouth.

♦ *The viewfinder*. Always check the position of the subject through the viewfinder. Look *around* the edges of the frame. Make sure there is nothing unsightly in the frame. Make sure there isn't a part of the background apparently sticking out of the interviewee's head. Check the contributor is not wearing anything that might be distracting, such as a striped jacket that could 'strobe' – cause a zebra effect – in the camera.

♦ *Shot size.* It's normal to have three prearranged shot sizes for an interview. A close-up (CU), a medium close-up (MCU) and a medium shot or mid-shot (MS) are typical (see Box 14.1). Start with an MS and change to an MCU during the second question, then go to the CU for question three. If the interview is getting interesting or the contributor is revealing something very personal, or particularly relevant, zoom in vision to the CU – but practise this first. The director/interviewer must allow time while asking each question for the cameraperson to change the shot size.

♦ *Look at the interviewer.* Ask the interviewee to look only at you and address all his or her answers directly to you. This means he or she will look just to the left or right of the camera lens, depending on which side you are sitting. This is the ideal position in the frame for an interview, as it shows a full face without the interviewee looking directly at camera, which would be 'cheesy'.

Shot size matters

One of the really big differences between a professional looking well-shot interview and something just cobbled together is the framing of the shots. You might think it is easy just to look through the viewfinder and make sure the contributor is in the frame. To obtain that professional look your shot sizes need to conform to the standard framing for each size of shot.

A selection of shot sizes has been developed that fit the TV frame naturally and can be edited together in a way that makes sense visually. This helps the viewer deconstruct the image and pick up on content.

Shot sizes are labelled to show their relationship to shooting a person. It is easier if you imagine you are filming a person standing up and wearing a suit and tie. Shot sizes are generally referred to by their abbreviations (see Box 14.1).

♦ A *big close-up* (BCU) shows just the face, cutting off some of the forehead or part of the chin, or both.

♦ A *close-up* (CU) is the person's face with the bottom of the frame along the line of the shoulders, just below the knot of a tie.

♦ A *medium close-up* (MCU) is slightly wider and the bottom of the frame runs just under the line of the top pocket of a jacket – sometimes known as the top pocket shot.

Box 14.1 Shot sizes

BCU
Big close-up

CU
Close-up

MCU
Medium close-up

MS
Medium shot
or
Mid-shot

Box 14.1 *continued*

MLS
Medium long shot

LS
Long shot

VLS
Very long shot

♦ A *medium shot* or *mid-shot* (both MS) cuts off at the waist, whether the person is sitting down or standing up.
♦ A *medium long shot* (MLS) cuts off a standing or walking figure around the knees.
♦ A *long shot* (LS) shows the person in full length, with the feet clearly in frame.
♦ A *very long shot* (VLS) shows the person or people quite small in the frame, with more dominance given to the setting.

Other standard shot sizes include:

♦ A *very big close-up* (VBCU) shows a part of the face, such as the mouth, or eyes, or even just one eye. This is popular with music video directors, and for post-modern looking documentaries.

♦ A *wide shot* (WS) is a wide angle of the whole set, or the scene being filmed. To get a wide shot that really looks wide you will need either a special wide angle lens, or to place the camera quite far back from the scene.

Cutaways

Cutaways are pictures that you can cut to during an interview so that the interview is not just one long talking head. Cutaways give you the ability in editing to cut away from the contributor at the point where you want to edit for content. They are preferably shots of what the contributor is talking about.

Whatever you shoot, make sure your cutaways are of something relevant. For example, if you are interviewing a cook, shoot pictures of the cook working in a kitchen.

Cutaways make the interview more interesting and therefore create better television. Frankly, unless you are interviewing a celebrity, you absolutely must have cutaways.

The most common mistake inexperienced directors make is not to shoot enough cutaway material. You need much more than you think. Construct cutaways in visual sequences. You need different size shots within each sequence, so that the sequences will cut together.

Shooting cutaways

♦ *Faces.* When filming the action shots of someone at work, or making something, remember to shoot close-ups of the contributor's face concentrating on what he or she is doing. This will make it possible in the edit to condense time. Someone making a wooden model might take 10 minutes or more in real time, but by cutting to the face this real time can be reduced considerably.

♦ *Shooting ratio.* Only shoot what you need. A contributor who is not a main player in the programme may be on screen for less than two minutes. There is absolutely no need to shoot more than a maximum of 10 minutes' interview with this person.

♦ *Cut.* Don't say 'cut' too soon at the end of a question, or particularly at the end of a sequence of action. You may need plenty of picture time to do a mix or other visual effect.

Box 14.2 Creative cutaways

I interviewed the famous Italian designer Alberto Alessi. Among many things for the kitchen, he has designed a whistling kettle and a squirrel nutcracker. He is seen here blowing the whistling part of the kettle. These shots were used in the opening action sequence to his interview.

♦ *Do the interview first.* Film the interview first, before you shoot related action. You will have a much better idea of what to film for cutaways after you have heard what the contributor has to say in the interview. Then you will know what extra footage may be needed to illustrate the interviews.

♦ *Wrap.* 'It's a wrap' is film lingo for 'that is the end of shooting for today'. It is a very final statement, which all crews and film technicians understand implicitly from the very first syllable. When it seems all the filming at a location is finished, don't immediately say 'it's a wrap'. Take a moment to think 'what have I forgotten?' Then check everything: your recce notes, the release form, the name and address of the interviewee. Finally, check with the camera operator that you have actually got sound and vision on tape. It is amazing how many people come back from an interview with no sound and just mute pictures.

Scenario 1

You are working on a documentary about ancient sites around Britain. You are making films around the country and you have arrived at Glastonbury in Somerset. The Tor is famous as an ancient site. You have set up an interview on the Tor and you need a variety of different shot sizes and angles to illustrate what the contributor is saying (see Box 14.3). You will also need shots of the interview that are wide enough so that the viewer cannot see lip sync. (see the couple framed in the archway in Box 14.3).

Scenario 2

You are working on a travel show for young people. You are going to interview Simon. In his gap year he travelled around the world and worked for a charity in India. What pictures are you going to use as cutaways to illustrate that journey to India?

Difficult. You can't just take off and go to India to get pictures. But think laterally.

♦ *Idea 1: stills.* Simon is bound to have some still photos of his journey and of his work with the charity. You can use some of those stills. If you are filming the interview on location remember to take the stills while you are there. Then film them against a flat neutral background on the floor, or propped up on a table against a wall. Film close-ups of people or buildings within the still picture. This is cheaper and easier than going to a rostrum camera.

Box 14.3 Glastonbury Tor

Try and shoot as many different angles as you can.

WS of Tor with dingle-dangle

MS of Tor

Postmodern WS

Box 14.3 *continued*

CU of Tor

Non-lip-sync. WS

♦ *Idea 2: bought-in pictures.* This is the term used for any video material that comes from an outside source. Talk to the charity Simon worked for. It is probably a large one like Oxfam and will have a publicity office. It is very likely that it will be able to supply you with moving video footage of the work it does in India. This may not be entirely appropriate but it may get you out of a hole. Good quality video footage from a recognized film library is very expensive, and probably not affordable on a low-budget programme.

♦ *Best solution: use pictures from both ideas.* Use some still pictures from Simon's collection and some footage from the charity. Ideally you would have talked to Simon before he went on his trip, and asked him to video his own footage of his journey, so that you would have this to use as

Fig. 14.1 Taj Mahal

cutaways. Beware that amateur video may not be very well shot, and you will only be able to use small sections.

If you are going to use a picture of a very famous building such as the Taj Mahal, make sure you have at least one shot that is the most obvious one, because this is what many viewers will expect. By all means shoot as many different angles as you can, but famous monuments are often only recognized from one memorable angle by people who have not been there. Television uses pictures as shorthand. The classic shot of the Taj Mahal in Fig. 14.1 tells everyone instantly that you mean India. You are not shooting a documentary on the Taj Mahal. You are just suggesting that this was part of the journey.

Filming interviews alert

You or the editor will rue the fact if you do not shoot enough action pictures of your contributor at the time. Always shoot more pictures than you think you need. Remember to shoot close-ups of faces and objects – it may take extra time, but it is cheaper and less embarrassing than going back for a reshoot.

Bluescreen

Using bluescreen involves shooting the interview against a blue curtain or a blue background. In postproduction the blue background is replaced by moving pictures of the director's choice. These pictures are often relevant to the subject of the interview and give an extra dimension to the interview.

With bluescreen, you do not have to send your reporter to Los Angeles to do a story on the Oscars. You can put her in a small studio specially designed for the purpose with all blue floor and walls. Modern sophisticated bluescreen studios allow the director to cut between close-ups and long shots.

Carefully selected pictures of Los Angeles will replace the blue and the reporter will appear actually to be there, in the heart of the city. She can even walk around and sit down on a bench on Sunset Boulevard!

This technique is also known as Chromakey. It is an effective and inexpensive way of adding production value to an interview. Carry a light blue background with you on location, and it is possible to shoot blue screen anywhere. A large blue sheet is perfectly adequate. Both the subject and the sheet need to be lit carefully to avoid highlights and hot spots.

Also remember that, if your interviewee is wearing blue jeans and a blue denim jacket, this blue will become part of the blue background that will be replaced. The results will be amusing, but may not be what you had in mind. During postproduction the software replaces all the blue it finds in the interview picture to create a composite image of the subject, with pictures overlaid behind the subject.

Incidentally, any colour can be chosen as the background to be overlaid. It tends to be blue for television and green for movies. I have never found anyone who can provide a satisfactory answer as to why this is.

☞ For more on bluescreen, see Chapter 36.

15
Lighting and sound for interviews

The easiest way to film anyone is to put him or her outside in broad daylight on a bright but overcast day. The light is not too strong to dazzle the contributor, and the reflected light from the sky provides nicely balanced lighting for the shot. This location may not, however, be ideal for sound, as there may be aircraft in the area, a busy road nearby, a disco or some other intrusive ambient sound.

Of course, you cannot just wait for the weather to shoot your interview, and you cannot ask Heathrow to suspend all flights for half an hour – unless you are Steven Spielberg.

So it is important that you know the basics on how to light an interview and which mics to use.

☞ For more sophisticated lighting set-ups, see Chapter 18 on three-point lighting, and Chapter 31 on lighting for drama.

Lighting for interviews

Digital cameras are very good at showing an image in low light level conditions.

As with all photography, clever use of light can enhance the image produced by the camera and therefore enhance your interview. You can use light to create a suitable mood sympathetic to the topic of the interview, or to 'lift' a face. But lighting a subject takes time, and you must have suitable lights and a power source.

Daylight

Daylight on a bright day coming through a plain glass window has the full range of colours in the light spectrum, and therefore gives you can excellent picture. For a standard interview with a digital camera you should position your contributor in a comfortable chair with a window to one side of the chair, but not behind it. The trick is to try and position the chair so that the daylight from the window illuminates the face and upper body of the subject. You need good diffuse daylight. Bright direct sunlight will be too bright for the camera and should be avoided. White net curtains are useful for diffusing sunlight.

This set-up will offer the camera a clear well-lit subject, but it may look rather flat through the viewfinder. Adjust the iris to compensate. Open the iris for more light and close it for less. Turn the subject slightly towards the source of light, or further away if it is too 'hot'.

> ☞ For greater detail on the manual use of the iris/aperture,
>
> see Chapter 24 on production equipment.

Lighting alert

- ♦ Don't sit your interviewee in front of a bright window or white wall. If you do you will get a very dark underlit face.
- ♦ Don't sit your interviewee with his or her back directly against a wall. Move the subject out at least a metre from the background.

Available artificial light

If there is very little daylight in the room, you will have to use 'available' artificial light. Close the curtains so that no daylight comes into the room. On this set-up you are going to use only the artificial lights in the room.

Office lighting

- ♦ If there is overhead strip lighting of the type found in offices, then you may be able to sit your subject in his or her usual chair and shoot the interview using the available light. Strip lights give a cold light, but it is usually consistent and casts few shadows.
- ♦ Always check very carefully through the viewfinder and ask the subject to move slightly to try and get more light on the face. For a quick interview, it will probably be alright.

Domestic lighting

- ♦ A room in a house is normally lit with domestic lighting, which is 'warm'. It can make interviewees look as though they have recently been to the Bahamas if it is too warm, so be careful.

- ◆ To get a brighter light, take light shades off lamps.
- ◆ Only use the overhead light as an overall source of lighting. It casts nasty shadows and makes people's faces look older and craggier. Your subject will not be flattered if you just use an overhead ceiling light.
- ◆ Put a side lamp next to your subject; it can be in or out of shot. Ask if you can take one from another room if there is not one in the room.
- ◆ Interviews generally look better on camera if the main light source can be seen to come from one side.

White balance tip

Do the white balance *after* you have set up the lights, not before. By pressing the white balance button, the camera will automatically adjust for the colours and the amount of light it requires for that particular location.

Film lighting

There is one way to be certain that your contributor is going to look extremely good on camera and that is to use film lights. You can hire a basic film light kit quite reasonably, which is usually three or four *redheads* (see Fig. 15.1). A professional camera crew will always carry three or four redheads.

A redhead is an 800-watt light mounted on a stand, which can be used in a 'flood' position or as a more focused hard light in a 'spot' position. This is the equivalent of eight domestic 100-watt light bulbs, so be very careful how many you plug into a typical domestic circuit. Always use an RCD – Residual Current Detector – as a safety precaution, and turn on film lights one at a time.

For perfect interview lighting, do a three-point lighting set-up. This can take some time to set up

Fig. 15.1 Redhead

Fig. 15.2 Film light with blue gel

to obtain the optimum balance, and many locations do not require it. You can obtain very good results if you use one redhead with blue gel as a 'fill light' (see Fig. 15.2), with the main light source coming from bright daylight through a window.

👉 For full details of a three-point lighting set-up, see Chapter 18.

Using a fill light

Position the subject's chair so that the main light source – a window – is on the right. Place a redhead out of shot on the left and raise the stand so the light is illuminating the left-hand side of the head and shoulders.

You will probably need the 'flood' position, but look through the viewfinder to check that the shadows on the face have been literally 'filled in' with light. Ask a helper to 'flash' the redhead – turn it on and off while you are looking through the viewfinder. You will see exactly how the redhead can 'fill in' the right side of the face.

♦ You now have to match the colour temperature of the redhead with the colour temperature of daylight. You do this with a blue filter or blue gel. This allows more blue light and less orange/red wavelengths to reach the subject. A blue gel is heat resistant plastic that you can buy in a roll. Ask for a medium density gel suitable for redheads.

♦ Attach the blue gel to the barn doors of the redhead with clips or pegs. It should cover the lens of the light completely with a gap all round the edges for the heat to escape.

> ### Lighting alert
> **!**
>
> Black or dark surfaces absorb light. The *Observer* newspaper's famous portrait photographer Jane Bown shoots her portraits against a black background using available light only, which gives an impressive Rembrandt look to the portraits. For television pictures, we usually expect to see the location where the interviewee is sitting, so darker surfaces have to be used with care.

Fig. 15.3 News interview

Lighting news interviews

There is another sort of interview where you cannot realistically do any of the above set-up. This is a news interview (see Fig. 15.3). The aim here is to get the interview with the subject in any light conditions whatsoever, as long as he or she is visible. Many news crews use a small film light attached to the top of the camera. Often it is the sound that causes the most difficulty. You just have to do the best you can and make sure you bring back some useable footage.

Location sound for interviews

It goes without saying that sound in an interview is vitally important. I have seen too many interviews with good pictures that were rendered useless because of lousy sound or even no sound.

Make sure you concentrate as much on getting the sound right as you do on getting the picture looking good. The two most important things you can do are to choose a good microphone, and then place it in the right position.

The right mic.

There are four main types of mic. you can use for an interview.

♦ rifle mic., hand-held or at the end of a boom/fishpole;
♦ personal or lapel mic.;
♦ radio mic.;
♦ stick mic., as used by a presenter.

Whichever mic. you are using, you need to be very careful that you do not pick up wind noise or handling noise.

Rifle mic.

A rifle mic. (see Fig. 15.4) is a very useful all purpose mic. to use on location – for example, Sennheiser MKH416 or similar. These mics are directional, and, as the name suggests, you point the barrel of the mic. towards the sound source.

Rifle mics are very sensitive to handling and wind noise. The mic. can be protected by mounting it in a cradle that allows you to handle and move it without getting 'mic. rattle'. The cradle is then put inside a plastic basket windshield to reduce wind noise. The basket can be further protected with a long-haired cover, which makes it ideal for exterior shoots.

The rifle mic. has many advantages.

♦ It can be used in a variety of situations.
♦ It is light and easy to handle.
♦ It is usually already rigged and therefore immediately available for action.
♦ It is often preferred for interviews because it is a directional mic.,

Fig. 15.4 Rifle mic.

and, if used in the correct way, can lose a lot of the extraneous sounds that can spoil a good interview. But do no expect it to filter out low traffic rumble or aircraft noise.

For an interview, you point the barrel of the rifle mic. at the mouth of the contributor – not the top of the head or the chin, but the source of sound – the mouth. The mic. should be positioned above the head, pointing towards the mouth and just out of shot at the top of the frame. Or it can be positioned below waist level pointing at the mouth and just out of shot at the bottom of the frame.

Personal mic.

A personal mic (see Fig. 15.5) is a small clip-on mic. that can be attached to a shirt, lapel or collar or hidden under a necktie. Sometimes it is better to use sticky tape to make sure the mic. is secure and will not move around. Personal mics are prone to handling noise from body movement or rubbing against clothing. Synthetic fibres may be particularly tricky and can even set up a static charge that affects the mic. They vary in characteristics and in operation, so always check before recording. Usually they are omni-directional and can be rigged pointing up or down. It is best to get to know just how sensitive your personal mic. is and where is the best position to place it. A personal mic. has a cable, which is either attached to a portable sound mixer or goes straight into the camera, where the sound level can be adjusted with controls on the side of the camera.

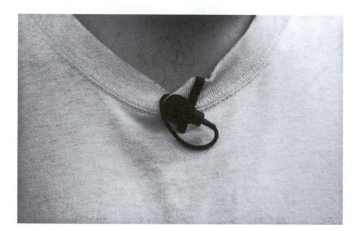

Fig. 15.5 Personal mic.

Fig. 15.6 Radio mic. on lapel

Radio mic.

There are many types of mic. that can be fitted with a radio transmitter. This is very useful for presenters or contributors moving around within range of the radio mic. – usually about 50 metres.

The most usual system for contributors is to rig a personal mic. on the lapel (see Fig. 15.6) with a cable to the transmitter out of shot in a pocket, on a belt (see Fig. 15.7), or attached to the body with sticky tape under the clothes. Attached to the transmitter is a short aerial, which has to hang down

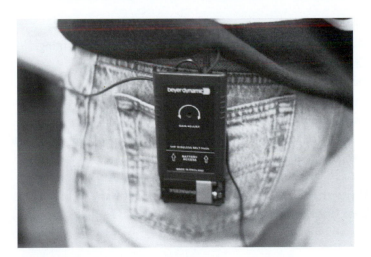

Fig. 15.7 Radio transmitter on back pocket

as straight as possible. The sound is picked up by a receiver connected to the sound mixer, or sometimes attached to the camera.

Always use the best alkaline batteries to power radio mics and change them regularly. You do not want to be let down by batteries in the middle of an interview. Radio mics are expensive and it may be better to hire them when necessary. Always check the mic. is working properly and at its stated range before leaving the hire facility, or handing over cash.

Stick mic.

A presenter who wants to talk to contributors often uses a 'stick mic.' (see Fig. 15.8). This is a robust, hand-held mic that does not 'rattle' and is linked by a strong cable to the camera. It looks the business on camera, but it has a very short range, and must be held just under the chin for best results.

Fig. 15.8 Stick mic.

☞ For further explanation on using mics, see Chapter 24.

Shooting interviews essentials

❖ Make your contributor look attractive with subtle lighting.
❖ Check that the mic. works.
❖ Do a white balance on set after lighting.
❖ Use three sizes of shot.
❖ Ask open questions.
❖ Check that you have the interview recorded on tape with good sound before you leave the location.
❖ Do as many cutaways of the subject as you can.
❖ Write thank-you letters as soon as you get back to base.
❖ Look at your rushes as soon as possible.
❖ For editing interviews, see Chapter 34.

16
Interviewing with a presenter

Working with a presenter gives you more possibilities and options at the editing stage but it takes longer to do the interview. You will have to pay a presenter a daily rate, and pay for his or her board and lodging if you are away on location.

Preparation

As the person who has set up the interview, you will need to brief the presenter about the person to be interviewed. This may mean providing background notes and bibliographic material about the interviewee. It will certainly mean providing the main questions. A good presenter will be able to formulate supplementary questions and pick up on points as the interview goes on. An accurate and comprehensive brief is important, so that the presenter feels confident he or she can handle all the answers, and help the interviewee to respond in a natural and interesting way.

You have two choices with a presenter.

♦ You can film the presenter in vision with the contributor, as a two-shot.
♦ You can film the interview with the presenter asking the questions out of vision, and then film the presenter repeating the questions when the contributor has left. These are known as reverse questions.

Presenter in vision with contributor

If the presenter is going to be in vision with the contributor, then you will be aiming to film them together as a two-shot. But you will also need single shots of the presenter and the contributor.

♦ Your presenter will typically have a stick mic. that he or she will thrust in the face of the poor interviewee. Try to keep the use of the mic. as subtle as possible.

- The cameraperson will go into single shots of presenter and contributor when appropriate, but this will become a difficult interview to edit.
- Cutaway possibilities will be limited. This means you really have to invent some cutaways in order to give yourself a chance to edit down the interview.
- During the interview the director can look for objects that are being demonstrated or handled, or anything that can be filmed later as a cutaway.
- You may ask your camera operator to go hand-held and 'follow the action' for something like a 'live' event.
- Write down at least two questions that the presenter can deliver again in a single shot. Yes, definitely write them down on a pad, as you will not remember them, although you will think you can.
- Other ideas include taking two or more wide shots making sure the presenter's and contributor's lips cannot be seen clearly. This is known as 'not in lip sync.' and any useful sound can be laid over the shot. Lip sync. means that vision and sound are coordinated exactly. If they are not, the viewer will see that the words and picture do not match.
- Discuss with your cameraperson how the interview has gone. You may find there were parts of it not covered particularly well. You can always ask the contributor to do an answer again in a single shot.

Presenter out of vision

You may be making a documentary where you want your presenter to ask the questions, but you largely want to see the contributors on their own without the presenter in vision. The advantage of a presenter asking the questions is that you can use the sound of the questions in the edited programme. This allows more flexible structuring of the programme.

Occasionally you can show the presenter in vision if it seems appropriate, but you are not limited by the presenter always being at every interview. There may be some interviews where your presenter is not able to be there to ask the questions. In this case, you could dub them on later, and you will have the continuity of one voice.

When you film the interview, you will need to shoot 'noddies' and 'reverse' questions with the presenter. These will be very useful in the editing.

Noddies

Noddies are silent shots of the presenter nodding or just slightly moving his or her head or even just looking thoughtful. They are used in the edit as cutaways. You will have seen these in news and current affairs programmes. I think noddies should be used only in an emergency, because they expose the fact that you do not have enough genuine cutaways. *In extremis* you can also shoot close-ups of the subject's hands, or the presenter's hands, to use as extra noddies. Frankly these usually make me squirm, but occasionally it is all you can do to create a cutaway.

Shooting reverse questions

Reverse questions are different. These are pictures of the presenter asking the exact questions as if to the contributor, and can help to make the interview more interesting by introducing the presenter in vision. They also work well as cutaways, and as ways of changing the subject or moving on to another topic. Also it is a way of using a shortened or more appropriate question, because you can rewrite it according to the answer which you will have already filmed.

- Make sure you have finished the interview and ask the contributor to leave the location, or at least to go and have a cup of tea.
- Move the interview chair to a position with a different background from that of the interview. You should not have to move it far. If you have set up lights, move the chair as little as possible so that you do not have to do a new lighting set-up. It can be just a question of changing one or two items in the background of the interview set, such as changing a hanging picture.
- Now set up the tripod, camera and sound to film your presenter sitting in the chair and asking the questions.
- The presenter must look to camera the opposite way to the interview. If the contributor is looking to camera right, then your presenter must look to camera left to preserve the fiction that he or she is actually asking the questions at the same time as the interview is taking place. Nobody believes this anymore, but you still have to stick with the convention, otherwise the viewer will be disorientated. Try and match the shot size as well.
- Now that your presenter is sitting down in the right place and looking to the correct side of camera, you can read out the questions that were asked. The presenter will repeat them as if he or she was asking them at the time of the interview. A good presenter will remember the inflection of the voice and the way each question was asked. Note it is up to the producer/director to have written down the questions.

Using a presenter to do interviews has advantages, but there are also disadvantages, mainly to do with costs. If you have to travel some distance or abroad to film interviews, it will certainly be cheaper to do the interviews yourself, unless you can persuade the presenter to become the sound recordist and assistant producer as well. Now that's a good idea!

17

Vox pops

Vox pops are a useful, if rather overused, programme tool. The idea is to ask a number of people one question about a topic. Edited together, the answers become a short, effective straw poll of views from a variety of different people about this particular topic.

This is not a representative or scientifically selected cross section of the general public, but it can be a useful way to set up a topic for discussion in a television programme. Vox pops derive from the Latin *vox populi*, meaning voice of the people.

Setting up

♦ *The question.* Choose a suitable 'open' question. You definitely do not want just yes-and-no answers for vox pops.

♦ *Avoid bias.* Be careful not to ask an obviously biased question such as 'Why do you think it is wrong to grow GM food crops?'

♦ *Aim for variety.* Phrase your question in such a way to get a variety of responses: 'What are your views on the growing of GM crops?'

♦ *Aim to get several responses from each person.* Ask the question in a different way if your first question does not get a very good response. 'Where do you stand on the GM crops issue?' If you are in a farming area why not try: 'Would you grow GM crops?' This way you should get a variety of lively replies.

♦ *Location.* Select where you are going to ask your questions very carefully. Think about the type of people who are likely to have strong views on your chosen topic. If the topic is the high cost of petrol, then a garage might be a good place to start. To balance the views of motorists, find some pedestrians and cyclists in another location.

Filming

♦ *Crew.* You need a crew of at least two people: one to operate the camera and the other to ask the questions and operate the mic. Use a stick mic. with a windshield.

- *Shot size.* Select a shot size suitable for your topic – probably a MCU. Remember one size fits all. You want all shots the same size.
- *Look both ways.* To be able to cut together a good mix of comments, film the interviewees looking to camera left and to camera right alternately.
- *Safety.* Remember that you must not cause an obstruction on the pavement with a tripod, or set up a potential hazard with trailing cables.
- *Be polite.* Nobody will talk to you if you are rude.
- *Introduce yourself.* Explain briefly who you are and why you are there. Ask people if they would mind taking part in filming for a particular production, then immediately ask the question. As you are not naming people, you do not need written consent, but they must agree verbally to take part.
- *Instant start.* Start the camera recording before you start talking to a likely victim. Some of the best material comes very early in a vox pop interview. You might get something humorous too, which is always a bonus.
- *Location.* Choose a suitable location where there are going to be lots of people. Outside a station or in a shopping area is often a good bet. If it is too noisy, try a little further down the road in a quieter street, or near a car park. Traffic or train noise could ruin your best comments.
- *Persevere.* Doing vox pops can be very dispiriting. Sometimes very few people agree to take part. It is cold and then it starts to rain. Don't give up. Try and generate some interest in the topic you are asking about – a few visual aids can be handy here. Give each location plenty of time to get going.
- *Timing.* Before work in the early morning and after work would seem obvious times to catch people, but it is not always a good time. People are in a hurry and may not always want to stop and talk. Lunch hour is better or Saturday morning.
- *Editing.* Vox pops are normally set up by commentary introducing the question. The responses are cut alternately between those looking camera left and camera right. You cannot cut a MCU looking to camera left with another MCU looking to camera left. (It is possible to flip the frame in the digital editing process but it is safer to get it right on the rushes).
- *Length of response.* You should aim for an edited sequence of one to two minutes, unless the answers are especially riveting.

Broadcasting

Vox pops should never be presented as a scientific or representative sample. Vox pops are a selection of views and opinions that can give an indication of how some people think, and that is about all.

Use vox pops as a friendly, casual and rather relaxed way of introducing a topic or getting some different perspectives. Keep it light-hearted and nobody will think the vox pops are an attempt to draw any conclusions about what the nation as a whole thinks about a topic.

18
Three-point lighting

The basic lighting plot for a person, or people, in a particular location is the three-point lighting plan (Box 18.1). This makes it the ideal way to light an interview or a dialogue scene with two actors in drama. It can be set up quickly and uses three lamps. Three-point lighting is so called because it uses three lights from three different points to illuminate a subject:

♦ the key light
♦ the fill light
♦ the back light

The key light

The key is the main light to illuminate the face and body of the subject. It is placed in front of the subject, but offset and slightly raised.

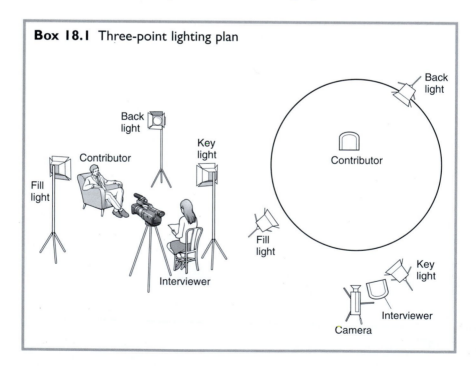

Box 18.1 Three-point lighting plan

We are used to seeing people lit from above by the sun, or by overhead lights, or from the side by a window or side light. Three-point lighting is a way of making a subject look as though he or she is lit naturally.

Lighting that is seen to be coming principally from the side and is slightly raised typically offers the best and most natural look for an interview.

♦ To light one person the key should be at an angle to the camera. It should shine into the eyes of the subject, and should be raised above the eyeline. The subject will want to have his or her eyes lit tastefully, but will not want to be dazzled. If the key is too high there will be dark shadows under the eyes.

♦ Getting the key light set correctly takes a little time at first – check for highlights and hot spots on the subject. If there are a few hot spots on the face the best way to deal with them is to use a dab of make-up powder to stop the shine.

♦ Lighting for interviews is about subtlety and restrained effects. Overlit subjects do not look as though they are in a naturalistic setting. This is not *Top of the Pops*!

♦ Use pegs or clips to stretch scrim (French tissue paper) over the lamp to create a softer light. You can use it over half the light for an even subtler effect.

♦ Adjust the intensity of the light using the spot/flood adjustment.

♦ Remember you are lighting for the camera, so keep looking through the viewfinder to check how the subject looks, and at all times liaise with the camera operator.

♦ Restrict any spillage from the lights by using the barn doors (four metal shutters to restrict the light – see Fig. 18.1), or a flag. A flag is a small metal square with a short pole that looks like a flag and can be attached to a lamp or lamp stand to stop a shaft of light reaching the subject.

♦ Digital video cameras are very sensitive to light, and work well in low light conditions. Don't flood the set with unnecessary light.

Fig. 18.1 Barn doors

The fill light

The aim of the fill light is to 'fill in' the darker areas that the key has not reached and to reduce contrast.

♦ The fill light should be a soft, diffused light. It can also be reflected light. By putting scrim over a lamp you are effectively increasing the size of the light source and creating a softer light.

♦ The fill-light intensity is typically about half that of the key light through the viewfinder.

♦ To reduce the intensity of the light, use scrim, or a diffuser, or move the light further away.

♦ The fill light is placed on the other side of the camera to the key and is as close to the camera as possible.

♦ Make sure the fill light does not show up more of the subject's face than the key light. This will not give good modelling of the face.

The back light

♦ The main purpose of the back light is to illuminate the back of the subject to create depth and solidity to the appearance of the subject(s). Also to give a lighting contrast between foreground and background. This gives a 3D effect and depth to your picture.

♦ In practice this means illuminating the back of the subject. This gives a 'glow' or highlight to the hair of the subject, and creates a pleasing effect.

♦ The intensity of the back light varies according to the subject. A woman with long black hair needs more light, and a bald man needs less.

♦ The back light is most effective if placed exactly behind the subject. This is not usually possible on location, so a compromise is necessary and it is positioned to one side.

♦ You can always make the light softer with scrim or a diffuser.

Check through the viewfinder that the back light is actually creating the effect you are looking for. Ask an assistant to 'flash' it – turn it on and off – to see there is a difference when it is on. It may need further adjustment.

Reflector

A reflector is one of the most useful pieces of equipment you can have in your lighting kit. It is used to reflect light from the sun or another light source onto your subject.

It can be a large piece of white polystyrene, which has to be held with a

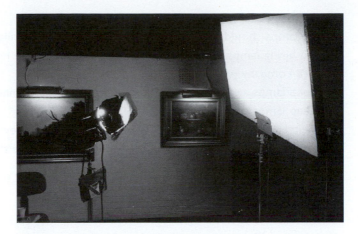

Fig. 18.2 White polystyrene reflector

clip in a lamp stand or by a helper (see Fig. 18.2). This is not very portable, so it is better to buy a fold-up type reflector that has a white or silver surface on one side, and a gold surface on the other. This reflector can 'lift' a face dramatically and naturally.

Location lighting essentials

- ❖ Take only one set of lights with you, such as a redhead kit. Use them sparingly to 'lift' a subject or highlight an object or person.
- ❖ Hiring lights for location use is expensive. Some locations do not have a suitable power source for large film lights of over 2000 watts. Generators are expensive.
- ❖ Balance your lights with the available light – use blue gel filters on tungsten lamps to balance for daylight.
- ❖ Use reflected light where appropriate to give a less obviously 'lit' set.
- ❖ Make sure subjects keep away from background walls and the background set.
- ❖ For exterior shots use a reflector, and avoid direct sunlight, except as a back light to make a halo effect around a subjects head and hair.
- ❖ Do a white balance on the camera after you have lit a scene. Remember to light safely.
  - ● Tape cables down with gaffer tape in areas where people walk.
  - ● Hang cables out of reach if you can, or use mats to cover the cables to stop people tripping over them.
  - ● Don't overload a domestic circuit. Make sure each lamp has a safety device such as an RCD (Residual Current Detector).

- Lamps get very hot. Use heatproof gloves.
- All lamps should have safety glass or a safety wire grille. If you are hiring lamps, check these are in place before you leave the hire company premises.
- Keep lamps away from curtains or other flammable materials.
- Keep lamps as cool as possible.
- Switch off or 'save' the lamps after each set up, and even after each take, if there is likely to be a long pause before the next take. The bulbs have a limited life span.

19
Magazine programmes

'For a young person interested in programme making, the best training ground is to work on a magazine programme ' – the words of a senior BBC producer who has worked on regular network magazine programmes for twenty years. I think he is right. On a magazine programme you have the opportunity to do everything. Nearly all genres of television have a magazine programme – current affairs, children's, art programmes, sport, consumer affairs, wildlife, comedy, entertainment and chat shows.

Working on a magazine show offers the best opportunities to develop and realize strong ideas. The short three-to-five minute items can often be made with a very low budget and can include drama and all forms of factual and entertainment programming. I worked on a one-hour broadcast magazine programme where all the film items had to be shot in just one day and then fully edited in another day. It was excellent training for trainees new to broadcasting.

Student television magazine programme

A magazine programme is also great fun to work on as a student. It is good training for later when you go into the media industry. Convince your University Students Union that the best way to reach the student population is to set up a regular student television magazine programme, and air it on campus in the bar before a televised football match.

Programme guests and contributors

Programme guests and contributors are different from interviewees that you film on location. Generally you will invite selected guests and programme contributors to take part in a television production that you are organizing or working for. They will be invited because they have something to say, or are experts in their field, or because they would be beneficial to the production. On the programme they might be asked to perform a task

Fig. 19.1 Student studio magazine programme, vision control

Fig. 19.2 Student studio magazine programme, sound control

(in say a children's programme), take part in a quiz, take part in a discussion or do a demonstration.

On broadcast television, guests and contributors are usually paid a modest fee. A first job as a television researcher will often involve working on a studio programme that requires you to find and check out suitable guests. This is why researchers have very comprehensive contact lists.

Here are some basic guidelines on getting good guests and keeping out of trouble, especially if you are working for a fast-turnaround magazine programme. The golden rule is check and double check to see if a person or story stands up.

Guests

♦ Always try and confirm a potential contributor's story before you invite him or her to come to the studio.

♦ Check details with friends, relatives or work colleagues if at all possible.

♦ Make sure guests sign a permission form – sometimes known as a 'blood chit' – giving the broadcaster (i.e. your employer) the broadcast rights over that particular interview. This gives only broadcasting rights, and other publishing rights must be negotiated separately or included in the form separately.

♦ For high-profile programmes make sure guests sign a form declaring that they will tell the truth, and not make false statements or false accusations against other people.

☞ For production forms, see Chapter 22.

♦ If you think there is something suspicious about a guest, tell a senior producer, ask for advice and ask for someone else to see that person.

♦ At all times make notes with dates and times or use a minidisc or cassette recorder to record conversations. This is not always practical, so always make notes anyway, and take a colleague with you if you can.

Privacy

♦ Researchers need to protect the privacy of individuals.

♦ Public figures are in a special position, but they retain the rights to a private life.

♦ Confine yourself to facts and avoid gossip.

♦ Always be very polite when dealing with public figures and ordinary individuals.

♦ There is no actual law of privacy in the UK, but there is in Europe and other parts of the world, so make sure you know local custom and practice if you are filming abroad.

♦ The Human Rights Act offers more protection for people's privacy. The Act states that everyone has the right to respect for his private and family life, his home and his correspondence.

Fig. 19.3 Studio camera operator

Magazine programme production 10-point master plan

1. *Audience*. Know the audience and you get the show right.
2. *Running order*. Choose the right story and run it at the right time in the programme with a good studio/film mix. Get the running order wrong and you are dead.
3. *Presenters*. A minefield in a war zone, why bother? You have to choose very carefully. Go for competence and professionalism rather than

Fig. 19.4 Auto cue operator

Fig. 19.5 Competence and professionalism are all-important for presenters, but glamour is an added bonus

glamour. Of course, if you can get all three, then you are very lucky (see Fig. 19.5).

4. *Three-minute story.* The three-minute story is still king – even if it is four to six minutes.

5. *Guests.* Go for guests who are interesting, energetic, hilarious, libellous (maybe not), fascinating and able to sing/dance/act/do somersaults and sail round the world – impossible? Not in a magazine programme

6. *Graphics.* Get the on-screen words right – titles/credits/stings/junctions/phone numbers/competition winners. Most importantly, spell the names of your guests correctly when you put their names up on the screen in a 'name super'.

7. *Budget.* Many modern magazine programmes have minuscule budgets, which means that all you can pay for are the costs of the show and expenses for guests. So make the most of freebies and go LIVE.

8. *Music.* If you are going to have music in your show – and I strongly recommend it – then you need a music policy. This means deciding what sort of music your audience like and want. There is no point in having a live punk band in a mid-morning magazine programme aimed at consumers at home. Remember that music incurs copyright costs, even for music videos.

9. *Ideas.* How and where do you get GOOD IDEAS – research is all. Good research means a good magazine programme – and the converse is also true.

10. *The buck stops here.* Have an executive producer to make all final decisions about programme content, but decisions should be made in consultation with the production team. Someone has to have the final say or you will never get on the air.

Magazine programme running order

Box 19.1 gives you a typical running order, for *Campus*, a 30-minute programme aimed at an audience of young adults.

Box 19.1 *Campus* running order				
Item no.	Item name	Source	Item dur.	Overall time
1	Titles	VT	0′ 25″	00′ 25″
2	Hello & welcome Presenters A & B	Live	0′ 30″	00′ 55″
3	Vox Pop – refectory food	VT	1′ 00″	1′ 55″
4	Guest Catering Manager Pres A	Live	2′ 30″	4′ 25″
5	Film what's on John	VT	1′ 30 ″	5′ 55″
6	Band	Live	4′ 00″	9′ 55″
7	Link Pres A to B	Live	0′ 15″	10′ 10″
8	Quiz Round 1	VT	3′ 00″	13′ 10″
9	Link Pres A	Live	0′ 15″	13′ 25″
10	Campus News	Live	2′ 00″	15′ 25″
11	Campus what's on	VT	1′ 30″	16′ 55″
12	Pres B + Two guests Student fees	Live	4′ 00″	20′ 55″
13	Sting	VT	0′ 05″	21′ 00″
14	Pres A emails/letters	Live	1′ 40″	22′ 40″
15	Band	VT	3′ 00″	25′ 40″
16	Trail for next week	VT	0′ 20″	26′ 00″
17	Pres A + student magician demo	Live	3′ 00″	29′ 00″
18	Goodbyes Pres A & B	Live	0′ 30″	29′ 30″
19	Closing credits	VT	0′ 30″	30′ 00″

20
Shooting script

Before going on location to shoot a sequence you will have gone through preproduction. Just as a reminder, you will have:

- ◆ prepared a treatment;
- ◆ produced a schedule;
- ◆ drawn up a budget;
- ◆ researched your production;
- ◆ carried out recces for people and locations;
- ◆ done a risk assessment.

You are now ready to do a *shooting script* and a *call sheet*.

What is a shooting script?

A shooting script is a personal document that varies from one programme-maker to another. It is a bit like a recipe for a favourite dish. It looks similar to many other people's recipes but it contains essential ingredients, and is structured in your own inimitable way. A good shooting script will outline the structure of your programme.

I cannot emphasize enough how important structure is to a high-quality well-crafted factual production. Whether it is a three-minute story, a 10-minute programme or a major documentary of 30 minutes or more, the way you structure your material is vital to getting the most out of that material.

A shooting script is created from the results of your research and the recces. Let's look at the ingredients first.

Before you start to create a shooting script you need to know:

- ◆ who is going to take part;
- ◆ where and when you intend to film;
- ◆ how many days' shooting you have;
- ◆ how much it is going to cost.
- ◆ what additional material you will need – for example, archive footage, music, graphics.

You will have picked your team and know:

- how many people are on the film crew – so much the better if it is just you and a couple of capable, hard-working, tolerant friends;
- what camera, sound and lighting kit you have available;
- details of transport, overnight accommodation, etc.;
- time scale of your production.

Shooting script structure

- A shooting script takes the ingredients of the programme and shows the structure of the edited programme.
- It details, at the very least, the opening sequence, the order of the interviews and the closing sequence.
- It brings together all the ideas you have been working on in your treatment and storyboard. It consolidates all the work you did in the research stage. It firms up the visual sequences you thought about during the recces.
- It is a written, or illustrated, version of the programme you have dreamed about making.
- You may have a very good idea in your head about how your programme is going to develop, but very few people can keep all their ideas in their head. By putting your ideas down on paper you are helping to structure them.
- A shooting script should not be thought of as written in stone. It is an organic, working document that will, and should, develop and change during the production. As you shoot material you will reassess and re-evaluate what you have done and what you are going to do.

Shooting script outline

- How is your programme going to start? Directors often write down a dramatic opening shot, and forget that it will last only a few seconds. They then think they have sorted the opening of the programme. An opening sequence must be a sequence – that is, a series of related shots, usually with spoken sync. sound or commentary. It should show how the topic or theme of the programme is introduced. It should set the mood and style of the programme.
- The middle part of the programme should be outlined in content form.
- The order in which you think the contributors will be placed should be written into the structure.

- Any extra material you want to include should be in the shooting script, including details of music and archive footage.
- The closing sequences may be crucial as the denouement of your story, or they may just conclude an interesting programme.

Shooting script example

Box 20.1 shows a shooting script for one sequence in a 10-minute programme called *Top Dog*.

Shooting scripts are very individual. This one explains the structure and contains notes and briefings. In this case there will be a hired camera operator and sound recordist. Neither will know very much about the programme – just what they were told on the phone. The presenter also needs to know what is happening in terms of the filming, even though she knows and has set up the contributors.

Box 20.1 Shooting script for *Top Dog*

TOP DOG Programme 1

Starters

Opening. Montage of dog shots from the three different dogs featured in this programme. Very short comments from owners describing their dog problem.

CU Cam left. Alison G. 'My dog lies all day in doorways. When anyone tries to pass he growls.'

CU Cam right. Joan D. 'Oscar is so lively, he pulls so much at the lead that going for a walk is a nightmare.'

CU Cam left. Jonathan B. 'Dylan is pretty good, until he escapes and goes binning.' (PICS of dog nosing around dust bins.)

Development

Main filming – three days with presenter

Interviews with Alison, Joan and Jonathan, who tell their full story of the problem with their dogs. We see Katie working with each dog and its owner. Big close-ups (BCUs) of each dog needed.

Radio mics for Katie and owners.

Interior and exterior. Katie does PTC (Piece to Camera) at each location on what she is doing to get over the problem.

Box 20.1 *continued*

Later filming
Return to each of the three locations for a half-day only to check on improvements in the behaviour of each dog. Katie reviews each dog's behaviour with owner. Very short interviews. WS owner and dog. MCU Katie.
Shots of dogs – all sizes – including 'locked-off' shots in garden.
(*Locked off* means the camera is locked in one position. The action takes place in the frame without moving the camera. This allows for invisible editing to make things appear suddenly in the frame or disappear.)

Final sequence
Fast PICS of changed dog behaviour patterns, with locked-off telescoped time shots.
Katie Voice-over to explain how improvements have happened.
Record on location, but may need to be dubbed later. Keep to short sentences.

Shooting general
Huge selection of shots of each dog, because continuity is always a problem with animals. Locked-off shots in gardens and BCU dogs – look for humour.
Alison. Do exteriors of house and interiors of doorways with dog in place. Try to get dog to growl on close up. Shoot Katie showing how to use hand signals and voice to control dog.
Joan. Main shots out for walk in local park – permission obtained.
Dog 3. See dog jumping over fence – he will do it if encouraged. Shoot Katie in large garden giving instructions to Jonathan on how to avert crazy behaviour.
Look for cutaways of Katie and Jonathan. Film Katie in WS with owner, but keep dog out of WS while training. Shoot MCU Katie giving instructions.
Music – specially composed by D. Stevens including dog theme for titles and credits – shots need to cut to music. Set-up – begging, CU wagging tail, CU panting, CU cute looks, etc. Leave time to do this.

The series is about how to improve your dog's behaviour, using a combination of canine and human psychology. It is presented by Katie, a professional dog trainer. The programmes are based on Katie's methods as she trains a representative selection of dog owners and their dogs.

This shooting script will be amended and improved after the first day's shoot. It will be issued to the two-man crew, and to the presenter, Katie, along with the Call sheet for Day One.

Box 20.2 Call sheet for *Top Dog*

TOP DOG
PROGRAMME 1	STARTERS	
PRODUCTION	Hot Dog Productions	
PRODUCER/DIRECTOR	John . . .	Mobile No. . . .
DATE	TUESDAY, 20 APRIL	
CAMERA	Max Headley	Mobile No . . .
SOUND	Ann Sadleman	Mobile No . . .
	Travelling together in Espace registration no. . . .	
RV	Katie's House	
	21 Hastings Road	
	Tel. . . .	
08.00	Pick up Katie	
08.10	All depart in Espace to South London	
09.00	Arrive Alison's house	
	43 St Margaret's Terrace, S. London	
	See map – set up in garden. Filming	
	Dog/Alison/Katie	
12.45	Lunch at King's Arms, Purley Road	
13.30	Interiors. Shots of dog. Interview Alison.	
17.00	Wrap	
18.00	Arrive back at Katie's house	

EQUIPMENT
DV digital camera
Tripod
2 radio mics + SQN mixer
Rifle microphone – do not use the mic. fixed on top of the camera under any circumstances, unless you have replaced it with a good quality rifle mic.
5 × 60 min. DV tapes
Lights: Redhead kit

The call sheet is created by the director/producer, or production assistant, or on a large shoot the production manager. It explains to everyone when they are needed and where. Note that RV means *rendez-vous*, which is French for a meeting. RV is the standard shorthand for the location where production and crew meet up.

21
Locations for filming

Finding locations suitable for filming is not as easy as you might think. It is best not to assume that any river bank, wood, derelict house, mountain or playground is a filmmaker's set. At least not until you have checked, because the sad fact of life is that someone does own it.

Someone or some official body may well own the very location where you want to film, but many places are open to a little polite persuasion, or the owner will rent you the location for a fee. But don't despair. There are still outdoor locations that are available free for unassuming, small-scale shoots if you look carefully.

When you have discovered or heard about a possible location, do not immediately go into negotiations with the owner. First you should do a preliminary recce.

♦ Always visit a location before filming. Take a notebook and a camera.
♦ You can use a Polaroid/digital/standard camera, or your digital video camera will probably take still pictures. Still pictures are much easier to handle at this stage.
♦ Take pictures of as many angles as possible, interior and exterior

What you are looking for

As a location finder and checker you will have several concerns.

♦ *Suitability.* Is the location suitable for the production brief?
♦ *Adaptability.* Try to find a location that provides many of the other locations specified in the script. For example: if you need to shoot a dialogue scene in a café, then choose a café which is not right on a busy main road, but which is in a quiet area, or is at least quiet when you close the door. If you need a kitchen scene as well, then find a café which also has a suitable kitchen for filming. You can do two key scenes in one location.
♦ *Access.* Can the production team and crew reach the location easily? This means can a truck or car get to the door and unload with ease.

Are there any obstacles to getting heavy kit to the place where filming will take place – room, balcony, roof, garden – that cannot be overcome or moved? If you are a very small crew with one camera you will still need to make sure you can get your tripod into the area. Do not rely on hand-held shots. They are harder to edit and can look unprofessional unless used in the right situation. For bigger productions you need access for chuck wagon (location catering), lighting vehicles, and mobile homes for costume and make-up.

♦ *Generator access.* If you are filming a drama, you may need a generator to provide power. A nearly silent film generator (jenny) is usually towed by a van, so you need to check that you can get a jenny reasonably close to where you will be shooting.

♦ *Parking.* You will need secure parking for several vehicles on site.

♦ *Distance.* Where possible you want the location to be within reasonable distance of the production base – that is to say, no more than a day's travel by car.

♦ *Overnight accommodation.* Even if you are filming only a reasonable distance from home/base, it could be a lot cheaper to stay the night. This will mean you can start filming earlier in the morning and do not have to spend time and money on travel.

♦ Check whether there is a pub/hotel/B&B that will offer preferential rates for a group. Also check what facilities are on offer. Remember film crews work late and get up early. Check if the hotel can do early breakfasts and late night snacks. Check whether the hotel can provide safe storage for kit and safe car parking for crew cars.

Exteriors

♦ *Photographs.* Always take a picture of any exterior you are going to use. The director needs to see several elevations. Do not rely on your memory.

♦ *The sun.* Check which way the sun moves across your location. A south-facing building will be in sun all day, but, conversely, if you are filming on the north side you will be in shadow. This is important for drama.

Interiors

♦ *Power.* You need to find out if the room/building you want to film in has a source of electric power.

♦ *Exact location.* Check the exact room in which you are going to do an interview or set up a sequence. Where are the windows? What is outside the windows? How loud is the air conditioning? Is there a reasonable background for an interview?

♦ *Space.* Check there is enough space so that you can work with a tripod and perhaps a couple of redheads. If it is a showroom or business, check that you are able to take a variety of shots from different positions.

♦ *Acoustics.* Is the room acoustically quiet and non-resonant? Stand in the centre of the room and clap your hands. See how long the echo lasts — in a church it is fine to have a long echo, but in a sitting room you do not want the acoustics of a bathroom. Listen for background noise.

♦ *Lighting.* Can you black out the windows, or put a light outside the window — this may be needed for drama?

♦ *Construction.* If it is a large space, like a night-club, what will you have to do to make it work for your production? You may have actually to build a structure like a special bar. Check the possibility of doing this and of course the cost.

Location permissions

Make sure you have signed permissions for wherever you are filming.

Public place

♦ If you are filming in a public place, no one can actually give you permission as such, but . . .

♦ It is a good idea to inform the local police if you are more than a one- or two-person crew. The Metropolitan Police in London do require advance notice of any serious filming to be given to the Chief Inspector at the local police station.

♦ It is a good idea to talk to the local police if you want to stage anything unusual. They can often be very helpful.

♦ You will certainly need permission to film in a historic setting, like the piazza in Florence in Fig. 21.1.

Private property

If you can obtain permission and afford the fee, private property offers the best bet, because you can have a free rein to create the scenes you want in the time you have (see Fig. 21.2).

♦ Make sure you get permission in writing from someone who has enough authority to give it.

♦ Make sure you agree the date and times of the shoot, and the names of cast and crew. Send everyone on the shoot a schedule and crew list.

Fig. 21.1 A piazza in Florence

♦ Agree a facility fee. This should be no more than about £25 for an ordinary location. For a famous location or country house, it will rise to more than £1000 per day.

♦ Keep a copy of the signed agreement with you throughout the shoot.

Action sequences

Special permission has to be obtained for action sequences with cars, and guns, even plastic replicas. Car chases that contravene the Road Traffic Acts are not allowed on public roads.

Fig. 21.2 Oasthouses at Sissinghurst Castle (National Trust)

You must not cause an obstruction

♦ Putting a tripod on a busy pavement could, in some circumstances, be considered causing an obstruction, if it blocks a thoroughfare.

♦ Filming in a busy street is best done with a hand-held camera.

♦ Take care that cables do not cause an obstruction or a hazard by crossing a public right of way.

♦ Make sure that lights do not cause an annoyance (shining in someone's window) and are not a danger to anyone.

Night filming

Residents in a street must be informed of night filming, which may affect them because of noise or lights. You can do so by leaflet or by telling them personally. Explain to residents, or anybody who may come into contact with the filming, exactly what you are filming and where.

Staged crimes

Filming of staged crimes must take place with these precautions

♦ Police are informed and invited to be present.

♦ Imitation firearms are kept out of public view.

♦ Residents are notified with the name and telephone number of the production company.

♦ The area is cordoned off and access is controlled by the production.

One production I know was shooting a thriller. They had permission to film on a public train, but forgot to inform the driver and passengers that an actor would be threatened with a gun. The driver was not amused when a terrified passenger pulled the alarm handle, and the train stopped. This very nearly cost a serious fine.

Cost

Most locations will charge by the day.

♦ *Rate.* Try and negotiate a daily rate that allows you a long day – i.e. 12 hours' shooting.

♦ *Security.* Some locations will charge for any personnel needed for security or to supervise use of the facility. Careful negotiation is needed to make sure you do not pay too much. Some famous locations are extortionately expensive.

- *Interruptions.* It may be better to pay a charge and have uninterrupted use of the facility, rather than try and squeeze your filming around whatever else is going on.
- *Government property.* You will need to negotiate in writing well in advance to film on government property such as hospitals, schools, social security locations, the Houses of Parliament or any government tourist site. It is really not worth the very serious hassle you will get if caught filming without permission on any land owned by the Ministry of Defence. It is forbidden to film even in the vicinity of some defence establishments.

Insurance

If you are filming on any premises other than your own, you will need to take out Third Party Public Liability Insurance. This can be taken out with most reputable insurers to cover a few days or longer depending on your requirements. It insures you and the production against liability, loss, claim or proceeding arising from the law relating to the production in respect of personal injury and/or death of any person and/or loss or damage to anyone's property due to negligence, omission or default by anyone working on your production.

If a member of the public trips over a camera or lighting cable and breaks an ankle then the production could be taken to court for negligence. This insurance will cover that sort of claim.

Also the law requires any company working in public places, or working with members of the public, to have public liability insurance.

Educational institutions should be able to supply a copy of their public liability insurance, which will cover students filming off the premises and working with members of the public.

- Take a copy of the Insurance certificate with you when you go on the recce because many locations will not allow you to film unless they are sure you are covered.
- A Third Party can be defined as someone not working for you or under contract to you; or as anything not owned by you.
- In the case of an accident, or if something is damaged, do not under any circumstances say or do anything to admit liability. This may be construed as an admission of responsibility. Talk to the insurance company first. And say nothing.

22
Production forms

Production forms include the Contributor's Release Form, the Contributor's Agreement, and the Location Agreement. There are also Actor's Agreements. Examples are given in Boxes 22.1, 22.2, 23.3, and 24.4.

Contributor's Release Form

The most useful form for any production is the Contributor's Release Form. All contributors who appear in any production that is going to be broadcast or shown to the public in any form – for example, as a video – must sign a release form. It is always better to get the form signed by all contributors, even if you do not anticipate that your video will be broadcast. You never know when you may want to use the material in a programme that will be broadcast.

The Contributor's Release Form covers all known rights in the universe. It is vital that you make sure you have all rights covered. Otherwise, when the broadcaster says that the interview is going to be put on its web site, you could find that the copyright for this contribution to be exploited in this way is not covered. The form also covers any subsequent uses of your programme for Internet distribution or any other exploitation as yet to be discovered.

Even if you are not going to sell your production to a broadcaster, it is still important to get all the contributors to sign a release form. It will save complications later, I assure you. For this, though, you need to use only the front page of the form. This is the page without all the small print and conditions.

Filming in public places

The only time when you do not require people to sign a release form is when filming in public places. This applies only to non-speaking members of the public who are filmed in public places going about their rightful business. Public places means streets and roads and shopping areas, and other areas owned by the community.

In private locations that admit members of the public such as public swimming pools it is not necessary to ask everyone in the pool to sign a release form. It may not be possible in a busy place.

The rule is that people should be aware that you are filming. They have a right to know what you are filming, and what it is to be used for – news, documentary, corporate video or your own personal use and they have a right *not* to take part. Sometimes a judiciously placed notice giving this information can avoid any difficulties.

If any people do not want to be seen in the film you are making, then they should be able to keep away from the area where filming is taking place. It should be quite clear where the action is happening and where it is safe to be away from the action.

Some people may be quite adamant that they do not want to be in your video. Respect their request and move to another area where they are out of shot.

In no circumstances should you tell anyone you can cut them out of the film in postproduction. You will forget who that person is and what he or she looked like and it will not seem important in the context of getting your programme made. This could land you in court. It is better not to film anyone who does not want to be filmed.

Filming in public places essentials

- ❖ Always get permission unless you are filming in the street.
- ❖ Make sure you have Third Party Public Liability insurance.
- ❖ Tell people you are filming and for how long and in what particular location.
- ❖ Tell them when it will be broadcast, or if the programme is for some other use, such as for educational purposes.
- ❖ Ensure people have the opportunity not to take part in the filming.
- ❖ You do not have a definite right to film people. As they are in a 'public place', the legal argument of 'privacy' would be hard to justify, but in some circumstances not impossible.
- ❖ It is prudent to ask permission from anyone who has been filmed in close-up or who is very obviously identifiable in any way.
- ❖ Ask parents for permission to film their children. Identifiable children cannot be filmed for broadcast without parental consent.

Using the production forms

All the production forms may be copied, or, ideally, scanned into your computer. Please note that, where it says The Company, you should fill in the name of your company or educational institution or broadcaster or whomever you are working for. Make sure they have a copy of each signed agreement.

♦ Use the *Contributor's Release Form* for contributors who are *not paid* and are taking part in any programme – for example, for an interview. Do not use for actors.

♦ Use the *Contributor's Agreement* for contributors who are taking a more major part in your programme and who may be paid for their contribution – for example, experts.

♦ Use the *Location Agreement* for any location. If no payment is required, then fill in the Agreed Fee line with: No Fee Payable.

♦ These are examples of forms used by a professional production company. Please note, contract law may vary in different countries.

Actor's agreement

Broadcasting Companies will have their own agreements and contracts for actors and performing artists. Independent production companies should seek advice on contracts from PACT for a major production. (PACT is the Producers' Alliance for Cinema and Television [www.pact.co.uk].) A contract for an actor is complex and should not be attempted without consulting a lawyer. See Box 22.4.

The actors' union Equity has a special low rate and special contract for actors working on student productions. Check with Equity and PACT on their web sites.

Accepting contracts and agreements

If you are thinking about accepting a contract from a production company, these are the things you need to think about.

♦ What interests must be protected and does the contract protect those interests?

♦ What are your liabilities in this contract? If things go wrong, what are you liable for? Make sure there is no clause that makes you personally liable for any service or costs. Be particularly careful that you are not being asked personally to guarantee a loan that is being made to your production company.

♦ Is the agreement or contract asking you to perform a task or tasks that are reasonable and 'do-able' in the time and under the conditions?

- If the agreement asks you to do something using your 'best endeavours', ask for this to be changed to 'reasonable endeavours'.
- Royalties are a very tricky area. Make sure that the other party has an obligation to collect and distribute to you any royalties or revenue derived from the production. Make sure they have an obligation to open their books to you or your accountant.
- Check what is defined by net profits. Will you receive a share of all net profits and if not why not?

Box 22.1 Contributor's Release Form

CONTRIBUTOR'S RELEASE FORM

Programme Title . . . . (The Programme)

Name of Company . . . . (The Company)

. . . .

Address . . . .

Description of Contribution (e.g. interview) . . . .

. . . .

Date of Contribution . . . .

Name of Contributor . . . .

Address of Contributor . . . .

. . . .

. . . .

Tel. No. . . . .

In consideration of The Company agreeing that I contribute to and participate in the above television programme, the nature and content of which has been fully explained to me, I hereby consent to the use of my contribution in the above Programme in accordance with the terms and conditions specified below.

Signed by Contributor . . . . **Date** . . . .

(Countersigned by parent or guardian in the case of a minor)

Terms & Conditions

I hereby agree that the copyright (if any) and all other right title and interest in and in respect of my contribution shall vest in and is hereby assigned to THE COMPANY (and this assignment shall operate to the extent necessary as a present assignment of future copyright) and that THE COMPANY shall have the unfettered right to deal with the programme containing such contribution or any part of it in any way it thinks fit. Accordingly I agree that the Programme incorporating my contribution or any part of it may be exhibited or other wise howsoever used or exploited (and such exploitation may include the exploitation of ancillary rights there in) in all media and formats throughout the universe for the full period of copyright and all renewals and extensions and thereafter so far as may be possible in perpetuity.

♦ What sort of control do you have over the conduct of the other party? What happens if they default on their promises or prove unable to pay you? Is there insurance to cover some of these possible difficulties?

♦ If you are offered a contract, it will be broadly in the other party's favour. If you do not like some areas of the contract or agreement, query them, and seek to change them or have them struck out if they cannot be amended to suit you.

Box 22.2 Contributor's Agreement

CONTRIBUTOR'S AGREEMENT

Programme Title . . . . (The Programme)

Name of Company . . . . (The Company)

Company Address . . . .

Tel. no. . . . .

Description of Contribution (e.g. interview) . . . .

. . . . **Date** . . . .

Name of Contributor . . . .

Address of Contributor . . . .

. . . .

. . . . **Tel. Nos.** . . . .

In consideration of The Company agreeing that I contribute to and participate in the above television programme, the nature and content of which has been fully explained to me.

I hereby consent to the use of my contribution in the above Programme in accordance with the terms and conditions specified below, and for the agreed fee.

Terms & Conditions

1 I hereby agree that the copyright (if any) and all other right title and interest in and in respect of my contribution shall vest in and is hereby assigned to The Company (and this assignment shall operate to the extent necessary as a present assignment of future copyright) and The Company shall have the unfettered right to deal with the programme containing such contribution or any part of it in any way it thinks fit. Accordingly I agree that the Programme incorporating my contribution or any part of it may be exhibited or other wise howsoever used or exploited (and this may include the exploitation of ancillary rights there in) in all media and formats throughout the universe for the full period of copyright and all renewals and extensions and thereafter so far as may be possible in perpetuity, without any further payments being made to me.

2 I understand that The Company is under no obligation to use the Contribution in the Programme.

3 The Company may without my further consent use my name likeness biography photographs of me and recordings of interviews with me to advertise & publicise the Programme in all media & formats throughout the universe.

Agreed Fee . . . .

Signed by . . . . **Date** . . . .

Box 22.3 Location Agreement

LOCATION AGREEMENT

Company Name

....

.... (The Company)

Address ....

....

........................**Tel. No.** ....

Programme Title .... (The Programme)

....

Owner of Premises .... (The Licensor)

Address ....

....

....

This document is to confirm the agreement with The Company and the Licensor in which the Licensor has agreed to make available to The Company the following premises on the following agreed dates:

Name of Premises to be licensed ....

.... (The Premises)

....

....

Agreed

Dates ....

....

Agreed Fee ....

Signed by a duly authorised representative for and on behalf of The Company

....

Date ....

Signed and agreed by the Licensor ....

Date ....

Box 22.3 *continued*

TERMS & CONDITIONS FOR LOCATION AGREEMENT

1 The Premises will be made available to The Company by the Licensor on an exclusive basis on the above agreed date(s), and on any additional days agreed with the Licensor.

2 The Licensor understands and accepts that The Company may need to return to the above location at a later date for further filming, if everything is not completed on the agreed dates.

3 The Licensor confirms that the Licensor will not make any objection in the future to the Premises being featured in the Programme, and the Licensor waives any and all right, claim and objection of whatever nature relating to the above.

4 The Company shall be entitled to use all film and audio visual recordings made in or about The Premises in the Programme as The Company may require.

5 The Company shall seek permission from the Licensor (not to be unreasonably withheld or delayed) if it wishes to make any structural or decorative alterations to The Premises. The Company agrees to properly reinstate any part of the Premises to the condition the Premises were in prior to any alterations.

6 The Company shall own the entire copyright and all other rights of every kind in all film and audio-visual recordings made in and about the Premises.

7 The Company shall be entitled to assign or license the whole or any part of the benefit of this agreement to any third party.

Box 22.4 Actor's Agreement

An Actor's Agreement should include the following:

ACTOR'S NAME	
PRODUCER'S NAME	
PRODUCTION TITLE	
ROLE	Character's name.
LOCATION	Include all location areas e.g. Scotland and New York.
FEE	Overall fee and possible royalties.
PAYMENT	How the money will be paid – e.g. in weekly instalments.
BILLING	How the actor is to be billed on the screen and in publicity.
ADVERTISEMENTS	Where and how will the actor's name appear in advertisements.
HOURS OF WORK	Typically 12-hour day for maximum of 6 days in any one week.
ACCOMMODATION	Specify the rating of the hotel or other form of accommodation.
TRANSPORT	Specify how the actor will travel to and from the location.
CATERING	Specify the catering arrangements – sandwiches, hot meals, restaurant.
COSTUME & MAKE-UP	Specify if make-up will be provided, and whether a make-up artist will be assigned to the actor, or whether he/she is to provide his/her own.
DRESSING ROOM	Will the artist have a personal dressing room on site or is it shared?
DURATION OF SHOOT	The beginning and end dates when the actor will need to be available.
CONSENT	The actor needs to consent to being filmed and recorded for the Production and to agree to all exploitation and world rights in all media.
COPYRIGHT	The actor waives any moral rights in the Production under sections 77 and 80 of the Copyright Designs and Patent Act 1988.

Box 22.4 *continued*

PUBLICITY	Specify what publicity will be expected in person. Actor will agree to use of the actor's name, likeness and recording of the performance in all media for the advertising and publicity of the Production.
LIABILITY	Clarification that the producer is not responsible for any loss or damage or injury caused to the actor, or the actor's property, during the making of the Production, unless caused by the negligence of the producer.
LAW	State the country under which whose laws the programme is being produced.
PREMIERES	The producer shall make best endeavours to get the distributor to invite the actor to premieres in the USA and the UK.
VIDEO	The actor will be supplied with a VHS copy of the finished production.

The filming day

23

You are in the storytelling business. You are 'recreating reality' (John Grierson) and you need to think and prepare.

Factual productions preparation

Before arriving at the location for your day of filming, you will have done a lot of thinking and preparing, but just check all the details are in place.

- ♦ *Schedule for each day.* Include a map of the location and directions on how to get there, where you are going to have lunch and details of where you are going to stay for the night if appropriate. Addresses must be accurate, with telephone numbers.

- ♦ *Crew list.* Include personal mobile numbers and registration numbers of vehicles.

- ♦ *Call sheet.* This will show who needs to be where and when. Use 24-hour time to avoid any confusion. Put in full location addresses, contact names and phone numbers. On a small production these details will be in the schedule.

- ♦ *Filming.* Say on the schedule what exactly you are filming – interview, action, background shots. Give some idea of what the filming is for – broadcast, corporate video, training film, broadband Internet – and say briefly what it will involve.

- ♦ *Release forms.* Check they are signed. If not, when will they be? Bring spare forms in case you need them. Also bring Location Agreement forms.

- ♦ *Video tape stock.* You will have to provide tapes on your selected format, unless you have hired a cameraperson who has agreed to bring the tapes. Even then, he or she may run out – it happens. Always carry spare stock.

- ♦ *Storyboard.* If appropriate.

- ♦ *Clothing for the occasion.* For wet weather, wear hat, wellies and water-proofs – always carry a warm weatherproof jacket. Wear decent shoes, or what are known as sensible shoes, or hard-wearing trainers. You will be on your feet all day, and the next and the next. A hat will keep the head warm on a cold day, or cool in the hot sun, so that you can think clearly.

♦ *Mini office.* Bring a supply of large thick pens to write on tape boxes, reporter's pad, pens, Blutac, sticky tape, a still camera, gaffer tape, mobile phone, laptop computer if you have one, spare batteries for anything that might need them – it will. Bring money – as in cash; there are always small things you need. You should buy your crew a quick drink at the end of a hard day, or perhaps offer coffee in the morning. The gesture will be appreciated. but you are not going to be partying every night. You will be too exhausted and too busy.

♦ *Minidisc or cassette recorder.* You will need this to record long interviews and hear them back in the car on the way home or in the hotel.

Filming alert
Have a clear idea of what you are going to film, and exactly how you are going to film it.

Shooting

Broadcast television tends to be rather traditional, and to stick to the established ways of doing interviews and filming stories.

Of course, you can experiment and try postmodern techniques, unusual camera angles or extreme close-ups. Make sure your producer or programme editor agrees and knows exactly what you are doing by showing him or her your storyboard.

Whatever you are filming, you will need more cutaways than you think, so film everything that is relevant and more.

Think up different angles. If you are filming a postman at work putting letters into sacks, then put the camera inside a sack and see the sack opening and letters falling in.

Walking shots

♦ It is useful to film your subject walking along the road and going into a house, but make sure he or she is coming towards camera, so you see the face.

♦ Try and think of an interesting way to introduce your subject.

♦ Suppose your contributor is a model-maker. Rehearse the subject picking the model up, turning it over with his or her face very close to the model. When you come to film, let the camera start with a close-up of the model, and develop to a wider shot of the model and the face of the subject. You could then slowly zoom in to the face. Repeat in a wider shot.

Panning shots

Most panning shots take too long for the sequence and reveal too little. The only reason to use a panning shot is if you start with something relevant and end with something more relevant – wildlife usually works, or one sculpture to another in a gallery, but otherwise forget it. Better to use several still shots to show a view or vista, then you can mix them together for a slower sequence or cut them for pace and energy.

Plan sequences

Think of a number of activities that your subjects can do and plan short sequences around these activities. Sequences need to tell a story with close-ups and wide shots – think of them as visual short stories.

If the shots are all the same size, you will not be able to make your story visually interesting. If you have a lot of activity in your film, then the interview could be shot on the same size of shot, rather than the more traditional change of shot for each question.

Working with a presenter

Place the presenter in different locations. Filming presenters 'talking and walking' gives pace and purpose to a scene. Wherever possible have the presenter as close to the action or activity as possible. Television thrives on getting behind the scenes, or getting somewhere unusual, or where most people cannot go.

If you are interviewing a building site crane operator, then, sorry, but your presenter has just got to go up in that crane – subject to safety regulations, of course.

Make sure you interview a main player, in any event. Generally, it is what the presenter says that matters, not what is going on behind him or her.

The filming day

♦ *Be punctual.* Turn up early – not on time, but before time. Production is the driving energy for the shoot. It is your idea; only you know exactly what you want to film.

◆ *Introductions*. Introduce yourself (yourselves) and explain to everyone what is happening today. What you are hoping to achieve. The first question a professional crew will ask is 'When is lunch?' The second is 'When is the wrap?' This is just another job for them. Try and make your shoot interesting and memorable – not for the disasters, but for the well organized and well-motivated day. Ask an experienced cameraperson what is needed from a director and the answer will be 'Someone who knows what he wants, and can explain that to me.'

◆ *Explanations*. Explain what your show is all about and what part has this day's shoot in it. Box 23.1 gives you a couple of examples.

◆ *Viewfinder*. The viewfinder is not just for the camera operator. Ask the camera operator if you can see each shot through the viewfinder.

Box 23.1 What is your programme about?

At the beginning of the filming day, you need to explain to the crew what the programme you are making is all about.

◆ Factual programme example

'This is a 10-minute factual programme about King Arthur. We are going to film King Arthur's grave here at Glastonbury Abbey. We need some exterior shots of the Abbey for the opening sequence. We are hoping to get a really nice sunset shot this evening. This morning we are doing the interviews.'

'Ralph Fiennes will be here at 11.30 for a short interview about his role in a new film about Arthur. Julia is our researcher, and she is collecting him from the station in Bristol. This is the shot number, and roll number we are on.'

◆ Mini-drama example

'This is a low-budget drama for inclusion in a factual programme. This is the first scene in a three-minute drama about the effects of cyberspace on an Internet addict. The progamme is a thirty-minute doc. Toby our addict is checking into a Cyber café for his daily fix. We start here in this park and follow him to the café. There will be a voice-over and music indicating his altered state of mind. Here's the voice-over script – it is quite short and we will record it later . . .'

'After lunch at the café we will have the staff as extras, and Emma is in charge of checking costume and make up.'

A good camera operator will always offer the director the opportunity to see the framing of the shot through the viewfinder. Try to include other members of the production in what you are doing. Television is a cooperative activity.

♦ *Monitor.* Do not be relegated to sitting behind the monitor. In fact I would not have a monitor on a factual shoot, but use it for drama only. Film Director Mike Leigh (*Secrets and Lies*) does not use a monitor on his film sets, as he says it distracts everyone from what they are doing. If the shot is not right for you, then seeing it on the monitor is too late. Explain what you want as you go along and use the viewfinder. Monitors are heavy to carry and heavy on power too. They need large batteries and take time to set up.

♦ *Hand-held monitor.* It is possible to plug a hand-held, battery-operated, miniature television into a high-end video camera. This can save time, and gives the director a good sense of knowing the frame size, and composition of each shot. The director can see what the cameraperson is seeing without disturbing his composition. The trick is not to say anything until the shot has been properly set up. The disadvantage is that the small screen is hard to see in daylight, and you need a long connecting lead that can get in the way. Also a small monitor cannot check colour balance or technical quality. It is, however, very useful if you are worried about the pictures you are getting recorded, and it could forestall a possible disaster.

♦ *Short breaks.* Filming is tiring and it is hard for everyone to keep concentration. Stop occasionally for short breaks, but they must be short. All the crew and cast will enjoy a 'Take Five' every so often. Some production assistants are very good at handing out sweets. Bring a thermos of coffee, or just call into a café for a quick comfort break. You will make up the time later.

♦ *Directions.* Travelling in convoy can be dangerous, so give all cars the directions and give them a time to be at the next location – do not say follow me. Keep in touch on the mobile.

♦ *Label tape/cassette boxes.* At the end of the day check that the boxes are labelled and numbered. *Never, ever* bring home an unlabelled tape or box.

♦ *Keep your camera with you.* On location, if you are operating the camera, remember that is not just an expensive piece of kit. It is your livelihood. It is your means of working – without it you cannot get your story or fulfil your brief. When you go to lunch take the camera into the pub with you – do not leave it in the car. At night take all kit into your home/hotel room, or other safe, locked place. Do not leave kit or tapes in the car overnight.

♦ *Rushes.* If at all possible quickly check the rushes the same night you film them.

At home or base

♦ *Watch your rushes* as soon as you can, and not later than a day after the shoot. Log best useable shots from the rushes and leave out bad takes, shoddy camerawork and anything you definitely do not want to use in your final edit. But be careful. Often material you think you can discard when you view the rushes turns out to be useful later on, so discard only the rubbish.

♦ *Paper edit.* Do a rough paper edit, getting some idea of the structure of what you have done so far.

♦ *What is missing?* Are you absolutely sure you have recorded everything you need from that location. Probably not, but maybe the shoot went well and you feel confident you can pick up other shots and sequences from the next shoot. Let's hope so. If there is any chance you will have to return, because of a technical glitch or for any reason at all, telephone the location contact and explain the problem. You may not be able to rearrange filming immediately but you have established that more filming needs to take place. There may be another way of doing it, which your contact might be able to work on.

♦ *Transcripts.* Arrange for interviews to be transcribed if necessary or paper edit them for content, and transcribe the essential sentences yourself.

♦ *Thank-you letters.* Write thank-you letters as soon as you get back and that means immediately, and it does not mean tomorrow. You will lose the impetus, something else will become important, and you will forget what each person did unless you write immediately.

♦ *Music.* Think about any music you might need. It could take a day or two to get hold of the CD, and clear the copyright.

♦ *Keep positive.* Congratulate yourself on a successful shoot – you deserve it. It is very important to keep positive, as programme making can be difficult. I was always grateful to a charming sound recordist I worked with, who, as we were driving through the rain to yet another difficult location, would always come up with the positive phrase 'It's all going terribly well'.

24

Production equipment

You and your camera

One of the benefits of using modern digital equipment is to that you can shoot good-quality, broadcast-standard pictures with low-cost equipment.

This chapter offers an introduction to the types of equipment you might use. Equipment is changing and improving all the time. There are many technical books that go into the technology and operation of broadcast equipment. This is not the aim here.

☞ For some suggestions for further reading, see Chapter 38.

A modern digital camera will be a camcorder.
- ♦ It will record and playback pictures and sound.
- ♦ It will have a Lithium or NiCAD battery.
- ♦ It will have a stereo microphone attached.

Low-cost television production with digital equipment still requires attention to the basic principles of camerawork. You are dealing with moving images that require light and need to be in focus and framed attractively.

Modern digital cameras will provide many automatic functions, but the more you understand the technology of your camera the better your filming will be. Automatic functions include:
- ♦ auto-focus;
- ♦ setting the iris/aperture and light level;

Fig. 24.1 Digital DV camcorder

Fig. 24.2 SONY DSR – PD150P

♦ setting the colour balance;

♦ providing a 'steady' feature;

♦ auto sound recording.

In many cases these will be effective and provide excellent sharp pictures, but it is important that you learn to override these automatic functions if and when the need arises. A more professional camera will give you greater flexibility (see Fig. 24.2).

Lens

Most digital cameras are fitted with a zoom lens that allows you to alter the size of the picture from a close-up to a wide shot, depending on the type of zoom lens. This works well for many situations, as you can select a variety of shot sizes without moving the camera. But you will notice that it is not only the size of the subject that changes; the background changes as well.

Depth of field

The depth of field is the area in the frame, both in front of and behind the point you actually focus on, that is also in focus. It is the range of distances over which the subjects in the frame are sharp.

The depth of field depends on:

♦ *The type of lens and its focal length.* A wide-angle lens gives greater depth of field. You can get more things in focus. A telephoto lens – the close-up end of the zoom – gives a restricted depth of field. This is useful for framing people when you want the subject to stand out from the background and/or throw the background out of focus.

♦ *The aperture.* On a dull day the auto-iris will open up wide to let in as much light as possible, but this gives less depth of field. On a bright day the auto-iris will close to give a smaller aperture but the subjects are better lit and so you will have a greater depth of field – more will be in focus.

Fig. 24.3 Glastonbury Abbey, showing depth of field; everything is in focus

♦ *Distance.* By varying the distance between the camera and the subjects, you can get greater, or less, depth of field. Put the camera close to your subject and you isolate it with virtually no depth of field. This technique is often used in wild-life programmes. The depth of field increases as the point you focus on moves further away from the camera.

♦ *Extensive depth of field.* For some situations you need everything in the frame to be completely in focus. You need extensive depth of field. These could be buildings, landscapes or crowd shots, where you want both the foreground and the background to be in focus (see Fig. 24.3). You need a small aperture and a wide angle to get those perfect shots. This usually means you need plenty of light on the subject, so that the camera's built-in exposure metre will offer a small aperture giving lots of depth of field. If not, try 'stopping down' manually.

Focus

♦ The focus adjusts the sharpness of the image.

♦ Put the camera on a tripod and zoom in on your subject's eyes to the maximum close-up position on the zoom. When you zoom out, everything will now be in focus at every setting – as long as you do not move the camera.

♦ Make sure you have experience of using the manual focus. Press the button on the camera to take the focus setting off auto onto manual. Use the focus ring on the camera to adjust the focus manually for a razor-sharp picture. Notice how small an adjustment you will have to make for the picture to go in and out of focus. Remember to switch back to auto-focus if this is the normal setting for you.

Auto-focus

Auto-focus will work well on most subjects, but can present some difficulties.

♦ If you are shooting a person who is particularly close to the background, the auto-focus may think it prefers to focus on the background rather than the subject. This will ruin the shot, as the subject will be soft (slightly out of focus). Solution: zoom in and focus on the eyes of the person.

♦ If you are shooting a person who is not right in the centre of the frame, the auto-focus is likely to sharpen up on something else in the frame. Solution: zoom in on the subject; focus, zoom out and then move the camera slightly to put the subject in the desired position in the frame. You may have to pan the camera slightly, but do not take it off the tripod.

♦ If you are shooting through a dingle-dangle (cameraperson's term for something hanging in the foreground of the shot such as a tree branch, or leaves, or even a wire fence), the auto-focus will tend to sharpen up on the branch or other foreground object, rather than the subject. This is a good example of when to use the manual focus.

♦ If there is a new movement in the foreground of the shot, the auto-focus may see this as a reason to refocus on this new object. Solution: zoom in to the old subject and refocus. This usually works, but if not you will have to go manual.

♦ When shooting in very low light, or at night, the auto-focus may experience difficulties in getting a focused image. Add more light or select manual.

♦ Shooting something through a glass window, or in a glass display case, may cause the auto-focus to 'hunt' – that is, go in and out of focus, searching for something to focus on. Go manual.

♦ Don't rely on your auto-focus to maintain a sharp picture as you pan on a rapidly moving object like a Formula One racing car. It may not be able to keep up. Going manual may not prove any easier, unless you are very experienced. All you can do is practise on as many cars as possible, and hope that when the Ferrari comes round you have got it right.

Box 24.1 describes an exercise for you to practise your focusing.

Box 24.1 Focus exercise

Choose a reasonably bright day. Put the camera on the tripod at the right height for you to look comfortably through the viewfinder. Ask three friends to help you. Ask friend A to stand about 5–7 metres away from the camera. Ask friend B to stand a metre or so in front of A. Ask friend C to stand a metre or so behind A. Zoom in as tight as you can to the head or head and shoulders of friend A.

Very slowly zoom out to a wide shot. Is everyone including the background completely in focus? Depending on the focal length of the zoom lens, it is very likely that friends B and C and the background will be hazy and out of focus. Why? Move the camera and tripod further back by a few metres. Zoom out to a full wide shot. All three people and the background should now be in focus. Why? This effect is due to the depth of field.

Exposure

♦ Experiment with the manual iris control. The iris, or aperture, controls the amount of light exposed to the camera. This will show up in the black-and-white viewfinder as increasing brilliance for opening the iris. By closing the iris the picture will simply get darker. Some cameras have a visual 'zebra' effect, which helps with obtaining an optimum iris setting.

♦ There is really no such thing as correct exposure. It all depends on the circumstances and the style of pictures required. It can be assumed that, if the flesh tones on faces in the frame look convincing and lifelike, then the exposure is correct.

♦ If you are shooting a rock band using coloured lights, you may want to create an overexposed effect with plenty of flashes and glitter. Conversely, if you are filming a white wedding, you may want to close the iris to a smaller stop to give better tonal shape to the dress. You are at liberty to be creative with your exposure. But remember the viewer needs to see what is going on – most of the time anyway.

f-stop

The iris is a diaphragm of overlapping, very thin sheets of metal, which can open or close to make a small or large round hole, or aperture, to let in light. The size of the aperture is expressed by an *f-stop* number. The largest and smallest *f-stop* number for that particular lens is marked around the outside of the lens.

♦ The smaller the size of the aperture, the larger the *f-stop* number.
♦ One of the smallest apertures is f/16.
♦ The larger the size of the aperture the smaller the *f-stop* number.
♦ One of the largest apertures is f/1.8.
♦ 'Stopping down' therefore means opening the iris to get a smaller *f-stop* number.

White balance

To get an optimum balance of light, and a good range and shade of colours, your video camera has a white balance button.

♦ Show the camera a plain sheet of white paper to fill the screen. For interiors place the piece of paper in the position where the subject is going to stand or sit. The camera should read the quality and amount of light on the subject, not in the room.
♦ Press the white balance button and the camera will adjust itself to the prevailing light conditions.
♦ Some cameras suggest you use the translucent lens cap to do the white balance. I prefer to use white paper in the area where you are going to shoot, as it tends to get a better colour balance.

♦ Remember to do a white balance for every different set-up.
♦ Remember to do a white balance when you move from an interior set-up to an exterior one.

Tripod

A good tripod is expensive but worth every penny. It is tempting to buy a cheap tripod, as there are so many on the market. Resist, if your budget will allow. When you are more experienced you will want to go out and buy the best-quality tripod you can find.

A good tripod will give you steadier shots even in a windy location (see Fig. 24.4). Wind can play

Fig. 24.4 Tripod

havoc with a small camera on a light tripod. A good-quality heavier tripod will survive all the battering and lugging around it gets. Better-quality tripods are more expensive because they tend to be made of durable, high tech. lightweight materials such as carbon fibre, to keep them light but strong.

Sound

Sound is such an important part of any production, it is surprising that some directors pay so little attention to it.

Modern digital cameras produce excellent pictures. But the quality of the microphone supplied with the camera is usually not nearly as good. Also a microphone mounted on top of the camera is nearly always in the wrong place to pick up the best sound.

Microphones

Most productions need a selection of microphones.

☞ For more on microphones, see Chapter 15.

Rifle mic.

The rifle mic. is probably the most important. It can be used in many situations. It is a directional mic. Point it at the mouth of the contributor and hold

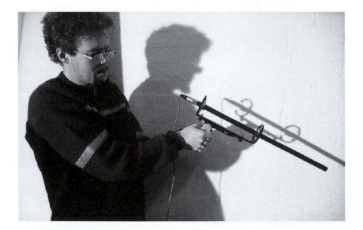

Fig. 24.5 Rifle mic.

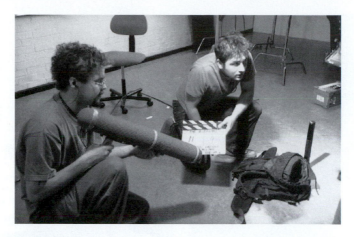

Fig. 24.6 Rifle mic. with windshield

it just out of shot. The sound will be high quality, clear, full frequency and with minimum background interference. It can be used with or without a windshield (see Figs. 24.5 and 24.6).

Personal mic.

A personal mic is clipped onto the lapel or under the tie of the contributor. It can be plugged straight into the camera or into a mixer

A *sound mixer* can mix a number of sound sources (see Fig. 24.7). The sound recordist will use his ears on headphones, and a meter to achieve a sound balance. He or she will make sure the sound does not over peak – that is, distort – or that it is recorded at too low a level (see Fig. 24.8).

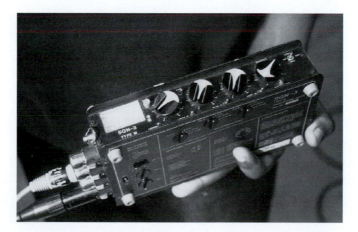

Fig. 24.7 Portable SQN sound mixer

Fig. 24.8 Sound recordist on location   *Fig. 24.9* Radio mic.

Radio mics

Radio mics are very useful if the contributor, or the presenter, is moving around a lot. This is a small mic. – similar to a personal mic. – that can be attached to a lapel (see Fig. 24.9) or even hidden under hair on the head. The mic. is attached with a wire to a small transmitter pack that is hidden in the back pocket or on a belt. A small receiver that the sound recordist has

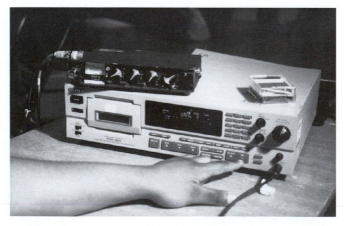

Fig. 24.10 DAT recorder with SQN mixer

attached to the sound mixer picks up the sound from the transmitter. The receiver can also be attached to the back of a camera. The sound, as well as being recorded onto the digital tape in the camera, can be recorded onto another format, such as DAT (see Fig. 24.10).

Sound tips

♦ Recording an extra sound track on another format such as DAT or minidisc gives more options during the sound dub in postproduction.

♦ Record in stereo at all times.

♦ Remember to do an atmosphere ('atmos' or 'buzz') track of at least one minute when on location. This is a clean recording of just the ambient sound with no movement or talking in any interior or exterior location where speech has been recorded. This will make for a smoother, more naturalistic final soundtrack.

25
Broadcasting ethics

Ethos is a Greek word meaning an accustomed dwelling place, a place where we can feel comfortable. Ethics has come to mean a code of conduct or behaviour that is the custom of the country where we live.

An understanding of ethical principles is essential if you are working in radio and TV.

- ◆ It is important to have some predefined standard in your mind when a quick and difficult decision is needed.
- ◆ If you have a personal code of ethics it means that you are more likely to have a level of consistency from one decision to the next.
- ◆ Working in the media, you are often asked to explain or defend your decisions in public.
- ◆ In the long run good ethics and good business go hand in hand.

Utilitarianism

Probably the most popular and clearest ethical principle is the theory known as *utilitarianism*. This theory suggests that a person should act in a way that produces the greatest possible ratio of good over evil. You should make a decision whose consequences will create the greatest good for the greatest number.

The fast-food example

A TV journalist has found out that a local and very popular fast-food outlet has been using beef that could be infected by BSE. The fast-food restaurant does not want this publicized. A local food inspector has filed a confidential report that the TV station has got hold of. The restaurant is a very big advertiser on the local TV station, and has threatened to cancel all advertisements if the story is run.

You are the broadcaster in charge of the news intake tonight. So what do you do?

If you were a utilitarian you would have to calculate the possible consequences. You have these choices:

♦ A Run the story.
♦ B Kill the story.
♦ C Run an edited version of the story without naming the restaurant.

♦ A *Run the story.* You would lose the revenue and possibly jobs, but your station would have good credibility, station morale would be improved (this station always tells the truth) and you would be warning the public of a health hazard.

♦ B *Kill the story.* Your station would continue to get lots of advertising from the restaurant and you would all keep your jobs for the time being. The fast-food outlet would stay in business and the public would not be warned about the potential health hazard.

♦ C *Run an edited version of the story without naming the restaurant.* This could have significant negative effects: your news operation would lack credibility, particularly if another TV or radio station did identify the restaurant. In the long run this might stop people tuning in to your TV station and so hurt your income. The morale in your newsroom would be badly affected and some customers might get food poisoning or worse.

So what do you do?

A utilitarian analysis suggests that you run the story because the overall outcome is more good than evil.

What has Aristotle got to do with it?

Aristotle in his writings put forward a theory of ethics rooted in natural law. As a scientist he noted that too much of something was as bad as too little, so the proper course of action was between these two extremes. Moderation, temperance, equilibrium and harmony are concepts that are important in his philosophy.

So, when Aristotle was faced with an ethical dilemma, he would identify the extremes and then find some balance point or mean that lay between them.

Fast-food example

♦ *Extreme 1.* Publish everything.
♦ *Extreme 2.* Publish nothing.

♦ *Compromise.* Aristotle might have suggested that a compromise would be to transmit the story completely but to allow the restaurant owner to make a reply to the charges – a solution often employed by the BBC. Indeed, the BBC must always attempt to provide balance in true Aristotelian style. This need not necessarily be in the same programme.

Cultural ethics

Cultural ethics theory is based in society and the culture of a nation, as opposed to nature. The basis of this theory is that an individual is shaped by his or her culture. Cultural ethics is popular at the moment. It suggests that the individual accepts the discipline of society, adjusts to its needs and customs, and finds that being part of the 'culture club' provides an ethical security. There are no universals by which each culture is judged. There can be many different subcultures within society with their own rules – for example, skateboarders may subscribe to a set of rules customized to their way of life and suitable for their sport.

Broadcasting

A TV or radio station should abide by the norms of the community and other businesses. In the fast food example, the local TV station might find out how other TV and radio stations have treated a similar ethical problem in the past. The manager could even talk to other managers to get advice on the course of action. In the BBC a manager or producer would ring a senior person for help. Never be afraid of asking for help over a difficult issue.

Situationalism

The ethical theory known as Situationalism argues that the traditions and norms of society provide inadequate guidance, because each individual problem or situation is unique. In a broadcasting situation, the general rule that 'TV newsreaders should always tell the truth' could be violated if the situation called for it. A broadcasting company could be asked to broadcast a false story to gain the release of hostages.

Back to the fast food

All this discussion of philosophy may not help you with the most urgent and pressing problem of should you run the restaurant story? Many things have to be taken into account.

♦ Was the local food standards inspector accurate in his findings or did he have an axe to grind?

- Are you absolutely sure that the leaked report is genuine?
- How much money will actually be lost if the restaurant cancels its advertisements, and could this be made up from another source?
- How serious is the danger of using meat that may or may not be infected with BSE? Very serious indeed, but are you convinced there is a genuine health hazard in this case?
- What is your position in this? Will you lose your job if the TV station loses this lucrative advertisement, or will you be rewarded for breaking a good story? Who decides?

What is the answer?

The truth is there is no one answer. It will depend very much on you and your personal code of conduct and behaviour. It will also depend on the code of behaviour set up by your employer. A Public Service broadcaster should be able to look up a well-defined set of staff guidelines on these sort of issues.

In all probability you will be able to pass on this sort of important decision to someone more experienced and higher up in the organization. At the very least, you will be able to talk to someone and seek advice.

But you may be surprised at how often you have to make a decision of this type on your own. Many digital TV stations broadcast 24 hours a day for 7 days a week, and there may be no one else around except you at 4.00 a.m. in the morning.

Practical ethics

It is really essential to have worked out a code of conduct to help you. Each of us will have our own sense of ethical behaviour.

Some people may feel quite comfortable about taking free gifts offered by a huge range of organizations from record companies to food manufacturers. In many cases you will not be alone in accepting 'freebies', and it is often considered quite normal.

A public service organization like the BBC will ask for all free gifts to be logged or sometimes not accepted. This may not be the case with a free baseball cap, carrier bag or pen from a well-known company. When it comes to substantial items such as personal gifts, or offers of free fares or tickets, then they should be rejected with polite thanks. By all means negotiate financial assistance or help in kind with your programme, but make sure it is all out in the open. Or the conditions are made absolutely clear.

As every journalist knows, there is no such thing as a free lunch. The trouble is you can never be sure the gift will not be used by the company to exert leverage on you. Free gifts can lead to far worse. Remember the case of Members of Parliament receiving free gifts for asking questions in the Houses of Parliament? You may think this could not happen to you, working in a small production company. But you may not be there forever, and companies have very long memories when it comes to seeking influence or favours.

Blagging

Student or very low-cost productions can accept the free loan of kit. Companies in the television business may feel that a free loan of equipment to a student production is in the cause of training. Many students wanting to borrow a camera dolly or some other piece of kit indulge in a little 'blagging' – the vernacular term for asking for something for free. Many companies are happy to help with kit on *bona fide* student projects without seeking any gain. Generally, the industry is keen to help if they have kit and it is not booked.

A code of conduct

Some principles that make a good ethical starting point for any broadcaster.
- ♦ Tell the truth.
- ♦ Behave justly.
- ♦ Respect independence and freedom.
- ♦ Act humanely.
- ♦ Behave responsibly.
- ♦ Don't cause harm.
- ♦ Keep all promises.

Action

Make your own personal list of ethical values.

Discussion 1

A TV station is contacted by a gunman who is holding hostages whom he says he will shoot if the TV station does not broadcast his demands – what do you do?

By the way. You have only five minutes to make your decision.

Discussion 2

Can you balance corporate profits against public service? Here are some common ethical problems in broadcasting that are a good basis for discussion:
- ♦ paying a DJ to 'plug' certain recordings (plug means play certain discs more often than others);

♦ politicians or businessmen trying to manipulate the news department;

♦ misrepresenting a TV or radio station's audience ratings to advertisers;

♦ not respecting privacy (the Human Rights Act passed in 2000 may provide some extra privacy for individuals).

Confidential sources

It can be very difficult protecting your valuable confidential sources of information. Some broadcasters have had to go to court because they have been unwilling to hand over rushes or notes that would give away the identity of an informant. Your employer should be able to help but always check you have the full support of your broadcaster.

Remember the source of inside information known as Deep Throat in the film *The President's Men*? Deep Throat was a real person who gave journalists inside information about the President Nixon Watergate scandal. To this day no one is quite sure who exactly is or was Deep Throat.

The future

One of the exciting things about working in broadcasting is that you are in the forefront of what is happening in the world of communication. This means some people who have an axe to grind, or who feel broadcasters have unjustly treated them, may target you. Even as a junior working on a small production you can still be 'got at'. Think about where you stand.

It is when you are working in the field that pressures are likely to be exerted. You may be working on your own as a cameraperson filming a whole range of incidents and events. You need to be aware that people will try to influence you.

BBC correspondent Fergal Keane, delivering the Huw Wheldon Lecture at the Royal Television Society Cambridge Convention, was already worried in 1997:

Remember the story of the TWA jet allegedly shot down by a US Navy missile? Rubbish as far as we know. Or hundreds of conspiracy theories floating around about the death of Princess Diana? What a pity if one-person single-camera journalism, far from pushing us into another age of enlightenment, were to return us to the rumour-ridden gloom of the middle ages.

Fergal Keane went on to say:

The danger is that the terror of being beaten by the opposition, the relentless hungering for success, can turn some in our profession into monsters for whom the claims of ego ultimately outweigh their commitment to the purity of the journalism. There is a lot of it about . . . executives must not allow the star system to become a carnival of ego slaves.

Something about libel

Libel is a word that strikes doom and gloom into the heart of anyone working in the media. But what exactly is libel?

The simplest definition is that libel is telling lies about someone. As you can imagine, it is rather more complicated, but if you stick to the facts and make sure you check everything, you are unlikely to be involved in libel.

It is important to know just what committing libel means because it is possible to libel individuals, groups or organizations. To commit libel a broadcaster would have to broadcast something that is *defamatory*. The courts normally apply these criteria to test if a statement is defamatory.

♦ Does it expose a person to hatred, ridicule or contempt?
♦ Does it injure the person in his or her profession or trade?
♦ Does it cause a person to be shunned or avoided?
♦ Does it reduce a person in the eyes of right thinking people?

This latter is perhaps the most difficult to prove.

Defence against libel

There are three principle defences against libel that a broadcaster could use. (You will, of course, need purse-sapping defence lawyers if you, or your broadcaster, are ever sued for libel.)

♦ *Justification*. This defence goes back to the original simple definition of libel as telling lies about someone. This is the defence that you are telling the truth. But you must be able to prove that what you said is true.

♦ *Fair Comment*. This is where your statement was made as a fair comment on a matter of public interest. You can show that the statement was an honest opinion that is based on fact on a matter of public interest.

♦ *Privilege*. Privilege refers to statements in broadcasts of court proceedings, or of parliamentary proceedings or of public meetings. The reports of these proceedings must be fair and accurate, and must not contain malice.

The best defence is to tell the truth and check that what you think is the truth is backed up by another source – not always easy to find, but you should try. And, of course, you cannot say something malicious about someone without the possibility of a libel charge.

Libel alert
It is not just you who might infringe the libel law. Any contributor on your programme or anyone taking part in a programme for which you are responsible must not infringe libel laws. Any libel would be your responsibility. This is as true for student radio and TV stations as for the BBC or CBS.

Drama and libel

You may have a brilliant idea to retell the story of a real person to make a television drama. If the person is not living, you should do your best to tell his or her surviving relatives what you intend to do. None has an automatic right to stop a programme going ahead. However, if there are serious objections against the making of the programme, the production may have to prove that there is a definite public interest in this programme being made. In most circumstances this is not necessary, but, if your brilliant idea is very controversial and possibly defamatory, then take legal advice. A living person may not want you to proceed with your project for all sorts of reasons. Some of these may not be valid and you can go ahead. If the programme offends the living person, it may result in a claim for defamation, which could result, in some circumstances, in an injunction stopping the programme going ahead. Being aware of these possibilities should not inhibit a production from going ahead, providing it sticks to the truth. But it is best to know what may happen before it does.

When a court case is *active*

All types of television programmes can be involved at some time with court cases. This means that you will need to know about *the law of contempt*.

When a suspect is arrested and charged with committing a crime, or when a summons is issued in a civil case, the case becomes *active*. This means there are restrictions on what a broadcaster can do. The 'active' period ends once sentence has been passed in criminal cases, and on judgment in civil cases.

If you are hoping to interview people in a court case or report on proceedings, there are things you must not do. You could risk contempt of court. This happens if you do something, or make a statement, that risks impeding or prejudicing the course of justice.

♦ You must make sure you do not broadcast pictures, or comment, that could influence people involved in the case – witnesses, jurors, lawyers. Details of evidence could fall into this category.

♦ You must not broadcast anything that could prejudice the case.
♦ You must not broadcast interviews with witnesses or have dealings with them that could prejudice the case, before the case is over.
♦ You must never speak to a juror about the case at any time.
♦ You must not speculate about the outcome of a case, or comment on a case due for retrial.
♦ You must not go against the court's wishes or report what a judge has said must not be reported.

Reading the tabloid press, you would be forgiven for thinking that contempt takes place every week. In fact, contempt of court is a very serious offence and rigorously enforced, but it can be contested.

Your rights

As a broadcaster or journalist, you have rights to be able to report cases that do not have reporting restrictions. You have the right to report a 'fair-and-accurate' account of court proceedings. But to use the defence of 'public interest' is of very limited value in contempt cases.

However, you need to be on the look-out for a sharp lawyer trying to invoke the law of contempt to stop the publication or broadcasting of something that is of genuine public interest.

If you have to work extensively with people investigating criminal activities or the courts, you will need to make sure you have a complete understanding of these issues.

26
Script writing

So you want to make a movie . . .

If the *Blair Witch Project* people can do it, so can you. It might be wise not to expect that sort of success just yet, but it's worth a go. There is one absolute essential. You must have a good script.

So what is a good script?

Tell the world

What do you want to tell the world? It is a good idea to have something you want to talk about or discuss with the world. This is not the frustration you get on the Central Line when the escalators have broken down again, and you really do want to tell someone something. That could make a reasonable item for a short comedy sketch, but it will not make a film.

You may just want to tell the world that you can write really good entertainment.

You may be good at chess and can work out the most fiendishly complicated plots, but can you write a script for a thriller like *The Usual Suspects*?

You are going to spend a lot of time and an enormous amount of effort creating a film. Even a 10-minute film takes days to write, produce and edit. You expect a large number of people to sit and watch your film, either in the cinema or on television or on the Internet. You owe it to your audience to create something you care about and believe in. Most important of all, you will get a better film if you really care about the theme of the film.

TV writer Kieran Prendiville, talking about writing for the screen, said: 'If you are going to write for television, don't be cynical. You really have to believe in the world you're creating.'

Theme

The theme is what you really want to say about love, relationships, the world, living in the city, vampires – in other words, about life.

The dynamic French director Luc Besson made his first film about his life-long passion for deep-sea diving – The Big Blue. This film was not an easy-to-watch wildlife film, but a strong forceful story about two world champion divers competing tragically for a final free-diving title. He wrote and directed a film about what he knew about and what he cared about. Luc Besson went on to make the very successful film The Fifth Element, in a quite different genre – Sci-fi.

Really study the themes of some favourite films. Find some common themes. Some films have at their heart the idea of a lone individual arriving in a community just at the right time to avert some sort of disaster. This is the theme of the famous western Shane, and it is the main idea behind the Superman and the Batman movies. It is the same theme with a few more people in The Magnificent Seven.

The story of how two people come together in love is, of course, a very strong theme of many successful films. It is an eternal human concern, and that's not a bad theme for a movie.

You may prefer to start even closer to home with your own experiences. Writers and directors like to set a film around an event in their childhood. The film Billy Elliot is set at the time of the 1984 miners' strike in Great Britain. The story of a young boy who wants to learn ballet dancing rather than boxing has an extra poignancy and edge juxtaposed with authentic events in the miners' strike.

Then there are thrillers and action movies, where a bank raid, as in The Thomas Crown Affair, kickstarts a film that becomes a sophisticated chase to discover who did it and why.

You may prefer a more thoughtful type of film that considers a particular area of human behaviour or reveals a truth about a character. The English Patient, for example, illuminates an area of human experience. This genre of film needs careful handling to work, but can provide a platform for a good actor or actress to shine in high-quality drama. Whatever theme you choose, you will need to develop the three crucial pillars of a good script: story, characters, setting – not so different from making a quality documentary.

Story

So, you have a theme, perhaps some ideas about interesting characters, a firm setting and the outline of a story. Good. You need to go into development – a state of mind and often inaction much favoured by Hollywood wannabes. Steer clear of soothsayers and friends who might want to put the kibosh on your idea, take a deep breath and lock yourself in a room with a computer. But read the next few pages first!

Development

How will your story develop? I suggest that you start with a 10-minute drama. This is an acceptable length for a 'short' and there are recognizable TV slots for this genre. It gives you time to create rounded characters within a satisfying story, and it can have just one linear storyline. There is no need for complex subplots, and you need only two or perhaps three characters for the 10-minute format. But you can say something worthwhile and create an impact with a well-wrought story. Also it is manageable in terms of filming resources and cash.

No matter how long you plan your drama, whether it is a 10- or 50-minute television drama, or a 90-minute movie, you will need to consider a variety of devices to hook your audience and create a really attractive story that has something to say, and films well.

Characters

You will need to develop interesting and arresting characters to deliver your story.

The protagonist

You need a central character, who will be the protagonist of your story. Your protagonist must have clear motivation to achieve his or her aim in the film. Motivation arises from inner character and experiences in the central character's past and present life. It can also arise from a deep desire for self-improvement, or freedom from all types of tyranny. But top of the list of main goals for Hollywood movies is the deep desire to have lots of money. If it is not money, then it is the consuming passion to 'get the ideal girl' or to 'get the apparently perfect man'.

Make your choice. Create a protagonist who can achieve a goal and try out a situation where he or she can be tested. Movies where protagonists do not achieve their goals by the end of the film have a habit of leaving the audience feeling depressed and downhearted. This may not be the best way to end your first film.

The adversary

The protagonist will usually have an adversary. This is a character who has the job of making it as difficult, and often as dangerous, as possible for the protagonist to achieve his goal. In a plot-led film such as a James Bond movie, there will always be a recognizable baddie. This is one character who personifies a 'bad' organization. The baddie aims for world domination, and the rest of us, who are of course goodies, have to be rescued by James Bond.

Setting

You will need to be absolutely clear in your mind where your story is going to be set. Clearly, if you are going to make a film called *Titanic*, then the setting is not just crucial; it is impossible to make the film without it. Setting is very important to the feel, mood and atmosphere of a film. Think of all those crime stories set in New York. Where would *The Godfather* be without New York?

Choose a location that you know you will be able to get to and use. A big city that you live near is fine, but you can also choose somewhere more intimate – a narrow boat on a canal. There are some definite advantages in setting your story at one flexible location. 'Whodunit' murder stories are often set in a country house. It makes the drama more intense and claustrophobic. Select an exciting and relevant location that is realistically within reach.

The treatment

Now it is time to get your story and characters together and write a treatment. This is a detailed outline of your idea. It is not the same as a treatment for a factual programme. It tells the story, showing clearly the structure of events. It will definitely show the beginning, middle and end of the story. This is the basic three-act structure. It is amazing how many people don't follow it, then wonder why nobody takes up their screen play.

Some movie producers think a story treatment should be just one sentence. It is not a bad exercise to see if you can put your story idea into one exciting sentence. Try it first with a film you know. The story of *The Usual Suspects* in one sentence – not easy.

Now try to write down the story of your film in a just a few lines. Does the premiss of that story excite you? If not, try another angle.

The full treatment

When you have a one-sentence version of your film, it is time for the full treatment (for a checklist, see Box 26.1).

It is a good idea to include in the treatment a page of dialogue to show that

> **Box 26.1** Treatment checklist
>
> ◆ Your treatment should answer these fundamental questions:
> ◆ Have you created a distinctive main protagonist who is a rounded, believable character?
> ◆ What is his or her goal?
> ◆ Who is stopping him or her achieving this goal?
> ◆ What is at stake and why?
> ◆ Where does the film take place?

you can write dialogue and that you know how to set out a script. This is more important than you think when it comes to showing a script to a potential backer or producer. Above all the treatment must show the structure of the film – what happens when and why. A well-structured film is often a good film. Check for yourself by looking at the structures of universally acclaimed films such as *High Noon*, *Notting Hill* or *The Insider*.

Script layout

Writing a screenplay or script for a film is more than just an excursion to the computer and typing out words using the default font – usually Times New Roman. The screenplay, as we shall now call it, has to confirm to certain industry standards and you break them at your peril!

While it is true that writing for television in this country is not so hidebound with conventions, you may as well follow the time-honoured US format and get used to it. Hollywood professionals use the excuse that they read hundreds of scripts and this format is easiest to read. Maybe.

The good thing about this format is that one page equals one minute of final screen time. This is most helpful in calculating the length of scenes and how long your piece will run on the screen. A 30-minute television script is 30 pages or about 6000 words.

The perfect screenplay

A television script or film screenplay has a new scene for each new location, and each scene has three important parts:

◆ a heading and a scene number;
◆ description of the scene;
◆ dialogue.

Heading

The heading informs the reader of the scene number and where the scene is set. Use capitals. EXTERIOR or INTERIOR; DAY or NIGHT. Also put the location in capitals on the same line. An example would be:

(Scene) 24. INTERIOR. NIGHT. HOTEL BAR. LEFT BANK PARIS.

You need to be consistent with what you call your locations. It is either a flat or an apartment, but not both. The names of places should be consistent. The left bank of Paris for example must not become just Paris.

Description

The description of the scene is always written in the present tense. Remember a film is viewed in real or present time. The description is written across the whole page under the heading and single-spaced.

You should aim to describe in as few words as possible anything that is relevant to the action or the plot. You do not need to describe details of the set, or what the characters are wearing, unless it is relevant to the action. If a character is wearing a coat to conceal a gun, then that is relevant.

Description of characters

On a character's first appearance you can describe significant aspects of the character's psychological and physical make-up. There may be unusual personality traits or physical features that are relevant to how the character behaves and reaches his or her goal. A private eye in your script might be young, clever, short haircut and in a leather jacket. This is relevant, because traditionally a private detective would suggest the Hollywood stereotype of rumpled suit, white shirt, tie and a shifty look in his eyes. Here is an example.

KELLY HAWK is young, clever and used to being top of the class. She is eager, with attitude. Kelly works for a dot.com start-up company and enjoys being in the thick of the fast, sexy world of new media. She has a tattoo in an intimate place, and expects her man to be successful, active and generous. Takes no prisoners, suffers no fools. Handle with care.

Dialogue

- ◆ Put the name of each character in capital letters, in the middle of the page.
- ◆ Use a reduced measure for the actual dialogue: you can do this by moving your left and right margins inwards, so that the lines are in the

middle of the page, but are ranged on the left – that is, all lines start at the same point. This makes the dialogue easier to read and stand out from the description and the heading.

♦ It is recommended that the left margin is 1.5 inches.
♦ Character's names, in CAPITALS, should be about 3.5 inches from the left-hand edge of the page
♦ Dialogue should be about 2.5 inches from the left-hand side of the page.
♦ You can add instructions for the actor that have a bearing on the scene. It might be *laughing* or *whispers or puts down phone*. Put these instructions in round brackets or parentheses at the place where they should happen.
♦ Put page numbers in the upper-right corner of the page.
♦ Stick to these rules and set up a template.

Font

The Americans insist on Courier font.

```
The  Courier  font  looks  like  this:  FONT:
courier 12 point.
```

It may remind you of an old-fashioned typewriter script, and that is exactly what it is. If you are working with Microsoft Word on a PC, I suggest that you use Courier New.

```
The  Courier  New  font  looks  like  this:  FONT:
Courier New 12 point.
```

It is virtually identical to the Courier font offered on a PC, but is much easier to use.

Here is an example:

```
KELLY
(slipping down another oyster)
Why do you bring me here. It's horrid.
The food's tacky. It's
out of touch this place.
```

In the UK it is acceptable to use the Times New Roman font with a 12 pt font size for television drama scripts. It looks like this.

The Times New Roman font looks like this: FONT: Times New Roman 12 point.

This is commonly the default font on many PCs, and is used in the UK television industry for scripts of all types.

My guess is to be optimistic and go for the Courier New Font in the hope that you might be able to send the script over the Atlantic. Margins are the same for both fonts.

Screenplay essentials

The last thing you want to do is make the reader really mad. You want to create a warm glow about your screenplay. Stick to the essentials.

- ❖ Always use the font Courier 12 or Courier New 12.
- ❖ Start a new scene for a new location or when time has passed in the same setting.
- ❖ Don't go out and buy a jazzy, coloured plastic cover, or indulge in any scary artwork on the front cover. Just the screenplay with no paper-clips or staples. If you are lucky it will be photocopied and shown around the office. They don't like ruining their fingernails picking out staples.
- ❖ Don't bind the screenplay in any way. Punch two holes and put it in a light see–through two-ring folder. The Americans use No. 5 round-headed brass fasteners and punch three holes. I find these very difficult to get, but if you want Spielberg to see it, you had better get those No. 5 brass fasteners.
- ❖ Your screenplay is not a shooting script. Do not put in any camera moves or suggest any shots unless absolutely essential for the action. Forget postproduction wipes and flips or other directions that are properly left to the director. You are just the writer at this stage.
- ❖ Your screenplay does not need a date, nor do you need to tell anyone that it is the first or thirty-first draft.
- ❖ You may think Brad Pitt or Julia Roberts would be ideal casting for your characters, but the reader would rather not know just now.
- ❖ All the reader wants to know is whether you can write, whether you have something interesting and a little bit different to say, and whether you can structure a story. The reader will also have at the front of their mind the very commercial notion – will this screenplay make me a million dollars. Cynical? Not really, just realistic if you are really think-ing of writing for films or TV prime time.

Writing a screenplay

Box 26.2 gives an example of a script that will be acceptable to British and American producers.

Box 26.2 Screenplay lay-out example

FADE IN:

EXT. A SMALL BUSY FISHING PORT.

Fishing boats weave in and out of pleasure craft. Slightly
run down feel. The fishing industry is only just making ends
meet. Boats look old and tired. A very attractive, expensive
modern cruiser stands out.

DAY — THE QUAYSIDE.

A smart ocean-going cruiser ties up at the quay.
SEAN in summer suit and carrying a flight bag hops out of the
back of the cruiser and walks quickly over to the fish market
area.

                         SEAN
          What you got for me?

                         JAKE
          Just come in. Six boxes. Scarce.
          Took time. Nearly lost 'em.

                         SEAN
          I'll have all six.
          Hope it's better tomorrow.

JAKE is a young successful fisherman who uses ultra modern
methods to catch high quality oysters. SEAN is his best
customer buying most of the catch and taking them by boat to
London.

INT. RESTAURANT — NIGHT

KELLY is sitting at a table with SEAN. KELLY is 24 with dark
hair cut in a fashionable short bob. She is dressed in a
little black number, with bare arms and shoulders. She throws
her head back and downs an oyster in one go. Then another.

                         KELLY
          Why do you bring me here? It's horrid.
          The food's tacky. It's
          Out of touch this place.

                         SEAN
          I like the people. They're over the top.
          They appreciate gracious living.
          Like you do.
          And the oysters are out of this world . . .

Box 26.2 *continued*

FLASHBACK
MONTAGE – OFFICE – CABIN OF A BOAT – BEACH – DAY
Sean is on the phone at his desk. Sea water churns around his
feet. The horizon is moving up and down as if he is on a boat.
The sky goes from vibrant blue to black. Sean is on a pebbly
beach gasping for breath.

INT. RESTAURANT – THE SAME EVENING

                    KELLY
          Where have you been?

She leans over and kisses him on the cheek. Then pulls his
tie hard so he nearly chokes. SEAN laughs in spite of being
held tight by Kelly.

                    SEAN
          You always want me twenty four seven.
          (coughs)
          I can't. I must let my mind go. I must see
          through the haze of that night.

EXT. AT SEA IN A BOAT – NIGHT

SEAN is driving the smart boat very fast. KELLY is at the
back looking out to sea. They are looking for someone.
There is a fishing boat in the distance. They reach it quickly.

                    JAKE
          I told you not to come out here.
          They'll see you.

                    SEAN
          Tell me it's not true. You must
          have found out more.

KELLY moves round to the middle of the boat so she can
hear. She is trying not to be seen.

                    JAKE
               (whispers)
          You couldn't have done anything.
          They wanted you. They wrecked your boat.

                    SEAN
          Who?

                    JAKE
          Ask them.
          (he points to a cruiser moored at a landing stage)

The opening

Whatever length of film you intend to make, you need a dramatic opening. This is part of the first act – the beginning. If you do not hook your audience in the first few minutes, you will find it much harder to keep them glued to the screen throughout. I find it best to write the opening last. You might have a good idea for the opening, but get your story worked out first, and then create an impressive opening scene.

American director Robert Altman explores, satirically, script writing and selling your script in the film *The Player*. Check out the beautifully composed opening sequence. It is one very long shot that sets up the story and the main characters, as well as containing the clue to the ending.

Pace

You will want to vary the pace of the action. Think of it as a range of mountains with just one or two very high peaks, some troughs and several smaller peaks. For an action film the protagonist will need to be thwarted a few times as well as revealing exceptional powers of recovery, and the ability to escape from the most impossible situations. In the best scripts the highest peak, or climax, grows organically out of the elements of the story. Periods of action can alternate with moments of reflection or character building dialogue.

Shape

The overall shape to the story is important and should have a pleasing symmetry. The opening should complement the ending, or mirror it.

In Bunuel's remarkable film *Belle de jour*, about a young, wealthy French wife – played with such conviction by Catherine Deneuve – who becomes a prostitute to try and absolve her dreams, the film has no music but begins with the rhythmic jingling of the bells of a horse-drawn coach. It also ends with the same jingling bells. This gives a clear and satisfying symmetry to a complex psychological film. This is known as 'closure' or narrative satisfaction and brings completeness to the story.

Foreshadowing

Foreshadowing gives the audience subtle clues as to what might happen later, or how a character might develop. It sets up possibilities that can be developed later. A cleverly developed scene can plant an unconscious awareness in the viewer of what might happen. You don't want to be too obvious and give too many hints and clues, but foreshadowing can lead to a more complete 'closure'.

Foreshadowing can include special skills that the protagonist has acquired previously, for example, Superman, or it might be great skill at cards. It might include close-ups of objects, or hints of trouble at certain locations. For films involved with the supernatural, there is often a place or site that has attracted supernatural forces in the past. A most unlikely character may supply this information.

Treatment of time

The great thing about writing a film or TV drama is that you can do anything you like with time. You can make everything happen within a 24-hour timespan, or you can extend it over 50 years like *Citizen Kane*. You just need to remember that everything the viewer sees apparently happens in present time.

Early cinema directors exploited time with great effect. Events appear to happen 'before your very eyes'. In fact, you can create any time period you wish – past, present or future – but it will all appear to be happening now.

You decide on what timespan would work best for your film. To create a claustrophobic, intense atmosphere where the characters are under pressure, set your film in a tight timespan. Gothic horror in the *Dracula* mode is often set over a contained timespan such as a weekend or one day.

Think carefully about the timespan you want to put your characters in. It can make a big difference to the pace and feel of your drama.

Backstory

Backstory is Hollywoodese for a character's past life. The difficulty for anyone starting from scratch is that you may know a lot about your main character, but the viewer knows nothing except what he or she looks like in Scene 1. So you have somehow to create a backstory for your characters, and certainly for your protagonist.

The backstory will show your character's internal desire and illuminate the reasons for wanting his or her goal, whether it is for ultimate power or love or that old war-horse money. Backstory may mean dropping into the script factual details about the past, such as where a character was born and grew up, as in *Forrest Gump*. It often works better if you can suggest a more psychological backstory, such as an inability to relate to the opposite sex owing to some trauma in childhood.

Incorporating backstory into the action

The problem remains as to how you incorporate these details and psychological traits into your script, so that they become part of the action. Even more important is how you realize them visually. Some films do this superbly well.

The French Director François Truffaut in *Quatre cent coups* tells the story of a 12-year-old boy who gets into trouble at school and runs away from home. We gradually get more insight into the claustrophobic repressed life he leads at home. Truffaut releases small packages of information in the film to show Antoine's deteriorating relationship with his parents and how this informs his behaviour. But we do not know until much later in the film that he is living with a stepfather and was born illegitimately. The viewer tries to work out why Antoine is running away and is so apparently disruptive. Truffaut releases this information at a point where it backs up some of the theories of emotional insecurity that we have worked out for ourselves.

It is a good idea to go easy on the amount of backstory you actually show. A character's actions, appearance and what he or she says should suggest indirectly what has happened in the past, and what the effect has been. The viewer should be able to build up a composite psychological picture of the character from hints and illusions rather than direct autobiographical detail, although some detail can be handy.

It is important to show how a character changes in the face of adversity or conflict. People can reveal their true nature through their conflicts. Drama thrives on conflict. You have only to look at the soap operas on television to see that. Truman in *The Truman Show* could not find freedom except though confronting his circumstances, and testing his theories that all is not what it seems. The choices your characters make help them to grow and become believable, rounded, human beings.

Flashbacks do sometimes work, but can look out of place. A cleverly constructed film may let the viewer work out whether what is happening on screen is a flashback or something going on in the character's mind at that moment.

Storyboard

A storyboard is the best way to see whether your film is working visually. You do not have to be good at drawing to make a useful storyboard. There are professional storyboard creators who will make your stick men and scratchy perspectives into a real work of art – at a cost. But they need something to work from, so don't shy away from having a go at a storyboard. The important word is *story* not *board*. A storyboard is a tool to help all the other members of the production work on what the director wants to see on the screen. In television drama and particularly a movie the director is very much in charge of what happens on screen; after all, it is his or her vision that will turn the script into a visual experience.

The storyboard will help all the other people needed to make the production aware of

♦ the action;
♦ cuts and dissolves;
♦ the period of the piece (is it modern costume or is the film set in the Sixties);
♦ the approach to scenic design, camera angles and lighting.

Once you have got your ideas into storyboard form, you need to make sure everything will work. Although it is often the director who initially does the storyboard, it may be reworked many times before it is actually used on the set.

It is rarely necessary to storyboard every single moment of the film, unless expensive special effects make it necessary. People take different things from a storyboard. For example, the lighting director will worry if he sees that some scenes have the main characters in large hats – it could be difficult to light faces under big hats.

The storyboard has a direct relationship with the script; both will be revised constantly, but it is the director's job to see that the storyboard is up to date. A storyboard is vital in the preproduction stage.

The storyboard should be as simple as possible, giving an outline of the action, with shot size, camera movement and a few indicative lines of dialogue. You should not draw a frame for every movement or action. An average-length scene of two pages might take up eight frames or one storyboard sheet.

☞ Creating a storyboard for a drama is covered in Chapter 10.

Realistic budget

Your setting must be realistic in terms of your budget and the time you have allowed to produce the film. Only set your film in the Caribbean if you have a family member who will put you up for the time it takes to make the film. Don't forget about the actors and crew. They need somewhere to stay too. Also, how much do you really know about the Caribbean? You may know more about Padstow or Brighton if you want a seaside location.

Write about where you know

At first it really is best to write about where you know, and to set your film or TV drama in locations that you either know well or can get to easily. If you are thinking about a Sci-fi setting, or creating an imaginary world, how will you do it?

I sometimes find that students come back from holiday with a sensational idea for their TV drama to be set in Ibiza or Thailand. It's very cheap out of season, they say. Yes, but it is also cold and does not look anything like it does in August. In fact, all they know about Ibiza is the beach and the interior of a few clubs. The clubbers' on–off romance with an ironic twist could look distinctly flat in an out-of-season resort.

If the plot needs an exotic setting, it is probably a James Bond film and needs rewriting. That may not be true, but you have to make sure that your story matches your setting. A domestic drama will work just as well in Willesden or Weymouth. It just depends where you are and what the plot requires.

If you do have access to a variety of locations, make sure the locations work for your screenplay. Make sure you use the stunning Scottish scenery or the rolling Sussex Downs to the advantage of the drama. If you have access to an unusual or startling location, you could use that as the springboard for your story (see Box 26.3).

I once had a student who was determined to set his final year drama in a disused mental hospital to which he had exclusive access. The trouble was he could not make his script work in this location. The story should grow organically out of the location. The characters should fit easily and unobtrusively into the landscape. The film *Notting Hill* is a good example of the symbiotic relationship between setting and plot.

Improve your script writing

You may find scriptwriting quite hard at first. You may feel that you can write good naturalistic dialogue but have difficulty with structure. Other people have lots of great ideas but just can't seem to get them down in a convincing screenplay.

Writing courses

One of the best ways of improving and expanding your skills is to join a writers' workshop, or go on an evening course. But please don't spend a lot of money on fancy-sounding courses hosted by a big name movie-writer. They can be entertaining, but not all that helpful. Local film or writers' associations may offer the same advice and not hit your bank balance so hard. There are full-time and part-time courses at universities and colleges in the UK and the USA. Try to meet other writers. Read as many scripts as you can.

Box 26.3 Use your location

Can this woodland scene on a snowy day in December spark a screen-play? Could something similar have inspired Charles Dickens to write *A Christmas Carol?*

Go to the movies

The best apprenticeship for a screenwriter is the most enjoyable – watch a great number of films and television dramas – but concentrate on the scriptwriting.

♦ Write down the plot.
♦ Make a list of the salient motivational aspects of each character.

- ◆ Work out how everything comes together.
- ◆ What is the structure?
- ◆ What works well and what doesn't?
- ◆ Why do some films take so long to get going, and others seem to kick in right away?
- ◆ Listen carefully to the dialogue; notice how little dialogue there is in some action films.
- ◆ Look for the rhythm of the film in terms of the dialogue: short quick dialogue between all characters, or longer speeches by the main protagonists and very little from any of the other characters.
- ◆ Watch and watch again.

You are now ready to write your own screenplay. Go for it.

A scriptwriter's essentials

- ❖ You need a strong original core idea.
- ❖ Each scene must advance plot, and develop character.
- ❖ Every line of dialogue should advance the plot or illustrate character or preferably do both.
- ❖ Story matters; plot matters; avoid deviations that slow down the action or the development of the theme.
- ❖ Create a dramatic opening scene.
- ❖ Find the 'right' setting for your characters.
- ❖ Write for your defined audience.
- ❖ Leave the audience satisfied. The ending is, of course, important, but it does not necessarily have to be 'happy' or 'conclusive'. The Italian director Fellini said about his films: ' I believe that everyone has to find truth by himself . . . that is . . . the reason why my pictures never end.'

The 10-minute short

The 10-minute short really is the best format for a first drama. It is also an excellent way to get your drama made and shown on terrestrial television, or even in a cinema. It is now possible to make a film on digital kit, and have it shown in a cinema using digital projection. This means that you do not have expensive transfer costs of at least £20,000 for a 90-minute movie to go from video to 35 mm film.

> ☞ The 10-minute short is explored in greater detail in Chapter 32.

The first independent film to be digitally released in the West End of London, *Second Generation* directed by Shane O'Sullivan, was shot on digital Betacam and premiered in November 2000. It was shot in 19 days and cost £40,000, with £15,000 postproduction costs deferred. Barco Digital Cinema offers digital projection, and it is now possible for filmmakers to direct and distribute their own digital films. There are many competitions and festivals around the world for short digital films. Box 26.4 gives you some guidelines to get started on a short.

Good luck!

Box 26.4 Shorts checklist

♦ You need an original core idea that is right for this duration. Not a shortened 20-minute drama or an extended promo.
♦ Every line and every word must fight for its place on the page.
♦ Every moment counts; every frame matters.
♦ Choose to see two or three characters develop in preference to a larger cast.
♦ Keep to simple settings that allow for character development and action.
♦ There is no room for the scenic establishing shot, unless it really does jumpstart the plot.
♦ Above all make sure you have a strong storyline with plenty of narrative thrust
♦ Don't be afraid of innovative ideas and off-the-wall characters.

27

Drama production

Creating drama is about imagination. It is about energizing the script with imaginative uses of locations, scenery and actors. It is about creating the right atmosphere for actors to show their craft. It is about finding the most entertaining and stylish way to create the aural and visual realization of what is in the script.

The drama production team

The members of the drama production team have similar names and role identities to the factual production team, but in drama what people actually do is different. The three key players are the producer, the director and the production manager.

☞ For details of a factual production team, see Chapter 6.

Creating even a modest TV drama involves many people (see Fig. 27.1). There is a lot of pressure to get complicated set-ups done quickly and efficiently, and

Fig. 27.1 Filming a close-up of a burglar taking contraband out of a bag involves the whole crew

the margin for error is small. The working day is rarely less than 10 or 12 hours and everyone gets tired.

If you are in one of the three key roles, you will have a happier team, and therefore get better results, if you respect the way people work and keep the lines of communication open at all times. Make sure everyone knows what is happening when and where at all times. Basically this means good scheduling, excellent organization and an ability to be flexible and pragmatic without losing your sense of humour. Good catering also helps smooth tired nerves; and whatever happens keep talking.

The producer

The producer's job is to get all the various elements together in preproduction, particularly the production team, script and budget, and to choose a director who is excited by the script.

The producer is always where the buck stops. The producer sets up the production and is the person who gets it all together from beginning to end. In a small production, the producer and the director may be the same person. The drama producer is involved with getting the initial idea off the ground and in selling that idea to a broadcaster or other interested party. The raising of finance for a production is traditionally the job of the producer.

In some creative teams the producer actually doubles as the production manager. That way, one person can keep total control over the budget. As the budget is unlikely to be anything other than minuscule, this is not a bad idea. It also frees the director to concentrate on directing actors and realizing the script. This works particularly well if the director has written the script.

The producer/production manager can then be a collaborative team member who can offer another pair of eyes to the production as well as looking after the budget, and do all the other things that need doing on a production. A person who is good at organization and hassling often works well with a creative imaginative person.

The director

The director is responsible for the overall look of the production, and for getting the drama in the can. It is a job that is both creative and organizational. It needs enthusiasm, determination, creativity and attention to detail. The director must be able to work with and inspire actors, and have a strong vision of what the finished film will look like.

The director's job starts with the script. He or she will help with the initial script breakdown and then mark up the script with any extra scenes or extra requirements. The director is involved in all stages of the production from initial planning to the final edit. He or she will be instrumental in the casting of the actors and have a say in selecting the key members of the crew. The director will explain to the crew, especially the cameraperson and sound recordist, how each shot should look. The director will block each scene, and rehearse the actors.

Experienced and respected directors do a lot of work on the script before coming near the set. They know exactly what they want, and have a clear idea of what each scene should look and sound like. They make extensive notes on the meaning and impact of each scene. They encourage the actors to interpret each scene in their own way using their talents and personality, and they make sure the interpretation fits into their vision of the whole production.

A director must have a very precise understanding of the meaning and resonances in each scene. This can be summed up as the *mise-en-scène* – what the director is putting into the scene. The director has the ideas and the imagination to 'lift' each scene off the page and realize it as a sequence of moving images. It is the production manager (PM) who does the actual day-to-day work required to make those imaginative scenes actually take place.

Assistant directors

You may also need the services of assistant directors (ADs).

First assistant

The first assistant is the director's most trusted and closest helper. He or she stays next to the camera, is the mouthpiece of the director and makes sure everything on the set is exactly as the director has requested. If there are to be white flowers in the vase, then those yellow ones must go and Props must somehow get white flowers, now. The assistant director tells the director when everything is ready, calls for QUIET or STAND BY followed by TURN OVER. This is a command to the crew to start the camera running. The director will then call ACTION to set the scene going, and this is the cue for actors to start to perform their lines or start their moves.

Turn over is a term from the early days of cinema, when you had to turn a crank on the camera to move the film though the camera. Somehow it has stuck, even when shooting on tape – probably because it is as good a phrase as any to tell everyone that filming is beginning, and everyone knows what it means.

Second assistant

The second assistant works closely with the first AD and looks after the needs of the actors. The second AD particularly prepares any extras for their role in the scene, and sets up crowd scenes. He or she also has the job of preparing everything for filming the next day, including making any changes to the call sheet.

Third assistant

On a large shoot, the third AD will help the second to deal with crowd scenes and extras. He and she can be a 'gofer' – someone to go and collect anything that is required – or driver, or may help with schedules. This is a good position for someone wanting to do work experience.

The production manager (PM)

This is a very rewarding job, which calls for formidable skills in managing budgets and organizing schedules. The PM will typically have worked with the producer from the beginning of the production, and an experienced production manager knows every aspect of the production process and is calm, practical and able to negotiate with everyone about everything. The larger the production, the more important is the role of the production manager. If the hotel is overbooked and the lunch does not arrive on time, then the production manager gets the blame and has to sort it out.

The production manager on a drama production has many responsibilities.

♦ *Kit.* Books all equipment, including hired-in lights, radio mics, camera dolly, filters or special equipment demanded by the production such as an underwater camera blimp. Even though the cameraperson may request special equipment and know where to get it, it is important that it is booked and paid for by the PM.

♦ *Budget.* Authorizes any expenditure. The PM is responsible for making sure the production is not overspent.

♦ *Safety.* Checks overall safety of cast and crew. Although the producer is ultimately responsible for all health and safety on any production, it is the PM who checks and takes care of safety on the set.

♦ *Risk assessment forms.* Makes sure that risk assessments forms are completed for all locations.

☞ For risk assessment forms, see Chapter 8.

♦ *Insurance.* Checks third-party insurance liability is in place.
♦ *Scripts.* Distributes scripts to cast.

- *Transport.* Books and confirms all transport.
- *Accommodation.* Books and confirms all accommodation.
- *Office.* Takes charge of finding a production office, arranging the rent and paying for all office expenditure, including phones and mobile phones.
- *Schedules.* Creates daily schedules and call sheets for cast and crew in consultation with the director.
- *Special requirements.* Books all special effects, stunts or essential set dressing in consultation with the director.
- *Release forms.* Arranges for release forms for contributors and arranges Equity contracts for actors.

☞ For examples of release forms and contracts, see Chapter 22.

- *Locations.* Secures locations and negotiates all permissions for all locations.
- *Police.* Seeks permission from the police for filming in the streets or other public locations.
- *Clear up.* Ensures all hired equipment is returned by chasing up cameraperson, lighting director or whichever crew member is responsible for looking after any piece of equipment that is missing.
- *Final budget.* Supplies all the detail in order to produce a final budget with the producer.

The job of the production manager is clearly a very important and a responsible job on any production. Realistically, the production manager and the producer work closely together from the start of preproduction to cover all the areas and ensure everything goes according to plan and to budget. But the producer and director will rely on the PM to do all the painstaking work of setting up each location.

Production assistant

The PA is an important role in any production. She – and it is nearly always a she – works on the production from the very conception of the idea right through to the, hopefully not bitter, end. There may be only one other person who does this – the producer/director.

A modern PA can also be a researcher, fixer and expert in writing contracts. She writes down time-code numbers and does paperwork. A PA can do location research and recces, and look after continuity during the actual shoot. The producer and the PA are the backbone of the production and can share certain responsibilities. The PA can look after the budget and take some of the responsibilities of the production manager if you want to keep the production team small and manageable. The PA should be paid according to her responsibilities.

On a drama there is usually much more to do in a short space of time, but it can mean that you do not have to hire the production manager until a few weeks later. A good PA is absolutely invaluable and sometimes hard to keep. I once produced a large drama with an absolutely first class PA who was lured away by the late film director Stanley Kubrick to work on his new film. Above all, the PA should always know what is going on at any one time. In a small production office the producer may be away, and the PA will be able to field calls and deal with all those people who need to call up the production office. In fact, she can be overloaded with too many mind-bending tasks, so it is important that a job description is agreed early on.

On the set the Production Assistant will fill in a log sheet for each scene. Small productions might be tempted to overlook employing a PA, but this really is a false economy. When it comes to postproduction, this log sheet will contain absolutely vital information, and save you and the production a lot of time.

You could also ask the PA to help with continuity. The first assistant and the director will also be involved in continuity, but the PA could take Polaroid (or digital) pictures of each set-up. These pictures are useful for checking make-up and set dressing as well as action continuity. The PA's pictures can make sure that the handbag carried by one character is on the same arm in the next scene. It is those little things that make a production look professional.

Runner

Other production jobs on a drama include a runner. The runner is the general helper who is willing to do those jobs no one else has time for. Yes, that does include making the tea, but the runner is also there to learn and observe the film-making process, and could well have useful experience and other skills to offer. After all, this is often a first job for a graduate entering the television or film industry, and the production should try to provide meaningful jobs for the runner.

Script breakdown

An early task for the PM is to break down the script into shooting scenes. Each written scene must be broken down into minute detail. This is usually done using colour marker pens for consistency throughout the script. Bear

> **Box 27.1** The railway carriage
>
> A favourite scene in countless movies, and very useful for meeting strangers, is one set in a railway carriage.
>
> In the script the scene will say INT. RAILWAY COMPARTMENT. That is all. For the scene to work in the film, it will almost certainly require exterior shots of the train speeding along the track and going under a bridge, and various other exterior shots. These are extra scenes that must be marked as such. Put each separate shot of the train as a separate scene when you do the breakdown. It is much easier to organize the shoot if you see these exterior shots marked as separate scenes. Also you won't forget them. A scene can always be cut if not needed. If you do need it, and you probably will, then it is there. In fact, you will be pleased when it comes to editing if you have more than one exterior shot of the train from several different angles. Believe me, you will be very relieved you have them as cutaways.

in mind that a script for a 60-minute television drama is at least 60 pages, long with possibly 100 scenes.

One colour will mark the characters in each scene. It is usual to give each character a number with Number 1 for the character with the most lines. Another colour will mark extras, and a third colour will mark all the locations. Use other colours to mark props and set dressings and other movable items specified in the script.

The script can be broken down into several new scenes if necessary. A scene is any action that has to be shot separately, or that requires cast and crew to move. Some scenes will not have been put in the script. You have to second guess what is needed or check with the director. See the example in Box 27.1.

Programme breakdown sheets

A breakdown sheet is created for each scene. List all the colour-coded elements under appropriate headings. Box 27.2 shows a breakdown sheet for a short 10-minute film called *Bikers*.

The scriptwriter

You may have to pay a writer for the screenplay. You will have to get legal advice on a secure contract with the scriptwriter to cover rewrites and any changes you may want to make during production.

Box 27.2 Breakdown sheet for *Bikers*

PRODUCTION TITLE	BIKERS
SCENE	2
PAGE NO.	5 (on original script to access the dialogue)
CHARACTERS (blue)	Jim (No. 1) Ellie (No. 2)
EXTRAS (pink)	
PROPS (green)	Scooter – Jim's Lambretta 2 helmets, 2 gloves
LOCATION (red)	Beachy Head downland area Public car park
SET DESCRIPTION	
EXTERIOR/ INTERIOR	EXT
DAY/NIGHT	Day
Special requirements	W/Angle Lens Access to Beachy Head Lighthouse for sea shot
COSTUME (purple)	2 pairs sunglasses his & hers 2 parkas – one with Target on back
MAKE-UP (yellow)	
Miscellaneous	

For all sorts of reasons, generally called 'financial restraints', you may find that you cannot realize every scene in quite the way the scriptwriter had in mind. Also you may have your own radically different interpretation of the script, or want to relocate some scenes or cut them out. Make sure the contract allows you to do this. Rewrites often do not become necessary until you are well into production. Negotiate with your scriptwriter before changing anything radically and try and get agreement for all changes. You want to keep your scriptwriter on your side throughout production. It is not usual to have the scriptwriter on the set during production. The scriptwriter's role in the production should be agreed at the contract stage.

On every type of production it is vital that the key players know exactly what their roles are, and the parameters of those roles. Areas that may lead to confusion and are potential trouble include: overspending, who is 'in charge' of equipment and talent, and – the one that seems to cause most contention – credits.

Drama production budget

How much everything is going to cost is always a thorny question. When you did your original treatment, you should have thought about the budget and entered a ball-park figure. Something along the lines of:

- ◆ 10-minute drama, two main characters, low budget, on location in two areas;
- ◆ four–five days shooting on DV.

If you are bidding for outside money, it is best not to be too cheap in the treatment, otherwise that is all the money you will get.

Now that you have the script broken down, showing all the elements of each scene, you can make an accurate production budget. Create a budget sheet on Microsoft Excel or other suitable software.

The production budget starts with all the costs for you and your production staff up to the time you start shooting. If you are working with friends or as students, these staff costs may be free. As soon as you try and make a film professionally, you will incur staff costs. Box 27.3 shows a typical production budget.

Programme budget

The programme budget will include all your actual production costs including postproduction (there is an example in Box 27.4). The headings can be further broken down, with another sheet giving exact details of: crew costs, accommodation and transport, costume, special effects, postproduction effects.

Shooting days

A difficult part of setting up a drama shoot is to calculate how many days' shooting you will need, and how many days travelling and servicing the shoot. The production manager (PM) will work with the director and producer to produce an overall schedule for the whole shoot and then daily schedules for cast and crew.

You have to allow for all manner of other things. You have to allow for contingencies such as bad weather or an actor getting ill, and for the failure of at least one piece of equipment. The more complex the shoot, the more you need to make sure you have back-up in terms of resources and time.

Working on the rule of thumb that you can shoot five minutes of edited

Box 27.3 Example of a production budget

Production Budget

PROGRAMME TITLE

Date.

Programme Budget £ . . .

Producer

	Budget est. per week	No. of weeks	Contingency	Estimated total cost	Actual cost	Saving or overspend	
Producer							
Director							
Production manager							
Production assistant							
Assistant producer							
1st AD							
Runner							
SCRIPT							
Contracts							
Research							
Mobiles							
Printing							
Photography							
Office telephones							
Postage							
Stationery							
Misc.							
Electricity							
Heating							
Rent							
Hire cars/taxis							
Transport							
Hospitality							
TOTALS							

Box 27.4 Example of a programme budget

	Budget est. per day	No. of days	Extra costs	Contingency	Estimated total cost	Actual cost	Saving or overspend	
Production Budget								
PROGRAMME TITLE								
Date								
Producer								
PREPRODUCTION								
Location days								
Travel days								
Cameraman								
Sound recordist								
Lighting director								
Camera assistants								
Overtime								
Night shoots								
Tape stock								
Hired in kit								
Props manager								
Props costs								
Costume designer								
Costume hire								
Set designer								
Set costs								
Transport								
Mobiles								
Location fees								
Per diem								
Catering								
Health & Safety								
Actors								
Extras								
Misc.								
POSTPRODUCTION								
Copyright								
Press & Publicity								
TOTALS								

drama in an average day, then a 10-minute drama will need only two days' shooting. This is definitely an underestimate. It takes a little time to get going on a drama shoot. You are more likely to need four days. A 10-minute drama is a condensed format, rather like a short story.

For a 10-minute film there may be up to 10 different locations. So you need to schedule more time. If the crew is inexperienced and you are working on a low budget – this usually means less people – then things will take longer. The PM will have to work out the most efficient and cost-effective way to get to and from each location.

Location scheduling

The first thing in location scheduling is for the PM to work out from the script which scenes to shoot at each location. All the scenes set at any one location need to be shot while the cast and crew are at that particular location. A good PM will also work out what else can be shot at the same location, in order to cut down the amount of travelling and the number of locations.

There may be a location manager involved. The location manager's job is to find suitable locations and, most crucially, obtain permission for the production to use them. The location manager may have gone to recce some locations. It is important to liase with him or her to make sure everything on the site is available for the production.

Some locations will specify that they are happy for filming to go ahead but only at certain times. These times can be quite anti-social, such as 5.00 a.m. on Sunday morning. Fortunately, cast and film crews are used to an early start, and the director may see an advantage in working with the particularly luminescent quality of the early morning light.

Box 27.5 gives a Schedule Example for a scene from a 10-minute film on bikers. The PM now has to arrange for cast and crew to get to Beachy Head and stay the night. He finds he can arrange overnight accommodation for cast and crew at discount rates at a friendly B& B farmhouse.

By careful planning and forward thinking, the PM has managed to find a location to shoot the place-specific scenes, and also a suitable location and time to do other necessary scenes in the bar and on the road. If only there wasn't this difficult scene on Tower Bridge that has to be done before 5.00 a.m. on a Sunday morning.

When filming begins the most important and most used paperwork is the call sheet. This can be a daily document, or it could be weekly, or it might cover the whole shoot. Choose whatever is most convenient, but actors and crew like to know where they will be as much in advance as possible.

Box 27.5 Schedule example for 10-minute film

A 10-minute motor scooter road movie:
BIKERS Scene 2: EXTERIOR. DAY. BEACHY HEAD. SUSSEX
There are four scenes set in and around the Beachy Head area in Sussex. Scenes 2, 4, 9 and 12. Also there are interior bar scenes that are not place specific and can be set at any suitable bar location. The PM knows there is a large hotel at Beachy Head with a suitable bar. There are three scenes set in the bar. Scenes 5, 7 and 14. He works these three scenes into his schedule.

There are also five scenes that require external shots of scooter riders on the road. The PM thinks he can do three of them on the quiet roads around Beachy Head. The bonus is the director will also be able to get spectacular views of the famous Beachy Head lighthouse. These could be useful in the titles or credits sequences.

Let's hope the weather is kind. If it is not good weather for Exterior shots on day one, he can do the Interior shots. There is a good chance the weather will be better on day two. With careful scheduling the team should be able to shoot 10 scenes over two days:

♦ four place specific scenes;
♦ three road scenes;
♦ three bar scenes;
♦ spectacular scenic shots for use in titles or credits.

The call sheet can be a complex affair, because it needs to contain a lot of important information. Box 27.6 gives a professional example that you can adapt, cut down or expand as you wish, and Box 27.7 shows a log sheet.

Marked-up editing script

The information from the log sheets will be transferred to a full version of the script ready for the postproduction process. This is usually done by the PA.

☞ For a more detailed account of the editing process, see Chapter 34.

The beginning and the end of each take is indicated. Takes have a designated colour. For example, red could be take one. The full dialogue script is marked with a line down the page from the beginning of the dialogue of each take until the end, usually in the left-hand margin. This line indicates the shot size

Box 27.6 Example of a call sheet that can be copied and used for any production

Page 1

«Programme Title»

CALL SHEET: «Call Sheet No.»	DATE: «Date»	
PRODUCER/DIRECTOR:		
PRODUCTION OFFICE: «Production Office Address»	UNIT CALL:	**07.00**
	B/fast (if required):	**08.00**
	LUNCH:	**13.00**
	ESTIMATED WRAP:	**19.00**
	COSTUME/MAKE-UP:	**07.00**
	ON SET:	**09.00**
	SUNRISE:	**06.45**
	SUNSET:	**19.45**

PRODUCTION OFFICE

CONTACT:

Box 27.6 Page 2

LOCATION 1:

CONTACT:

LOCATION 2:

CONTACT:

EATING AREA: «Eating Area»

Breakfast:

Lunch:

Unit contact:	Location Assistant	Name	Tel. No.
	Runner		
	Runner		

LOC	SET	SCENE	INT/EXT DAY/NIGHT	CAST No.	SUPPORT No.
1	Street	1, 2	INT DAY	1, 2	1, 6

Box 27.6 Page 3

CAST No.	ARTIST (Artist's name)	CHAR. (Character's name)	PICK UP	ARR.	MAKE-UP	WARDROBE	ON SET
1	John L.	Romeo	06.30	07.15	07.30	08.30	09.00
4	Celia K.	Juliette	06.30	07.15	08.15	09.00	09.50

NB: Actors to arrive early to talk through scenes

Box 27.6 Page 4

No.	SUPPORTING ARTIST	Role	Phone Number	On Location	On Set	Approx. Wrap
				00.00	00.00	00.00

PROPS:

(Put in scene numbers with the props needed.)

Box 27.6 Page 5

REQUIREMENTS:	As per requirements
Camera Dept:	As per requirements
Lighting:	As per requirements
Sound:	As per requirements
Costumes:	As per requirements
Make-up:	As per requirements
Grip:	

TRANSPORT Driver: *Name* Tel.	**Details of who is being picked up and at what time.**
Driver: *Name* Tel.	e.g. To p/up those required from production office @ 08.30
Driver: *Name* Tel.	
Production Vehicle: *Name* Tel.	

Rushes:	To be dropped off by «RushesRunner» @ «Rushes Address» «Rushes Tel.»

Extra Information:	

Box 27.6 Page 6

<u>**LOCATION**</u>   e.g. No Smoking

<u>**INFORMATION**</u>

R/V point   Details of meeting point

Parking   Details of parking arrangements

Power   Details of source of electric power e.g. generator

Police   «Police contact name & tel. no.»

Hospital   «Address of nearest hospital»

Box 27.7 Example of a log sheet

TITLE OF PROGRAMME

LOG SHEET

SCHEDULE – Date

Time code IN	Time code OUT	Scene No.	Description
00.00	00.00		
00.00	00.00		
00.00	00.00		
00.00	00.00		
00.00	00.00		
00.00	00.00		
00.00	00.00		

NB For a log sheet, you need only minutes and seconds and not frames for the time code.

and the extent of any dialogue or continuity errors and the exact duration of each take for that scene.

This marked-up postproduction script is a visual record of where all the takes begin and end, and includes notes on which take the director liked at the time. It is, therefore, easy for the editor to see which are the best takes to use in the edit.

Dealing with people

This may be a low-budget production, where the production and crew are working for no pay. Sometimes in this situation one or two people promise to give their time and then fail to give as much time as is required to see the production through. It may be thought necessary by the key production personnel to 'sack' someone who is not pulling his or her weight. This sort of situation should be handled by the producer as sensitively as possible. Always give a warning first and offer the person a second chance. Make it absolutely clear that, if this person still arrives on set late or does not turn up, then that means he or she is no longer working on the production and will not be named in the credits.

Crew and staff contracts

I find that it is a very good idea to have a simple contract for all production staff and crew on any 'no/low-budget' production. This contract to everyone stipulates the following:

- ♦ your role and your areas of responsibility on the production;
- ♦ the person you work to – for example, the production manager;
- ♦ the number of working days you will be required, and between which dates;
- ♦ the credit you will be entitled to if you complete the contract;
- ♦ the condition that, if you do not fulfil your role as defined and agreed, you may be asked to leave the production with no on-screen credit.

This should be signed by each member of the team and kept by the producer. It is a good idea to ask all members of the team to write their own definition of their role in the production, and have this agreed with producer, and put in the contract. If a dispute arises about who does what, it is easier to resolve if everyone has written down a job definition.

28
Mise-en-scène

At this point it is worth a short diversion to check that what you are setting up will make sense to your audience. There is little point in making a film if it will not interest and entertain an audience. One of the most important ways of holding an audience's interest is to make sure all the visual elements in your film fit together in a meaningful way. This is known as *mise-en-scène*.

Mise-en-scène is a French term that literally means 'put in the scene'. It means what the director and the production team have put in the frame to give meaning to that scene. In a drama, unlike a documentary, every single item in a scene has been carefully selected to be there.

In a good film all the visual components will complement the story and the characters. That Chinese table lamp in the foreground is there for a reason (see Box 28.1). It is Chinese for a reason. It is, if you like, an extra visual clue. It shows something extra about the character's background. *Mise-en-scène* includes the staging of the action and the techniques used to shoot the scene. When you are planning a scene, check that these elements all contribute towards the meaning of your scene.

The setting

♦ *Location.* Is it interior or exterior? Actual location, or a set constructed in a studio? Authentic or stylized; heavily dressed or natural?

♦ *The props.* The props should contribute to the ongoing action – for example, the shower curtain in *Psycho*. They should also indicate the overall mood or atmosphere, and indicate psychological or interior mood of character; as an example, a mirror often indicates a character 'looking at' his interior state of mind.

♦ *Costume* plays an important part in defining genre such as comedy, horror, science fiction or gangster film. Costume is crucial in defining period (year) or time or fashion. Costume is used to help define the overall 'look' or style of a film.

♦ *Make-up* is concerned with either making characters look natural or making them look non-natural – as, for example, in *Star Trek*. Make-up is

Box 28.1 *Mise-en-scène* example

In this scene from a film, the Chinese lamp and Chinese vase carry a lot of significance, initially to do with the fact that the protagonist has lived in China. But the scene carries more meaning. Loaded with symbolism, the lamp and vase convey the oriental feel to the film, and the intricate 'Chinese-puzzle' nature of the plot. The director has carefully chosen these two artefacts so that they can be strategically placed on the set, and help infuse the scene with hidden meaning.

important in keeping the characters realistic, even if they are aliens. On feature films 'hair' is a separate job done by a specialist hair designer. On television make-up do hair as well. Make-up can smooth over imperfections or skin blemishes and can define an actor's or actress's 'glamour quotient'. (It is currently fashionable for women, and invisible for men.)

Lighting quality

The quality of light on a film defines the texture of the picture. Hard lighting gives well-defined shadows from a key light suitable for *film noir* or for evoking moods from fear to mystery. Soft lighting, or diffuse illumination, is associated with romantic scenes and candle-lit dinners. Warm lighting using warm coloured gels can be used to create a 'fireside' effect that suggests a comfortable, cosy environment and an inner warmth to the character.

Lighting direction

Frontal lighting eliminates shadows for clarity and truthfulness. Side lighting is dramatic, emphasizing facial features. Back lighting is used to create a silhouette effect, especially if the sun is the back light. Also it gives a subject a three-dimensional feel with a sense of depth. It is often used to highlight hair to heighten romance.

Lighting source

Check whether lighting is natural and comes from the sun, or a mixture of natural and artificial light, or is just artificial light. Filters can be used to give coloured light effects to stimulate reality – for example, in a night club – or for artistic effect. Remember the overall purpose of film lighting is to make things look better. It is an art. That is why the best lighting camerapersons and television lighting designers are in such demand.

The acting

Acting is more than just the portrayal of character. It is the way the viewer interacts with the plot and theme of a film, or television drama. The acting is the way into most films. Appearance, gesture, movement, facial expression, sound, commitment and integrity are all part of an actor's armoury.

Beware of using 'realism' or 'believability' as a criterion for judging an actor's performance. Many films and TV dramas do not set out to be realistic – for example, *The Wizard of Oz*. Notions of what is realistic change rapidly with time. What is acceptable to one generation will appear wooden to another.

29
Directing drama

On a drama production the director really gets into his stride when shooting begins, although he or she will have been involved in many aspects of the production so far.

Cast contracts

You, the producer/director, have held auditions. You have chosen and contracted the cast. You should now write a contract to all members of the cast, even though it might be for minimum-pay parts, or even no pay, or postponed payment. You should contract the actors for the number of days they are required and compensate them for their expenses. A daily inclusive expense claim should be agreed in advance, based on a basic rail fare. You should provide food for cast and crew.

On larger budget productions there is a wonderful service called location catering. This is a comprehensively equipped trailer with dedicated staff who can produce a wide range of, sometimes exotic, meals. This is costly. It is more cost effective, but more work, for the production to provide simple meals for the cast and crew while on location. Sometimes friends and helpers can be persuaded to supply good quality sandwiches. In the contract it should be stipulated that meals will be provided by the production and no *per diem* will be paid. A *per diem* is a daily allowance for personal subsistence costs while on location.

Read-through

The first time the cast and the production team will get together formally is at the read-through. This is a good occasion for the producer to introduce the whole production team, and the key members of the crew such as the lighting cameraperson and the sound recordist. The cast will respond better if they know who is doing what. The director will outline his vision of how he would like the production to look and maybe fill in some key locations.

It is important to create a sense of being a team working together on an exciting project. Everyone knows there is going to be a lot of hard work ahead and some very early mornings and a few late nights. The key players on the production will work hard to create a real sense that the production is well organized, that everyone knows what they are doing, and that everything is going extremely well. It may be your first serious production and the budget may be very small, but if you can convince the cast and crew that this show will be a cracker then you will have wholehearted support throughout.

Rehearsal

Try and do an outside rehearsal before filming begins. It helps everyone to get to know each other and it helps the actors. Scenes do need rehearsal.

Directing rehearsal

You, the director, will explain a little about the drama, but leave characterization. The actors will build their own picture of their characters. Be firm about learning lines, but encouraging. It is best not to overpraise, or to worry about someone who may not be so good at this stage.

Put yourself in the position of the camera and move around as the camera would move. Take the rehearsal from there, so the actors know where the camera will be. Concentrate on moves first, then learning lines and then details. Be positive in your approach. Speak quietly. Let the actors do any shouting if necessary.

On the set

The director should try and rehearse the actors while the crew are setting up the lights and getting the camera in position.

This is where the director will block the scene according to the storyboard or according to memory. The storyboard will show the camera angle and the framing of a particular shot as it will appear in the final edited film. This is where the little frames sketched by the director on his or her script come in so useful. They will show the breakdown of shots within the scene.

The director shows the actors which door to come in, where to sit and what particular movements are essential to the scene. An experienced director will allow the actors plenty of freedom in interpreting the dialogue and characterization involved in the scene. This is what actors are trained to do, and they do it very well. After all, you chose these actors because you thought they would interpret the script in the way you imagined it.

Directing rehearsal is about giving encouragement, preparing the right circumstances and allowing the characters to develop and be illuminated by the actors.

Being the director

The director has the responsibility of interpreting the script and staging the production. The director is responsible for everything that appears on the screen, although many decisions will have been made in consultation with the producer. In a modern low-budget production the producer and director are often the same person. In this case it is a good idea to give budget responsibility to the production manager or the production assistant. This way you can help each other stay within budget, or raise extra money if it is needed.

The director may have some elaborate ideas that are not realizable owing to budget constraints. This is not always a bad thing. The lack of a big budget can spur a director to create ingenious ways of realizing a scene. By the time it comes to 'turning over' the first shot on the first day of filming, everything to do with setting up should have been resolved.

Being a drama director requires a balance of skills. You need to be able to work with actors. If you have experience in the theatre, that is very helpful. It is no surprise that two of the best theatre directors working in the UK have gone on to make successful films – Stephen Daldry with *Billy Elliot* and Sam Mendes with the extremely successful Oscar-winning *American Beauty*. Directing for cinema or television requires an understanding of just what can be achieved and what works best in this medium. Stephen Daldry has spoken about the steep learning curve of making his first film, although he was very experienced at directing actors. There are so many other things that you have to make happen.

Filmmaking is about imagination, and the director has the chance to create a world that will excite an audience's imagination. How do you it? You could do worse than start with a few guidelines that other directors have found to be successful.

Composition

The director's job is to realize the script onto the screen for the benefit of the viewer. It is also to intrigue, sometimes to indulge and generally to entertain the viewer with a good story and memorable characters. The successful drama director uses a variety of techniques and strategies to carry the film to the audience. One of the most important is the visual composition of each shot.

Composition consists of shot size, lens angle, camera angle and the way

Fig. 29.1 Over-the-shoulder MCU

these elements add meaning to the content of the frame. For example, the over-the-shoulder two-shot is effective for an intense dialogue scene (see Figs. 29.1 and 29.2)

Camera angles

High-angle and low-angle shots add surprise and visual interest. An overhead shot can give the audience a dramatic overview – perhaps seeing the spy listening at the door. A very wide-angle lens can give a scene enough distortion to create a sinister and disconcerting effect.

Fig. 29.2 Over-the-shoulder two-shot, wider angle

The camera set at an angle and placed low down can look up at a character and make him look evil or very powerful. The tilted frame was a favourite device of Hollywood B movie directors to let the audience know there was something distinctly fishy about the character or what was happening in the scene. You can use both these devices to increase dramatic tension, and convey extra meaning to a scene.

Sound

Sound is a very important way of adding drama and meaning to a scene. I am really talking about extra sound — sound that is added in postproduction to heighten tension, induce a feeling of terror or just give a greater sense of 'reality'.

If you see a car swerving fast around a corner, you expect to hear that tell tale screeching sound so common in films. It is amazing how often exactly the same sounds are added to different feature films for similar actions in entirely different locations. Action movies seem to use a very limited number of sound effects, but that is part of the attraction. It is part and parcel of the genre.

☞ Sound is discussed more fully in Chapter 24.

Don't skimp on sound

It may seem obvious, but it is amazing how many people ignore the need for high-quality sound on a production. So many low-budget films are ruined by bad sound. If you cannot hear easily and without straining what the actors say, you do not engage with the story, and all that nice framing goes for nothing. In the cinema, sound is most important to our enjoyment of a film. So do not be parsimonious on sound resources for your production.

Sound essentials

❖ Always record the best-quality location and sync. sound that it is possible in the conditions. Postproduction cannot improve bad-quality original sound. It can improve good-quality, clean original sound.
❖ Record in stereo.
❖ Use the best mics available.
❖ Do not use the mic. mounted on the camera.
❖ Remember to do a one-minute atmos track, or buzz track, for each location. Record it in stereo. Do the atmos track with set dressing in place, and even some people on the set, or it may sound very empty.

❖ You will record all the sound on the camera, but it is useful also to have a separate recorder. You can use this to record the atmos tracks, and not have to worry about the camera being there. If you want excellent professional quality, use a DAT recorder. But a reasonable quality mini-disc recorder also provides good-quality digital sound.

❖ *Stereo.* Make sure the left and right sides of the stereo mic. represent the left of frame and the right of frame respectively. Obvious, but it can easily be recorded the wrong way. Mark which side is which on the tape/cassette box.

❖ Ask the sound recordist to record any extra sound effects you know you will want on the DAT or minidisc. Always record effects in stereo. It could be possible for the sound recordist or an assistant to do this while you are setting up for another shot that can be recorded on the camera.

❖ Wherever possible use a mic. on a boom, or fish pole. You will need a boom swinger. This will give a better sound perspective, as the boom will move with the camera for the wide shot or close-up.

❖ Sound kit for drama
  ● SQN stereo mixer;
  ● Sennheiser stereo mic.;
  ● Extendable boom, or fishpole;
  ● DAT or mindisc recorder;
  ● Long lengths of XLR cables;

Fig. 29.3 Using a hand-held reflector

- Two lapel radio mics.;
- Lots of spare batteries;
- Headphones.

Lighting

♦ Light subjects first using the three-point light plot. If necessary, use small lights to illuminate the set.

☞ For three-point lighting, see Chapter 18

♦ Use reflected light (see Fig. 29.3).
♦ Most cinematographers agree that drama locations look better if not overlit. But you do need to see your subjects lit attractively to show their features and keep your audience attentive. There are no prizes for being the prince of darkness!

30
Three-way shooting

Shooting with one camera, you typically need to cover a scene in three ways to ensure you have the shots you need and can make the scene work in the edit. If we take a scene where there are two characters with dialogue, then the scene needs to be covered by three shots – a wide shot of the whole scene and close-ups of both characters delivering their dialogue. This will allow for overlaps and 'listening' or 'reaction' shots when the scene is edited.

Your fundamental concern in directing drama is to make sure the whole scene is covered with enough shots to be able to edit it in a meaningful way.

You can also think about camera angles and shooting style, but if the scene is covered by three-way shooting you know it will cut together.

In the example described in Box 30.1, two characters are talking at a table in a café, and the action involves a third character who comes in and joins them with some good news.

The café scene

To shoot this scene in a traditional way you will need to shoot the scene three times. The actors will have to perform the scene three times with exactly the same movements and delivering the dialogue in exactly the same

---

Box 30.1 Café scene

SCENE 10 INTERIOR. DAY. CAFÉ
Anne and Isabelle are sitting at a window table discussing how they are going to raise the money for their forthcoming trip to California.

Angelo comes into the café and sits down at the same table and puts three aeroplane tickets on the table. There is much excitement and hugging as he explains the bizarre circumstances in which he obtained the tickets.

way. This scene can then be edited into a smooth, seamless sequence of dialogue and action.

A good director will shoot and edit a scene like this in such a way that the viewer will not notice the influence of the director or the editor. The viewer will be so captivated by the plot, the characterization and the naturalistic performances of the actors that the illusion of real time and real people will be preserved for that cinematic moment. You can expect competent actors to have learned their lines by the time it comes to shooting each scene. It is still important to rehearse on the set.

The wide shot

The camera position is chosen to view the whole scene as a wide shot (WS).

♦ The two female characters, Anne and Isabelle, are sitting at the window table opposite each other, but quite close, otherwise there is too big a gap between them.

♦ They are clearly composed in the frame to be the main subjects.

♦ The director wants to see a wide view of the main area of the café to give the feeling and atmosphere of the venue. He wants to show it is daytime, and that the café is busy but not bustling.

♦ It is important to see the doorway to the street, as Angelo will come in through this door in a hurry.

♦ In this wide shot the camera will see the street through the glass window. There will be hangings and signs on the glass, so that the daylight in the street does not 'burn out'. The street will not be prominent.

♦ The film lights in the cafe will have blue gel sheets to balance the daylight coming through the large glass windows.

This wide shot can be used as the master shot taking in all the action. The action in the scene can be covered in other ways – perhaps by using all close-ups, or steadycam. If you are confident that this is how you want the scene to look in the final edit, then do not waste time with the master or wide shot. But are you absolutely sure you can do without the wide shot?

Scene I. Take One

The actors have been rehearsed while the lights are going up and the crew is preparing. The rehearsal has gone OK; the lights are set and the camera is ready. The sound recordist has discreetly placed personal mics on the table in front of Anne and Isabelle. Angelo is wearing a hidden radio mic. The sound took some time to do. The actors are ready and rehearsed. The cast and crew are concentrating hard. One last technical rehearsal to check camera and sound are getting the right pictures and the right sound. Then, Turn Over and Action.

The scene runs smoothly until near the end, when Angelo comes in and trips over the carpet. Much laughter and a sense of relief all round. The carpet is taped down. The atmosphere on the set is a fine balance between serious and intense concentration, and relaxed professionalism.

Scene 1. Take Two

All goes well but Angelo comes in too early. He says he did not hear the cue line. This is where you need people. Yes, there is a first AD on this shoot. She can go outside and cue Angelo. If she wears headphones with a feed from the sound mixer, she can hear the dialogue, but the cable is not long enough. More cable needed.

Scene 1. Take Three

No glitches, but the director feels the performances have 'gone off' owing to the short break. He asks Angelo to hold back the tickets until he has sat down. This will make the single shots around the table look better and allow for an edit to compress time within the scene.

Scene 1. Take Four

Everything goes well this time. Everyone is happy. 'Let's move on to the single of Anne,' says the director.

So the WS is in the can. The PA has taken the time-code numbers for each take. The director watched the wide shot on his small personal monitor, but for the other scenes will watch performances of the actors nearer to the set. He knows the framing is right and is now concerned about the actual impact of the scene. He is already thinking about the next shot. Even the cameraman thinks the shot went well, and, amazingly, sound are happy too.

Reset for the next scene

The crew start resetting for the next shot. The actors relax. It goes dark. Somebody turns the café lights on. People in jeans emerge out of corners and from behind and under tables.

The lighting cameraman is in deep discussion with a corpulent guy in jeans who is wearing large gloves – that's the freelance Sparks (electrician).

The sound recordist is putting something cold down the back of the actress playing Anne. She is looking at her script and does not seem to notice she is being wired for sound.

Large lights on stands are moving around the room, seemingly by themselves. The table is being pulled away from the window so that on the next shot the camera will not see people moving in the street.

The camera assistant picks up the tripod and moves it to behind Isabelle's chair. She puts the camera on the tripod and lines up the shot. A soft light lamp with blue gel and scrim is moved next to the camera — this is the fill light for Anne's single shot.

The set looks bright and sharp. Dust can be seen reflecting in the light beam of a small 800-watt lamp. The café table is dressed with clean coffee cups, a bowl of sugar sticks, paper napkins and a small vase of silk flowers. The PA asks the actress for clarification of the lines, as she thinks there was a change.

Move on

A new director might feel that to get a scene right in just a few takes means that the scene could be performed better. Avoid this way of thinking. Keep up the pace. People work better if they feel that good work can be accomplished without resorting to dozens of takes. Experienced actors are used to getting things right first time. Keep the set energized. Move on just as soon as you can.

Keep up with the schedule

The director sets the pace and rhythm of work. He or she will work with the production manager to make sure the schedule is kept to. Try not to slip behind schedule. Not only will the costs go up, but cast and crew will lose enthusiasm and energy. Of course, things happen that are out of your control, but a good production team will have minimized the chances of long delays.

The single shots

The next shot will be an MCU of Anne sitting at the table and saying her lines (see Fig. 30.1). She has the most dialogue. The camera has been moved and the lighting adjusted. Make-up has done some minor touching up. The actress knows her lines and she will remember what to do. She may ask the PA about a small point of continuity. Was her cup of coffee put down at this point or later?

The cameraman frames the shot and asks the director whether he likes it or whether he would prefer the shot to be tighter. Yes, the director would prefer the shot to be a little tighter. The director asks Anne to bring her hand

Fig. 30.1 MCU Anne

with the coffee cup nearer to her face, so that it is included in the tighter shot.

The director asks for a run-through. The actress runs through her lines as for a performance. Angelo is now at the table and we hear his lines. In fact, we see the whole scene apart from Angelo coming in through the door because that action is not in shot. There are some minor adjustments to the lights and the scene is ready to be recorded. Suddenly everything is ready to go.

MS Anne is in the can.

The reverse single

Anne is in dialogue with Isabelle. Isabelle has some lines but is mainly listening. The whole scene must be run again. This time the camera is on an MCU of Isabelle (see Fig. 30.2).

The cameraperson and the PA make sure the shot is the same size as the single shot of Anne. The framing must match perfectly, as these two shots will be inter-cut. Anne is looking camera right. Isabelle must therefore look camera left.

Eyeline

The single shots have to be framed to cut perfectly with the two-shot. The continuity has to be perfect. The eyeline of each actor in the single shot must be at the right height and angle. Nothing looks worse than a wonky eyeline.

Make sure the camera is in the right position to be at the eyeline of the

Fig. 30.2 MCU Isabelle

actor who is responding to the dialogue. This may require a little bit of cheating to make it convincing.

Crossing the line

Not crossing the line worries a lot of people when they start filming. It is really not so difficult. It is just like watching a football match. You buy a seat to a football match and you sit on one side of the stadium. The two goals are to the left and right. You could be watching the match from the position that the main cameras take when they televise a match.

The blues start off kicking from right to left, and the reds from left to right. At half-time they change sides. As long as you stay in the same seat, the players will change round playing from the opposite ends after half-time, and it will all make perfect sense to everyone in the stadium.

The main TV cameras stay the same side of the pitch throughout the match.

But if you moved to the opposite side of the stadium at half-time, the players would not appear to change round. You would have crossed an invisible line that could be drawn down the middle of the pitch from one goal to the other.

This is not a good idea from a television point of view. It confuses the viewer and upsets our notion that the cameras are seeing the game in a seat we might have taken if we had been there. Also, if a camera on the other side of the pitch offers a wide shot that is then cut with a wide shot from one of the main cameras, the players will appear to be playing towards the wrong goal.

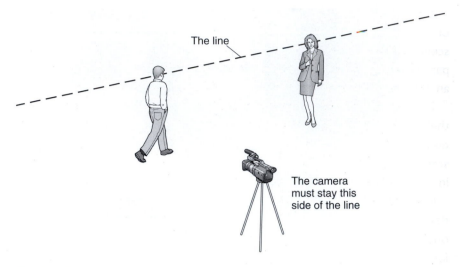

Fig. 30.3 Crossing the line

In television drama production you draw an invisible line between the eyes of each actor in a dialogue. The same rule applies in documentary between the eyes of the interviewer and the contributor. When you shoot the single shots of each person, you must stay the same side of that line. By not crossing the line the characters look as though they are talking to each other, and not to someone else outside the frame.

The camera must always stay the same side of that invisible line, and not cross over on to the other side. In practice, this typically means not moving the camera behind the head of either character, but always shooting from the same side (see Fig. 30.3).

Getting the message

So far the scene has been covered in three ways, so that you are certain you have all the shots needed to cut the scene together:

♦ a wide shot of the entire action;
♦ a single shot of one character;
♦ a single shot of the other character.

You will need to ensure that:

♦ all three shots will cut together to make the scene work in the film;
♦ the action is the same in each shot;
♦ that there is continuity in dialogue, lighting and set dressing.

But does this convey the meaning of the scene? Is the emphasis right?

It is, of course, impossible to say just what is going on in this scene without seeing and hearing the dialogue. But what we can say from the way this scene has been shot is that the character Angelo appears to have a minor part as he only appears in the WS. But when Angelo delivers the tickets it is an important moment.

The two young women can realize their goal in the film – to escape from their tedious, menial jobs and start a new life in California with Anne's newly discovered father. Angelo, her cousin, has had to pull off a daring Internet scam to get the tickets. His role in the story is pivotal. This may be conveyed in the dialogue, but it is not visually clear.

A fourth shot is needed. The director wants to see Angelo come in the door and hurry over to the table and deliver his important opening lines in one smooth tracking shot. This has been planned and the crew are setting up for it.

When should you film a shot like this? Just after doing the master shot would be ideal. The lighting would be set up for the wide shot and this might save time. On the other hand, the tracks have still to be laid, so the actors may prefer to do their single shots before the more difficult and time-consuming tracking shot. In the end it will be up to the camera operator and the director to make a decision based on their experience and the local circumstances.

Camera dolly

A professional camera dolly is a platform with four wheels that runs on tracks. A camera is mounted on the platform usually with the operator sitting with it. The idea is that camera and operator can be moved together along the tracks to record a smooth moving shot. A jib arm can be mounted on the dolly so that the camera can also move up and down with a smooth action.

There are less sophisticated, and much cheaper, dollies for lightweight cameras that work surprisingly well. A light four-wheeled platform carries the tripod and travels on plastic piping tracks. The floor surface needs to be flat, and you can get a good tracking shot for low cost and less setting-up time. Good for interior use.

Try and beg or borrow a camera dolly and tracks. A tracking shot can look very professional and give that classy 'film' look to any television drama. But it can be costly in time and resources, so don't go to all that trouble just for the sake of one shot if it does not contribute to the meaning of the scene.

The tracking shot

In this café scene above the tracks have been laid for the camera to move round behind the table and up towards the door. This shot requires good teamwork and coordination. Lights have to be moved and marks put on the floor using gaffer tape. The camera will be moved on its dolly by a grip. The cameraman will sit on the dolly and operate the camera, while the grip pushes the dolly along the track. He may have help, but he is in charge of gently hitting the exact mark where the camera will stop, and ensuring the smooth camera movement necessary for this type of shot. The shot is rehearsed several times. This sort of tracking shot will take time to set up. It is important to rehearse the actors and crew with the camera in place. It has to look absolutely right, otherwise it will look awful.

Steadycam

There are many different ways to film a scene with three characters set in a restaurant. Television and film dramas that want a modern, fluid quality create a tight-knit, intimate world by not using the three-way approach. The framing is close and often takes place within one developing shot.

This approach works well using steadycam and digital cameras to shoot in low, naturalistic light conditions. Steadycam offers a lot of fluidity, and it is difficult working with a hand-held camera when you want to have long takes on close-up shots.

Instead of shooting a scene three ways with a WS and single shots, you can concentrate on close-ups of the actors, or two-shots. The intimacy of the characters is mirrored in the way the scene is shot with tight close shots. The characters interact within a tight frame. This works well in Widescreen, where the screen ratio is 16:9. Conventional television works with a 4:3 format. Terrestrial television channels now require programmes to be shot using the 16:9 format, or a version of it.

The professional Steadycam is used on movies and throughout television for factual programmes and drama. It is a wonderful tool and can create marvellous sequences in the hands of a trained operator. The Steadycam System is basically a special body harness with the camera attached that the operator straps on. This allows the operator to move and shoot at the same time by checking the shots not through the camera view-finder but with a small conveniently positioned monitor typically at waist level.

The wonderful thing about Steadycam is that the shots are completely steady, and are very smooth, giving a fluid, gliding movement to any scene. Steadycam is good for chase scenes, as it can go virtually anywhere. Some directors prefer to use it instead of tracking shots.

There are budget versions for smaller cameras that operate very well. Make sure you practise before filming that chase sequence across the roof tops!

Cinematic framing

Scenes in a television drama shot on 16:9 format can be more 'filmic'. You can use framing more commonly seen in the cinema. Many directors feel the 16:9 format offers more natural framing not only on exterior scenes but also with dialogue shots.

One way to do this is to frame your dialogue shots with both characters in the frame. You see one character on one side of the screen, and the back of the head or the shoulder or the side of the body of the other character (see Box 30.2). You can have at least two sizes of this type of shot. A close-up of the full face of one character, with the side of the head and a little shoulder of the other. You can have a medium close-up, or a wider mid-shot, showing most of one character with part of the back of the other.

This type of framing can give urgency and dynamism to the relationship between the two characters.

Cut off

Using the widescreen mode on your camera, this style of two-shot can be achieved relatively easily. Actors are trained to keep their head absolutely still while reacting to another actor who is delivering his or her lines. But there is the problem of 'cut off'.

Cut off is the area around the edges and the inside of the frame that is not visible to the home viewer. High-end cameras have this 'safe' area marked on the viewfinder. You can hire monitors that can switch between the 'safe' area and the full frame captured by the camera. Make sure the shot is composed so that the action is within the 'cut-off' lines in the viewfinder or on the monitor.

Some broadcasters demand that programmes are shot in widescreen but have a 'safe' area for the important action within the frame. This is for domestic viewers who are not viewing on a widescreen format television. It

Box 30.2 Over the shoulder two-shots

These two matching over-the-shoulder two-shots will cut together.

is important to make sure you know what is the 'safe' frame size recommended by the broadcaster. It may be necessary to use black tape to make a letterbox effect on the monitor screen to make sure the framing conforms to the required standards.

31

Lighting for drama

The best and most effective lighting for film or television drama is both a science and an art. It takes considerable talent, and many years of experience to understand and know how to 'paint in light'. You have to know the possibilities and parameters of the medium in which you are working – film or the digital video domain. You also need a large budget, a dedicated crew and a lot of specialist lights to create the sort of beautiful lighting seen in films like the period drama *Shakespeare in Love* or the classic *Citizen Kane*.

It is no wonder that the best lighting cameramen, directors of photography (DOP) and cinematographers are in such demand. They can make a film or television drama look like a million dollars just using light and their camera. You may aspire to make beautifully textured and lit films, but start with what you have.

Why do we need lighting?

Try the exercise outlined in Box 31.1.

Daylight with the sun shining on a clear day offers full spectrum light that helps create a three-dimensional image on a flat screen. Blue skies mean blue seas, white surf and superb landscape – vistas with depth and clarity. The trouble is you cannot set all your dramas in outstanding landscape in a sunny climate, or you would have wall-to-wall westerns.

You don't need a lot of expensive lights to create an effect. A single candle can produce enough light to film two people at an intimate, romantic candlelit dinner. But if you want depth, clarity and

Blonde

> **Box 31.1** Exercise
>
> Take your camera outside and look through the viewfinder at an object or person. Look at how the light falls on the subject and locate the source of light. If the sun is out the main source of light will be the sun. There will also be a second source of reflected light – the sky itself.
>
> A person's face will show strong light coming from overhead and one direction – that is, from the sun. The other side of the face will also be lit, but the light will appear to be less powerful. You should be able to see facial features in a way that suggests a three-dimensional face and head. This will work well only if the sun is not directly behind you, but more over your left or right shoulder.
>
> The natural sunlight has illuminated the subject both through the direct light from the sun and from reflected light from the sky to give natural modelling to the face.

'naturalism' in your pictures, especially those interior scenes, then you are going to have to add some extra lighting.

Paint with light

Lighting can do so much more than just illuminate a scene. It can direct the viewer's attention to a person or object. It can create depth. It can make performers look so much more attractive. Lighting is a wonderful way to create mood and atmosphere. Soft light can be seductive. Harsh light can make an ordinary room into a disturbing and destructive environment with overtones of fear and desolation. Light is the filmmaker's pallet.

The television picture responds well to lighting for depth. Somehow it is more satisfying to watch television pictures that have depth and subtlety. We want to see three-dimensional characters leap out of finely detailed back-grounds straight into our living room. We don't want to see annoying hotspots on faces and foreheads, or nasty shadows on the walls.

Above all we want the lighting to help us understand and enjoy the fantasy that has been put on the screen before us. It must not intrude, but it must do its job.

Zebra

Digital cameras typically have an aid to getting the light levels right in the frame. 'Hot spots' on a well-lit subject or scene are to be avoided if possible.

There are some exceptions, such as a night-club scene, or where an effect is desired that allows the image to burn out in places. The 'zebra' effect in the viewfinder is a way of showing when part, or all, of the frame is too 'hot', or is too bright for the overall good of the picture.

If a small part of the picture begins to zebra, that shows you that there is a slight hot spot there. There is no need to adjust the lighting or the aperture if this is a very small part of the picture — perhaps a nose or the top of a bald head. That is fine. Adjust nothing and know that you will have a well-lit picture — everything else being equal. If the whole frame zebras, then you do need to make adjustments, either to the aperture or to the way the lighting is set up, or possibly both. Experiment with different lighting conditions so that you know exactly what degree of zebra is right for you.

Naturalism

This is a difficult term that can mean different things to different filmmakers. In lighting it comes from the idea that a scene from a television drama should be lit in a way that recreates a natural situation.

One definition might be: naturalism is a look that appears to most people to be something they know and can relate to, because it relates to a scene lit naturally. Lighting should be subtle for a naturalistic look. Much television drama is set in the everyday world of today. The filmmaker is attempting to create a recognizable world with characters that would not look out of place in the town where you live.

Reality

I have deliberately not used the word 'real'. Each person has his or her own sense of 'reality'. The world the Spanish film director Luis Bunuel created in his films was often not naturalistic, but it had a very definite 'reality'. Genres such as Sci-fi and Horror have their own sense of what is 'real'. One of the exciting things about filming a screenplay is that you can create your own sense of reality.

Reflected light

To obtain a naturalistic look to a scene, create a reflected light source. Reflected light comes from a bigger light source offering softer light.

- ♦ *Sunlight reflector.* For exterior scenes you can use a sunlight reflector. This can be a specialist 'fold-up' reflector. These are coated with a reflective white, or silver, or gold surface. The gold surface gives a warmer light that can be used to create a romantic effect. A reflector is useful as a fill light where the sunlight is providing the key light. If the sunlight is providing back lighting for a sunset shot, then the reflector can 'lift' the face of the subject.

♦ *White polystyrene.* You can use a large sheet of white polystyrene held up by clipping it onto a light stand. In India, where they make a large number of movies using the abundant sunlight, you see film workers carrying white stand-mounted reflectors on their backs from one set up to the next – one worker to one reflector. They also use huge white reflectors measuring two metres by two metres. This large reflective area gives a very good soft light source. Incidentally, if you see someone carrying a black umbrella on a film set in India, it is not because it is going to rain, but to keep the sun off the director or a star actor. It is a prized job to carry the umbrella for the director and the star actors. The large sheet of white *poly*, as it is known, can also be used on interior sets. Point a light at the poly and it will create enough naturalistic reflected light to light a reasonable working area.

♦ *Bounce light.* You can even use the white walls of the room to bounce the light off, but make sure they are white and not cream or magnolia. Your characters' faces will look rather ill if the wall is not pure white.

Hard and soft light

♦ *Hard light* is direct light from a concentrated source. Direct sunlight is hard light. Sunlight at midday is hard light that casts well-defined shadows. In filming, hard light is used to create a sharply defined image, and as a distant light source, such as outside a window, to indicate daylight.

♦ *Soft light* is diffused or reflected light, as you would find on a cloudy overcast day. Light from the sky is soft light. In filming, soft light is useful as a 'fill' light, as it does not create shadows. Modern lighting directors tend to go for soft lighting sources to create a more naturalistic look.

The area to be lit

Before setting the lights, make sure the director and the lighting cameraperson have agreed on the area to be lit. The main characters and the centre of the action should be in a position where they can be lit. Keep the characters well separated from background walls, or other flat areas of the set. This way you will find it easier to use the lights for good 3D modelling. The idea is to avoid unsightly shadows. Of course, if you are shooting a *film noir,* creepy shadow effects can be desirable.

Check that there are no hanging objects such as an overhead light that could cast an unsightly shadow over the scene. Check that when the characters move they move within the agreed area that has been lit.

Lighting the café scene

As a lighting example, we can take the café scene from Chapter 30. Just to remind you, there are three actors and no dramatic action, stunts or pyrotechnics. It is an important scene in the film. It must be lit properly and naturalistically.

♦ The lighting cameraperson has to consider that the scene takes place next to a big street window. The table where the action takes place is in the window of the café.

♦ Two characters are sitting at the table.

♦ The third character Angelo comes in through the door from the street.

♦ The natural light for the table is coming from the daylight out in the street. Let us assume it is a typical British day in summer – bright but not sunny.

♦ The daylight from outside has to be matched with a key light positioned right next to the window to light the faces of the actors at the table.

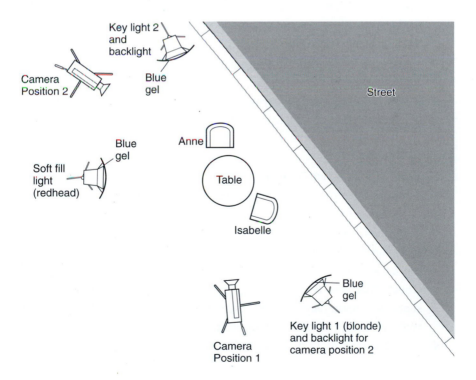

Fig. 31.1 Possible lighting set-up for café scene wide shot

Ideally there should be two key lights – one for each actor at the table, but the second key would be visible when Angelo comes in through the street door. A possible lighting set-up is shown in Fig. 31.1.

Lighting essentials

- ❖ Use the three-point lighting system as your basic lighting design even if the key light is the sun.
- ❖ Use the light sources you have available to create effects and make your actors look good.
- ❖ Light quickly and efficiently. Try not to move lamps too much. Make each lamp work in several different ways
- ❖ Do a white balance for each different lighting set-up.
- ❖ Keep the sun over one shoulder and not directly behind you. This will not dazzle the subject, and will help 'model' the features.
- ❖ Use reflected light for a naturalistic look.
- ❖ If a light is too hot and creates hot spots on an actor's face, put a layer of scrim over the barn doors.
- ❖ Carry make-up powder to dab on noses and foreheads. This is not a silly idea: it is often an easy and quick way to stop 'flaring', and could help you in many situations from interviews to love scenes where a 'flare' is inappropriate.
- ❖ Watch out for flares from shiny objects and reflective surfaces such as mirrors.
- ❖ If you are using natural daylight and artificial light, remember to put blue gel on the film lights.

Safety essentials

Keep safety in mind when using film lights. Make sure all light stands are safe and no light is near to an inflammable surface – the major fire at Windsor Castle was thought to have been started by a light too near to a curtain.

- ❖ Tape down cables with gaffer tape.
- ❖ Make sure all film lights have safety glass or grilles before taking them out on location.
- ❖ Check that the power source can handle the wattage. Domestic supplies cannot handle more than 3000 watts on one socket. One redhead is 800 watts. One blonde is 2000 watts.
- ❖ Always use an RCD on all electrical supplies.

32

The 10-minute short

So, you have a beautifully written script that has been lovingly revised, and is ready to go. Let's say it is a ten-minute short. This is a very good length for a first or second film. It is popular with industry professionals because it shows you can create a story with a beginning, middle and end, and realize it on the screen.

British film director Ridley Scott (*Alien* and *Blade Runner*) puts his name behind a competition called *Sci-fi shorts*. You have to submit a script for a 10-minute sci-fi short. Scott says: 'There was nothing when I started. And this is a great incentive. My message is have a go, just do it.' The 10-minute short really can be a passport to getting work in the industry. First you have to make it.

Let us imagine that you are the director and writer. You will probably be the producer as well. Television production is collaborative and involves a great deal of teamwork. In the case of a low-budget 10-minute drama shot on digital equipment, it is better to work with a small committed team.

A 30-minute drama would involve more people because there would be more scenes, a bigger cast, more locations. This all involves more complex servicing. More people to transport and more equipment. That means more problems. It is also more exciting. Working on a big movie with dozens of people is a creative and a very rewarding way to earn your living. But it is not at all easy to get that first break.

More and more people are working outside broadcast television and the big movie system. They are creating their own digital films for Internet consumption or digital distribution. Keep it simple. Less is more.

Phase one

It is the first meeting of the production team. All you have at this meeting is a script. You may have an overall budget. Let's say you are a small production team of three people. The ballpark budget will have been worked out at the treatment stage. Around the table will be

- ♦ the director/producer/writer – you
- ♦ the production assistant;
- ♦ the production manager;
- ♦ the lighting cameraperson, called in for the afternoon session;
- ♦ possibly a runner or other general assistant.

At this meeting the team will primarily be involved in the following.

- ♦ The script will need to be broken down, scene by scene.
- ♦ The script should also be discussed in detail, to discover what can be done, what might not quite fit and what does not make sense.
- ♦ Casting may be mentioned.
- ♦ Budget is always important and will need to be discussed.

By the end of the meeting you will have a fairly detailed breakdown of the locations, some ideas for the casting for each scene and a better idea of how the budget will stretch to cover everything, or not as the case may be. Remember:

- ♦ Adapt and be flexible: these are the watchwords for this meeting.
- ♦ You all need to go home feeling you can do the film on the budget and in the time allocated.

Phase two

You as the producer/director, the production assistant and the production manager get together to break the script down fully and do an overall schedule. The script will be broken down into scenes in terms of characters, locations, crew, costume, make-up, props, and so on.

Each character – and therefore each member of the cast – will have a list of the scenes in which he or she has lines to say, or needs to be present. Any extras needed will be indicated here scene by scene. Scenes will be grouped by location and shooting day.

The production manager will be working on props lists for each scene – suitcases, costume, binoculars, whatever the director specifies. There will also be special requirements for each scene – for example, 'in-vision' cars, or other specific location requirements such as a telephone kiosk or bus shelter. The breakdown of each scene will be under headings such as these.

- ♦ *Locations.* All scenes and their locations will be marked and grouped together.
- ♦ *Essential props and ongoing props.* One character might smoke a cigar in several scenes or carry a briefcase. The script may have forgotten to say this, but the props must be given to the actor for each scene in which they are required.

♦ *Costume.* Any costume changes essential to the story will be noted. Does a character age prematurely, or have an injury that goes from one scene to the next? (An actor with a plaster on his face because he has sustained an in-the-script injury always seems to me to look excessively silly – see the movie *Proof of Life.*)

♦ *Special effects and Health & Safety.* This includes explosions and anything to do with fire or water, as well as other situations that need to have a risk assessment – such as working at heights, in extreme conditions, or even in very tight spaces. All locations must be risk assessed.

♦ *Special equipment.* You may need something like an underwater camera – for example, a blimp (protective cover) for a small DV camera that can be used underwater can be hired for a very reasonable daily rate.

♦ *Continuity.* An important and difficult area for the production manager and the production assistant is to make sure that there is seamless continuity of every single thing that will be seen on the screen, from one scene to another. The PM must be totally on top of this before shooting begins. Continuity can let down a short, or it can show how impressive your team can be.

Phase three

You need to cover a lot of ground over the next few days. It may even take longer.

You will try and decide on the following.

♦ *Crew:* lighting cameraperson, sound and camera assistant if necessary.

♦ *Equipment.* What do you have already and what needs to be hired or begged or borrowed? Decide who will fix this and by what date. Check cost and availability of kit for any tricky shots requiring a different type of camera – for example, a car rig with miniature cameras.

♦ *Locations.* Decide who will fix locations and get permissions. The production manager and the director should visit and confirm all locations. It is always better for two people to recce locations.

♦ *Casting.* Ideas for casting, including secondary roles, need to be finalized as soon as possible. Use the publication *Spotlight* to find actors. It is now available online, but you have to subscribe to *Spotlight* to access its online lists. Some libraries have copies. Casting is a time-consuming process.

♦ *Auditions.* Make a definite date for auditions. Once a list of possible cast has been agreed, the production assistant should be in charge of organizing the auditions, inviting performers and chasing them up to make sure they are coming. The audition day can be a long stressful day. If you need more than one day, try and make the second day as soon after the first as possible.

♦ *Props and costume.* Sort out any difficult props or specific costume requirements. You may need to have mock firearms, or any other props essential for the action. There are usually some essential props, ranging from wigs to wire cutters. Who will be in charge of props? Will you need a specialist props person or can the PA do it? Will you need to hire costumes and will you need a costume person to look after them and fit them?

♦ *Transport and office expenses.* The PM is in total control of the budget for everything. Phone bills, mobile phone bills and photocopying will eat up a lot more than you think and need to be rigorously controlled. Transport costs must all go through the production manager.

♦ *Schedules.* The production manager should now be able to start doing daily schedules.

♦ *Production.* You should now be ready to shoot your 10-minute short. Good Luck.

Postproduction

33 Desktop digital postproduction

Postproduction is the process that takes place after you have shot all relevant material for the programme. It is everything you do after the production phase of the programme.

This can be a very complex process involving high-end digital equipment to enhance and recreate sequences for a film like *Titanic*. It can also be a relatively inexpensive and cosy experience done in your own home on your computer.

Experienced and controversial filmmaker Ken Russell now makes low-budget films using a DV digital camera. He edits at home with a computer desktop editing system. Non-linear digital editing has truly democratized filmmaking.

A moment of history

It is interesting that it was not until the early 1920s that Russian film students discovered the real power of film editing. The filmmaker Lev Kuleshov was running a filmmaking class with students, including one called Pudovkin. Running out of film stock, the students tried re-editing films that they had already produced. They tried a number of different ways to edit the films.

Perhaps their most significant success was with a famous Russian actor, Moszhukin. They filmed three identical close-up shots of Moszhukin. Then they intercut these shots with three different images – a little girl, a woman in a coffin and a plate of soup.

Pudovkin wrote up the experiment. He described how audiences were amazed at the actor's ability to convey a variety of emotions depending on what he was looking at. Love for the little girl, sadness and compassion for the death of an old woman, and hunger and anticipation of a good bowl of wholesome soup. In fact, the actor had been directed to have an unemotional and blank expression on his face. He had no idea what he was supposed to be looking at.

The experiment showed Pudovkin that separate images are like individual words that impart their full meaning only as part of a sentence. Separate images take on a different meaning when placed next to other images. The concept of film editing was born. The idea that by juxtaposing different images it is possible to tell a story and create dramatic tension works for both documentary and drama productions. An audience will search for meaning and credibility in a sequence of images.

Understand the editing process

Whatever role you are taking, or are going to take, on a production, it is important to know something about the editing process. Knowing how the pictures will eventually fit together will help with all the production processes. It is well worth doing a quick editing exercise to familiarize yourself with the kit available to you, and with working out just how pictures and sound can be put together to tell a story.

Look at any music video to see the power of editing. See an artist apparently singing in the middle of a busy street in New York. It is night. Cars go by in front of and behind the singer in blurred streams of coloured lights. The singer appears to be standing in the middle of the busiest traffic in the world. It looks beautiful and dangerous at the same time. In fact, the singer is miming the song in a studio down the road against a bluescreen. The effect is possible only with the use of sophisticated digital effects in postproduction.

☞ For more on bluescreen, see Chapters 14 and 36.

Postproduction is now largely a digital process where pictures and sound are manipulated and rearranged to produce the final programme. This includes any digital effects or extra material needed to enhance the programme. Computing power has changed the way films and television programmes are edited.

It is now possible to create the most spectacular and awe-inspiring pictures with advanced digital technology. But be warned: these effects are not just extremely expensive; they are also very time-consuming.

Because of the power of modern computers, it is also possible to repair many 'mistakes' made during shooting. For example, a scene that was filmed under water in a swimming pool could be digitally enhanced to make the sides of the pool invisible, or to make it seem as if the action took place in open sea or in a coral reef near a desert island. The same warning applies though: this is very costly. Why? The kit needed to manipulate images over and above average editing costs hundreds of thousands of pounds and exists only in postproduction facilities houses. Kit such as Quantel Edit Box and Quantel Hal, or Flame or Smoke, is available in facilities houses. It is possible to hire a digital effects (DVE) suite with an editor, but think in terms of well over £1000 a day at 2001 prices. Dry hire, or hiring just the equipment without an operator, for basic digital editing is much more reasonable.

Digital editing kit

There are several dedicated postproduction systems used in the industry. The most well known is Avid, which has become almost industry standard in the USA and the UK. Other systems that run on MAC or PC platforms are also widely available. Final Cut Pro is Apple's system, and there are many more for PCs. Adobie Premier is popular both professionally and for home use. Other systems include Speedrazor and Fast Edit.

In all cases you will need a great deal of computer memory to produce broadcast-quality pictures and sound. But it is possible to produce high-quality short films with a good home computer and some extra disk storage space. Digital video editing is getting easier, more available and more affordable. Recent developments mean that many new computers are being sold with video editing software (see Fig. 33.1).

◆ *PCs.* Microsoft's Windows Millennium Edition (ME) operating system has digital editing software built in. Digital video pictures and sound can be recorded and the images manipulated. You will still need plenty of computer disk space to make a 10-minute video programme, but the software is fine and works well.

Fig. 33.1 Desktop editing

- *Apple.* Apple has created the iMovie 2 software, which is standard on Mac computers. You can do normal cuts and dissolves as well as transitions and exciting digital effects with this software.

- *Adobe Premiere.* There are many editing software packages available, but, if you are going out to buy one, then Adobe Premiere is sensibly priced and works well in most situations for Mac and PC. This is tried-and-tested editing software that can do everything most people will need to make a drama or documentary up to broadcast standard (see Fig. 33.2).

- *Firewire.* To transfer your rushes from your DV camera to the computer you will need a Firewire. This is a smart connecting lead developed by Apple. Firewire ports are standard on Mac computers, but can be used on PCs as well. Firewire is rapidly becoming the industry standard, taken up by major camera manufacturers such as Canon, Sony, JVC, Sharp and Panasonic. The big advantage of firewire is that there is absolutely no loss of picture or sound quality in the transfer process to and from the computer.

- *Cameras.* The best quality format for desktop digital editing is the DV format. This DV family includes mini DV and, at the professional end, DVCAM.

  Check that your DV camera is firewire compatible and has a suitable DV port built in to the camera. The technical term is an IEEE-1394 port.

- *DV capture cards.* You can get low-cost DV capture cards that work very well for home editing, but most will not be able to give full-screen video on your computer screen. The pictures are digital and high quality, and it is possible to see two pictures side by side – essential for editing.

- Better-quality and more expensive DV capture cards include hardware CODECs. These will display full-screen video on the computer screen.

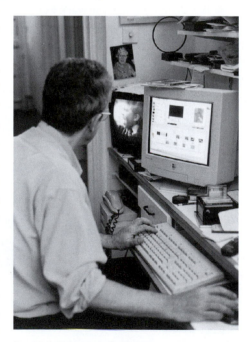

Fig. 33.2 Editing on Adobe Premiere

- *Sound.* Most sound cards will work with the DV firewire system. The sound card should have SP/DIF digital input and output facilities.
- *Sound monitoring.* The tiny speakers that come with computers are not up to the job of monitoring good-quality sound for video. If you are going to do sound editing, then you need a good-quality sound amplifier and speakers. If you have a decent hi-fi system, you can link it up to the computer and use that. But do not deprive the rest of the family of their one and only stereo sound system!
- *Broadband.* Broadband is the new lightning fast method of sending all sorts of information via the Internet. (It does require a special broadband line to do this.) This includes moving video pictures of high quality. Many Internet users will benefit from this new technology, because web sites will be able to deliver video as well as the usual web content such as audio, text and graphics.

Computer storage

The way pictures are stored onto tape is called compression.

- DV format uses a standard compression ratio of 5:1.
- Video needs about 200Mb of disk space to store one minute of moving pictures and sound.
- A five-minute television programme will need at least one Gb of disk space to store the programme. But . . .
- When you edit, you will be putting much more video material into your computer than the final duration of the programme. You will also need disk space for the rushes. You usually digitize about five or six times as much material as you need. So a five-minute programme will probably need at least six Gb of disk space.
- Realistically you should go for as much disk storage as possible. Perhaps a minimum of 10 Gb extra disk space with an optimum forty or more Gbs.
- Ideally you should go for a very fast disk drive suitable for coping with moving pictures. This is known as an SCSI drive.

Time code

When you press the record button on your camcorder, numbers representing each frame, second and minute will be recorded onto the tape. This is *time code.* It is essential in the editing process. It allows each frame to be identified by its discrete number.

- Consumer DV will 'pick up' the time code from the last shot on the tape, provided there is no break in recording. This does not mean that you cannot stop recording and turn off the camera. It means that when you start recording again you must make sure you 'pick up' – that is, record over – the last few frames previously recorded on the tape. This will 'pick up' the time code of the last few frames and continue numbering the new frames you are recording.

♦ Difficulties arise because each separate tape can record the time code with the same numbers. Roll one of your production could have a time code of 00.12.22.15 of your production. Exactly the same timecode could appear at a similar point on Roll Two. When the editing software calls up the number, it could have two sets of the same numbers to choose from, which would confuse it terribly.

♦ To get over this, the editing software renumbers everything that is digitized into the computer with a new set of time codes. The operator can set the time code so that each tape is numbered separately to avoid confusion, adding another set of digits for the roll number. But the original time code will be lost.

♦ The video editing process works by accessing each picture and its recorded sound via the time code.

♦ Professional cameras allow the operator to put in 'user bits' to the time code sequence, and customize the numbers for each roll of tape. Then it is possible to go through the editing process with the original time code for each roll of tape.

♦ The advantages for preserving the original time code are that you can use the desktop editing system to do an off-line edit. On completion of the off-line edit, an EDL (Edit Decision List) can be produced.

♦ An EDL is a complete list of all the time-code numbers in the order in which they have been edited. It is an accurate record of all the decisions you made during the editing process. You will need appropriate software to produce an industry-standard EDL.

♦ Most online edit suites will have equipment that can read an EDL. This will be able to read your EDL and automatically conform a master tape from your original rushes tapes.

Video editing

Linear editing

Until the late 1980s, video postproduction was linear. With linear editing the pictures and sound are compiled in a line from the beginning to the end. The beginning of the programme has to be at the beginning of the tape, and each sequence in the correct order. Sequences can be re-recorded in the right place, but quality is sacrificed. It is not possible simply to drop in some extra pictures and sound, without going back to the beginning and starting the edit all over again. It is rather like dominoes: you cannot break the sequence and you can only add on at the end.

Non-linear editing

Computer non-linear editing changed everything for video. In fact, it brought editing back to where it had been with film.

With film editing you can hold up a strip of film, look at it, turn it upside down, add another strip of pictures to it. Then you can put back the strip of film at any point in your programme. You can take out a few frames here and a few frames there to adjust for time without having to re-edit the whole programme. You can work in a non-linear manner. This is how computer editing works.

Just as on your computer you can take out a word or a paragraph from the page you are writing and paste the words elsewhere in the document, so you can do exactly the same with pictures and sound in an editing software package.

Video editing – you have the power

The art of storytelling relies on a good story, and the way the story is told. The story has to be in the right order and it has to be told with an assured delivery, varying the pace and rhythm. There need to be light and shade with climaxes and quiet periods. These are the skills needed for video editing.

In the case of making television programmes, it is in the postproduction process that the final programme is fashioned, but only if everything else is in place. Good editing can make everything in the production look better, but it cannot rescue a bad script or disguise terrible camerawork.

You do hear directors say, often rather hopefully: 'it can be sorted out in post.' The truth is Yes and No. And more often than not, the answer is No. Certain technical adjustments can be made to the picture, but there is absolutely nothing you can do with off-mic. badly recorded sound – except record it again. This is often not possible or not practical or just not affordable.

Poor acting cannot be disguised. Badly framed shots can be reframed to a certain extent, but you should not rely on this being an improvement that will transform your programme: it won't. Poorly composed shots can be altered but may still remain poorly composed. Sequences without those vital close-ups cannot be miraculously saved in postproduction.

The professional route

It is perfectly possible to shoot your programme on a small camcorder and obtain broadcast-quality pictures and sound. To be sure of broadcast-standard quality shoot on a DV format camcorder. Your rushes will be recorded digitally and will not lose quality with later transfers.

However, for all or part of the postproduction process you may choose to go down the professional route. Some producers prefer to shoot on a digital format and then edit on a desktop editing system, but do a final 'tidying-up' edit in a facilities house where you could also do captions and titles.

Sound is always tricky. You could do all the picture editing on a desktop, and then go for a professional sound dub. Alternatively, you may prefer to do an off-line edit on the desktop system and go for a professional online sound and picture edit. It all depends on the budget.

Postproduction budget

Postproduction will be a major cost in time and resources for any production. Your major resource will be the time required to finish the editing process and all the other things you need to do to produce a completed programme.

This book is about making satisfying and interesting television programmes as reasonably as possible. So the ideal and most cost-effective postproduction is with your own computer and editing software. Box 33.1 gives a breakdown of what you need to budget for if you are not doing your own editing on a digital desktop editing package.

Professional editing costs

♦ *Off-line editor.* Hiring an editor and off-line Avid suite will cost upwards of £250 per day. You can negotiate a weekly deal that will usually give you more hours for less per hour.

♦ *Online editor.* Online editor and edit suite with DVE and Aston or Collage on-screen caption generator will cost upwards of £150 per hour.

♦ *Tape.* Tape costs can be higher than you expect. Online suites in facilities houses usually record onto a high-quality digital format such as Digital Betacam.

♦ *Sound dub.* This will be at least £150 per hour and a 30-minute programme will take a day unless it is very straightforward.

♦ *Contingency.* Allow contingency time in days, and money to pay for extra travelling costs, etc.

Box 33.1 Breakdown of editing costs

Action	Costs	Rate
Transfer rushes with burnt-in timecode	Tape costs Transfer costs	Per hour
View and log rushes	Personal Time	
Paper edit	Personal Time	
Off-line edit – dry hire	Per hour	
Off-line edit	Editor and edit suite hire	Per day
Online edit	Editor and edit suite hire	Per hour
Sound dub	Editor and sound suite hire	Per day
Final tape master(s)	Cost of digital master tapes – digi-beta for high quality	Per tape
VHS copies	Duplication fees	Per hundred
Publicity	Letters; well-designed publicity hand-outs or brochures; launch screening	

- *Health warning.* Postproduction always takes longer and costs more than you expect. You may have to add up to 15 per cent to your original postproduction budget.
- *Time.* Leave lots of time before your delivery deadline. Start postproduction as early as you can.
- *Allow time for changes.* You may have to show a rough cut or a tidied-up first version of your programme, to a client, an executive producer, or the other members of your group. Allow time to make all editing changes that may be requested by a client before you go to the online suite.

Transfer rushes

Transfer rushes from your camera format (could be DV, DVCAM, DVCPRO, digital video 8, Digital-S or analogue formats such as Betacam SP) to a format such as VHS so that you can view them at home. Ideally you should be able to view the rushes with time code in vision. This means that you will need to have the rushes transferred with burnt-in time code, which has to be done with extra equipment. An editing company or TV facilities house will provide this service.

A straight transfer can be done easily by linking your camera through a Scart lead to a VHS recorder, but there will be no in-vision time code. Working with desktop editing, you can transfer your rushes directly to your editing software. This is known as digitizing, although if you are shooting on DV the data are already in a digital format. Digitize only the rushes you need, to save disk storage space.

34

The editing process

Figure 34.1 shows the typical options available in the editing process. The director of the production is responsible for producing a paper edit that is in fact the cutting order for the 'rough cut' of the programme. Even though no physical cutting takes place with video editing, these film terms are still used.

Editing film

Editing film is an analogue process (see Fig. 34.2). The editing starts by syncing up the sound with the picture. The picture is recorded in the camera on film, but the sound is recorded on a separate recorder onto tape or DAT. An ungraded print of the film and sound track is literally cut at the join between two frames and stuck together with transparent sticky tape or special cement. The film is viewed on a flatbed editing table called by its trade name, a Steinbeck.

The editor joins the film together in the chosen order to create a first 'assembly'. This means that the material is assembled in the order of the paper edit and includes everything that is relevant. The next stage is a 'rough cut', where the programme is long, but the material is in the right order.

The rough cut is reviewed and changed, and when all changes are agreed the editor then produces a 'fine cut'. This is reviewed and further minor changes made to create the final version of the programme.

With film, the negative is then cut by a 'neg-cutting' company to match frame by frame the final version of the fine cut, including fades and dissolves. It is returned to the editor as an 'answer print'. This requires the editor to check and agree a definitive 'answer'. The negative is returned for final adjustments and then a very high-resolution graded print can be taken from the cut negative. This is known as the 'show print'. Nowadays, the film rushes are likely to be transferred, and then edited off-line on digital editing equipment such as Avid or Lightworks, so doing away with any actual cutting.

Digital desktop video editing adopts the same process. A paper edit is created by the director, who works by himself, or with a video editor, to

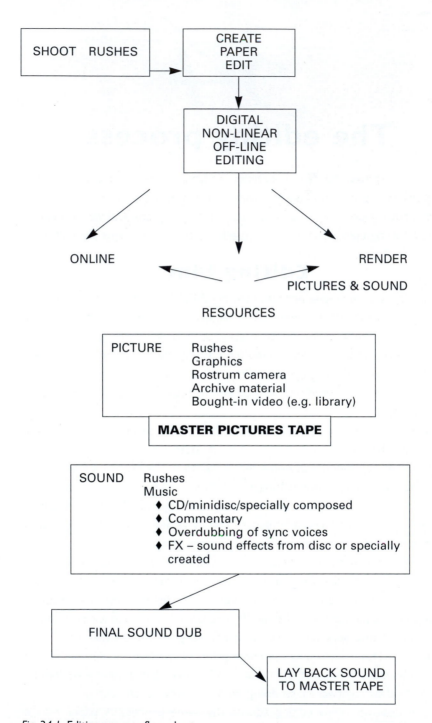

Fig. 34.1 Editing process flow chart

Fig. 34.2 Shooting on a 16 mm film camera

create an assembly and then a rough cut of the programme. This is reviewed and changed to create a fine cut.

From rushes to fine cut

View the rushes

If you are viewing on VHS, the rushes will need to have time code in vision, so that you can identify each frame. You can digitize your rushes into the computer and view them with the time code generated when you transfer from camera to computer.

You will need to have burnt in the time code on the picture actually to see the time code in vision. Commercial editing facilities companies will offer to transfer your rushes to VHS with in-vision timecode, for a fee.

Log the rushes

For any programme, even an item of three minutes' duration, it is worth logging all the rushes, so that you have a record on paper of everything you have recorded. It is often much easier to find a particular shot from a list on paper than to shuttle through all the rushes. It is amazing how elusive that particular close-up can be.

You can log the rushes by viewing them on the computer. You will feel that you want to get on with the editing, but at the very least make a record on paper of the sequences and shots you want to keep. You will not regret the time put in at this stage.

Logging the shots is a really good way of viewing the rushes. It helps you work out what shots work and what do not, and reacquaints you with the material. With most video editing software you can label a sequence of shots or any selection of frames with an appropriate name. This should be logged on paper with the time codes. Choose names that help you remember what is in the sequence. It is not a good idea to label the first sequence you have shot as: Interview 1 or Exterior A. Much better to go for: Paul interview opening, or WS Ferrari 1.

Then expand on paper with notes what the interviewee actually says in the interview. It may seem like a chore, but the more detail you have on paper the quicker you will be able to find the shots you need, and therefore you can be more creative in the editing.

The paper edit

The paper edit is the cutting order for your programme. When you have viewed the rushes, you are in a position to think about and write down your ideas on what will go where in your programme. This will almost certainly not be the final order for all the sequences in the programme. The paper edit is a starting point, and will probably cut together to make a programme that is too long. This is normal.

Of course, you will have thought about this before and during the shooting.

For a documentary, you will know how many interviews you have and in what order you think they should go. You may have worked out and filmed a snazzy opening sequence, but what happens after that?

♦ You will need to work out the shape and structure of your programme before going into editing, especially if you are working with an editor.

♦ You will need to have transcripts of any long interviews. Do the transcripts yourself or send them to specialist transcription services.

♦ Mark up the transcripts with the passages that you want included in the programme. Number each passage and put that number with the IN and OUT words in the paper edit. This is more important than getting the time code right.

♦ Mark the IN and OUT time code of all shots or sequences with a brief description.

♦ If you are working with an experienced editor, he or she will offer all sorts of ways of putting a sequence together. Use your editor's creativity. A good editor will bring a great deal of useful experience to any project. Do not be too prescriptive with your paper edit. Leave some areas for the editor's creativity.

♦ If you are editing the programme yourself or with a friend, then still be flexible in your approach. It is virtually impossible to get the whole programme assembled in the best possible way at the paper edit stage.

♦ Create a cutting order – the exact order in which you want the sequences to go together. Box 34.1 gives you an example.

The first assembly

You have done a cutting order on paper. You now have to create on your desktop system an assembly from the information in the paper edit. The most important aspect of this video assembly is to include all relevant material, and to try and get the content generally right, even if it is not in the correct order.

The result is usually a very long programme – maybe twice or even three times as long as it should be. This does not really matter, as it is not a cut as such, but an assembly of all the material. However, if it is way too long, then you will have an extremely difficult job in getting it down to time.

The rough cut

The next stage is to create a version of the material that is more, rather than less, in the correct order, and is only slightly overlength. At this stage it can be difficult to discard material that you have become attached to. Eventually you will have to be ruthless and cut out any loosely framed shots, or irrelevant material. You may have to change around the whole structure of the programme. The weakness of a sequence sometimes only becomes apparent when it is juxtaposed with another visually stronger sequence.

Sometimes you realize that a point has been made twice, or someone else in another part of the programme has said the same thing but in a more interesting way. In a documentary you may have to drop characters completely, or prune their contribution dramatically. In a drama you may have to drop cherished scenes. You will almost certainly have to look for ways to 'speed things up', as editors are fond of saying. This means using the audience's ability to accept the compression of real time in all types of television programmes, and in all sorts of different circumstances.

An example is a scene where a character gets out of a car in front of a house. The next shot shows him coming into a room inside the building. It could also show him actually in the room about to interact with another character. This cut needs to be in keeping with the editing rhythm of the film, and to work seamlessly.

Box 34.1 Cutting order example

PROGRAMME TITLE

DIRECTOR

Contact Nos

PRODUCER

Contact Nos

Number of Rolls of Tape

Programme Duration

DESCRIPTION	IN/OUT WORDS	IN TC	OUT TC	COMMENT
Seq. I WS Red Ferrari enters cam. Left turns to cam and stops. Paul carrying briefcase gets out. Exits cam right	Sync FX	01.03.24	01.04.17	Add music from CD1
Seq. 2 Paul and Linda 2Sh Develops to MS Paul	Interview Paul See transcript section A 'I started writing number one hits in the eighties. . . . OUT . . . flowers in the rain was at number I for 4 weeks.'	02.06.18	02.07.02	Run opening words under WS of Ferrari Fade in CD5 Flowers from refrain CD5 Flowers
Seq. 3 Rain sequence	CU daffodils mix WS pine trees, cam spins clockwise Mix BCU time lapse flower opening			Fade music To rain FX

Fig. 34.3 Editing on AVID

Commentary – first version

A rough version of the commentary can be written at this stage in a documentary. In fact, it is a good idea to do so. To complete the rough cut, write notes with the main gist of what will be in the commentary. This may not be word perfect, but the essential information will be accurate.

It is not a good idea to use all your best shots at once. It may be better to leave the information about say a castle until later, when the superb shots of the castle can be used to more dramatic effect. It might be better to leave out any mention of the castle at this stage in the commentary.

This is the sort of dilemma that can be mulled over at the rough-cut stage. But you do need to have some commentary to work from. It is easier and quicker to change existing commentary than to have to write it from scratch.

35
Editing interviews

You have filmed your interview. You have checked the quality of both picture and sound. You have labelled the tape box with the interviewee's name, date of the interview, overall duration and the name of the producer/director or whoever did the interview. You should also name the programme or series for which the interview has been made.

You have also labelled the actual digital tape(s) with the name of the interviewee and the name of the programme – so many people forget that the tape will become separated from the box: it is vital to label the tape.

Now you are ready for digital postproduction. Fig. 35.1 outlines the procedure.

Log the rushes

Box 35.1 shows an example of an interview rushes log sheet.

Write down on a log sheet the IN and OUT words of the question – you

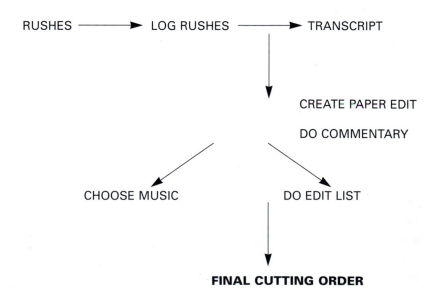

Fig. 35.1 Editing interview flow chart

Box 35.1 Interview rushes log sheet

PRODUCTION TITLE

THIS.ITEM

PRODUCER

IN WORDS	OUT WORDS	IN TC	OUT TC	COMMENT
What did you do . . .	. . . the Taj Mahal?	01.02.24	01.03.07	
I first saw the Taj . . .	. . . the last time.	01.03.09	01.04.12	good answer

Log sheet template
It is a good idea to create a template on your computer for a log sheet.
You can fill it in as a hard copy or directly onto your computer. Keep a
print-out with the original rushes tapes.

will need to know it – and the IN and OUT words of each answer. Also put
the IN time code in minutes and seconds and the OUT time code. You may
have to transfer the rushes to VHS, but if you are using a digital camera you
should be able to see the time code on your screen (see Box 35.2).

Why bother to log all the shots? Because it gives you an easily accessible
record of everything that you have shot, it makes finding shots a great deal
easier when you get to the actual edit, it gives you time to see everything

> **Box 35.2** Time code
>
> Time code looks like this. **01. 03. 48. 20**
> - ♦ The first number is the video ROLL NUMBER. **01**
> - ♦ The second number is MINUTES **03**
> - ♦ The third number is SECONDS **48**
> - ♦ The last number is FRAMES **20**
>
> Don't use the frames when you are logging rushes or paper editing.
>
> Just in case you have forgotten: 60 seconds in a minute and 25 frames per second for video in the UK. (Feature films run at 24 frames per second.)

that you have shot, and it allows you some thinking time. It saves on digitizing space later.

Do not go straight to the off-line edit; log your shots first. You won't regret it.

The paper edit

The paper edit is a very important part of the postproduction process. It will save you aeons of time in editing. It will make you think about the structure of your interview, and let you see that structure in a linear, visual way which is hard to do when you are in the edit suite. It will help you edit the interview to time.

For long interviews it is a good idea to get *a transcript* of each interview. There are various ways of doing a transcript, including sending an audio tape of the interview to a specialist transcription service. This can be expensive, as it is costed per thousand words.

If you have the time, you can do the transcript yourself, for no cost at all. All you need is a computer with a word-processing package and a means of listening to the interview. This could be audio cassette or minidisc or MP3. You need to dub your rushes onto a recorder/player that can be easily controlled with pause and play. Listening to interviews and then typing what has been said requires an audio machine with the flexibility to rewind and repeat sections.

Once you have made a transcript of your whole interview, it is easy to move the various answers around with the cut-and-paste functions on the computer. Or you can literally cut and paste the printed transcript to structure the interview as you wish.

You now have the exact words of the interview in a rough but structured form. Is it the right length? It is probably too long. At least you can now start off-line editing with a good idea of how you want this interview to begin and end and what will be in the middle.

The French film director Jean-Luc Godard famously remarked that a film 'should have a beginning, a middle and an end, but not necessarily in that order'. This is something to bear in mind when you are structuring interviews or indeed the whole programme.

Interview structure

Doing the paper edit should help answer these questions.

- Does the structure of the interview wholly engage the viewer?
- Does it have a beginning, middle and end?
- Have you discarded the unusable parts of the interview – the retakes, the inaudible sections, the coughs and splutters, the silences?
- Do all the answers carry the story forward?
- Is there a worry about jump cuts and are there other pictures to put over them?
- Have you done justice to your interviewee?
- Have you thought about how you will use the interview in the programme or video?

Ready for the edit

You are nearly there.

Check the shot list to make sure you have enough cutaways to cover the jump cuts and to make the interview interesting.

- Now is the time to view the rushes again, especially the pictures you think will work with your structured interview.
- Write down the time code of these pictures and put the selected pictures with the most suitable words on the paper edit.
- Make sure you have enough pictures. Hopefully you will not have to reshoot.
- Also compose an *edit list* of required pictures to put over the interview. You do not want just talking heads. This is a separate list of each picture sequence with its time codes, to help you find the pictures when you start editing.

Music

You may need music to go with your interview. Choose the music to complement your interview, not just because you like that piece of music. Make sure you have cleared all the rights and that you have a copy of the CD, or a tape of the specially composed music.

Final cutting order

You should now have a final cutting order. This has all the information you, or an editor, needs to produce a first version of your interview. Given the time constraints of most productions, it will be an advantage if this version is very close to the final version. Of course, all sorts of things can happen.

Executive producers might view your first version and recommend changes. These may or may not be improvements in your eyes, but you can always try them out and then see if the executive realizes your version was better. It is usually best not to argue but to do the changes and let him or her decide which version works best. It could be yours.

If you have composed a comprehensive final cutting order and have a complete shot list, then making changes is not going to be a problem. Enjoy the edit.

Commentary – final version

Once the edit is complete, you are ready to finalize the commentary. This can be the hardest part of the production so far, because the commentary has two main functions. It fills in information that has been left out, and it adds extra material to add value to the programme. The proper function of commentary is to complement the visuals.

♦ It is important to write to the pictures you have, rather than make the pictures fit words you have written previously.
♦ Write in short sentences. Avoid complex clauses.
♦ The difficulty is in getting the timing right. The rule of thumb is 'three words equal one second of screen time'.
♦ Don't rush commentary. It sounds unprofessional.
♦ Allow time, or breathing space, for the sound you have already edited to do its job and be complemented by the commentary.
♦ The basic rule for writing commentary is to be brief and to the point.
♦ Do not state the obvious, or describe what can be seen in the pictures. The commentary should add extra information or opinion.
♦ Make sure that any complicated information is broken down into easily digestible bite-size chunks. State what, when, where and why.
♦ Statistics are always hard to take in on their own. Make them as easy to grasp as possible. Instead of saying 'one-fifth of the population' say 'one in five of the population'. One-third is better than 33.3 per cent. Round

up decimal points and fractions by saying 'nearly 40 per cent do not take sugar in their tea' or 'almost one-third of all car drivers'.

♦ Commentary is usually in the present tense. If you find yourself writing about the past, make sure the pictures support it – for example, archive film.

♦ Before recording your commentary onto tape, it is vital to rehearse it with the edited pictures on VHS. You may find you have to cut down what you have written to fit the gaps. Do not think you can talk quickly – it won't work!

A few lines of typical commentary might run like this:

> *Paul Peters is unknown outside the music industry. But he is more successful than many better-known faces on Top of the Pops.*
>
> *He lives with his second wife, Linda, in a castle in Herefordshire – a long way from the glitz and glamour of the world of pop music. He records all his music in his own state-of-the-art sound studio.*

This is to cover an opening shot of Paul's Ferrari pulling up outside his home, which cuts to a two-shot of Paul and his wife Linda. It sets up the interview and gives the names of the interviewees, so it is an important piece of commentary. It leads into the many shots you have of the recording studio.

Check that the actual words fit the relevant pictures, and that the commentary is not too long. Short sentences lead to crisp commentary.

Commentary essentials

❖ *Complement the visuals.* Commentary should complement the pictures and expand the viewing experience.

❖ *Short sentences.* Write in short sentences.

❖ *Three words a second.* It takes three words a second to read commentary. If you have five seconds of pictures then you have only 15 words to play with.

❖ *Read aloud.* Read your commentary aloud. You are writing a piece that will be read aloud on the programme. Write as you speak. The piece must sound like a conversation, rather than an article for a newspaper that is read aloud.

❖ *Pace.* Leave 'breathing space' at the beginning and end of a piece of commentary to allow the natural sound to register, and to avoid that rushed feeling of a densely packed programme.

❖ *Information and reasons.* A good commentary provides additional information, and gives a deeper understanding of the subject.

❖ *Simple language.* Keep to simply stated statistics and avoid overcompli-cated fractions and percentages. Use simple language such as 'one in five people' instead of one-fifth.

❖ *Match words and pictures.* Wherever possible, match the commentary words with relevant pictures. Do not describe what is happening in the pictures, or repeat what is about to be said in an interview.

❖ *Avoid the obvious.* Make sure you have not written something that is obvious from the pictures.

❖ *Audience.* Always bear in mind your audience, and for whom you are writing. Never write down to your audience

❖ *Clichés.* Try and avoid all clichés such as 'at this moment in time' or 'at the end of the day'. Also avoid self-conscious back announcements such as 'and that was Trevor in jovial mood'.

❖ *Progress.* Commentary should always lead the programme forward. Only comment on something that has just happened to clarify a point or to identify something that is important to what comes next.

❖ *Specialist language.* Some scientific language in a documentary about volcanoes is acceptable as long as it can be understood by someone who has little scientific knowledge but a lot of interest in volcanoes. The viewer should never feel patronized but should feel some new knowledge has been gained.

❖ *Voice of the programme.* Commentary is the voice of the programme. It must be accurate, clear, direct and simple. It must be free of racism, sexism or ageism.

36
Creative editing

Where to cut

You wouldn't cut together two shots of someone looking the same way would you? You wouldn't cut together two wide shots of people would you? Look at the example in Box 36.1. Where would you cut to the closer mid-shot of the man?

♦ *Cut before he sits down.* It will work if this is his only line standing up, but the scene continues with an argument. You will have to go back to the wider shot when he eventually sits down or stick to closer shots of both men. This could make the scene too static, and will not show how the dominance changes from one character to the other as the argument progresses. Could be messy.

♦ *Cut after he sits down.* Too late, the impact of the line has been missed. It could work if there was first a cut to the closer shot of the businessman. It is important that the actor does not deliver the line as he is sitting down. The man could sit down and deliver his line in close up from a seated position. But the rhythm and impact of the scene may be wrong for this stage in the conversation.

♦ *Cut on the action.* The cut is on the action of sitting down. This continues the pace and energy of the scene and concentrates on the main character. For maximum flexibility the line can be delivered at the most suitable point before he sits down or after he has sat down.

Box 36.1 Cutting

Wide shot. A young man enters a room, walks across the room to the big desk under the picture and sits down opposite a wealthy businessman. He now has his back to the camera. His line is:

'*You're making a big mistake. Take your money out of my business and your reputation will be in tatters.*'

Box 36.2 Cutting a walking sequence
You need at least three sizes of shot for this sequence, MS, MCU and CU.
To make things easier, you could ask the characters to stop and then you
can cut to the close-ups. Check continuity for each cut.

Cutting on an action is a rule that always makes for a good edit. There are
other benefits. Cutting on the action can often hide poor continuity. It can give
style and a better sense of timing to a scene, as well as pace and movement.

Sometimes when the action is continuous, you need to be able to cut while
people are walking and talking (see Box 36.2).

Jump cut

A jump cut in drama is a cut from one frame to the next where there is no
obvious and smooth link between the action in each frame. It can also occur
where there is a glaring continuity error between the two scenes.

Sometimes this can be effective, because it makes the viewer metaphori-
cally jump and think why did that happen. The jump cut has become a handy
tool in the hands of a postmodern director like Jean-Luc Godard. He uses it
intentionally to jog the viewer into remembering that the film being shown
is not reality, but an artefact that needs deconstructing by the viewer.

In a normal television programme a jump cut is used by an editor only as a very last resort, when the scene cannot be made to work in any other way, and even then it is dodgy – unless, of course, it is intentional.

A jump cut in a documentary is the result of editing a single shot of a contributor in an interview where there is no alternative shot size, or suitable cutaway. The subject appears to jump in the frame from one position to another, which disturbs the smooth flow of the interview.

What has typically happened is the picture editor has cut the interview for sound and taken out a few words in the middle of the interview. So the picture jumps when it is played. Some directors like to put a short mix in here to denote that the interview has been edited, in the hope it will give a greater sense of 'honesty' to the programme. I fear that this technique, apart from looking ugly, does not actually fool anyone.

An interviewee who 'umms' and 'errs' or hesitates a lot is a nightmare to cut, and can lead to a succession of jump cuts where the editor has edited the sound to make it flow. This would be unwatchable as a coherent interview.

It is dilemma if there are very few cutaways to paste over the jump cuts. One solution is to 'slowmo' any relevant material of the interviewee so that you have twice as much material to paste over the joins. Or you can paste over the jumps any pictures that are in any way relevant to the subject of the programme. This is known as wallpaper, and can get you out of an awkward editing situation, but may not enhance your programme.

Music

Filmmaking is a process of communication rather like writing, but you have both sound and pictures as your communication tools. An audience reads a film or a television programme, and looks for clues and signposts to help process the information. Music is a valuable way of communicating with the viewer.

Adding music can change the way a viewer 'reads' a scene. Music works on the viewer's emotional reaction, and affects both mood and atmosphere. The right music used in the right place can be extremely effective in enhancing the way a viewer reacts to a factual piece, or a scene in a drama.

Music is added at the edit, but best thought about before the shoot. A piece of music may be selected before shooting, but it is only when you hear it alongside the pictures that can you judge if it actually works in the context of the programme. Production music from a music library is recorded specifically to accompany pictures – but not, of course, your pictures. Choose sensitively and don't go for the obvious.

Adding music essentials

❖ *Appropriate.* Make sure the music is appropriate to the subject of the piece. No point in adding the overture to Bizet's *Carmen* to a programme about the south of France. I know Bizet is French, but his opera Carmen is set in Spain.

❖ *Emotionally accurate.* The music should evoke the feeling and emotion suggested by the pictures. An obvious example is to have lyrical, calm music to go with pictures of a beautiful, tranquil landscape.

❖ *Mood.* In drama, music is very good at showing the mood of a character in a scene or sequence, and may contrast with the pictures to suggest inner turmoil in a character. In documentary, the director can create a mood for a sequence by adding music that evokes that mood. For example, fun and gaiety can be evoked with upbeat, optimistic, light, jazzy music.

❖ *Transition.* Use music to help the transition from one sequence to the next. A sequence may start with a complete change of location and you want to signal that this means a change of mood as well. Choose the music to do this for you.

❖ *Punctuation.* Music can be used effectively to signal the beginning of something new in your programme, or the end of something, or even a pause in the middle.

❖ *Preparing the viewer.* Music can be used to help the viewer prepare for what is about to happen. An audience knows that when you hear music like the slow, deep dah dah dah from *Jaws*, something dangerous is about to happen.

❖ *Cut to the beat.* Lay the music down first and cut to the beat.

❖ *Copyright.* Using commercial CDs? Fill in a form with all details. Make sure that the CD can be cleared for whatever use your programme is intended, such as broadcast, corporate or educational.

☞ For more details on music copyright, see Chapter 37.

Editing music

It is relatively easy to connect a CD or minidisc player to the desktop editing system. It is then straightforward to digitize the selected music into the system. Music is viewed as an optical representation of the musical cadences on a linear display on the screen. It takes a little getting used to at first, but after a short time it is possible to identify any point in the music and make an edit at that point.

Adding music to factual programmes

Lay the music down first and then add the pictures. Cut the pictures to the beat of the music or to just off the beat, whichever sounds best, but don't mix the two. Keep to the beat or to just off it.

The temptation is to cut the pictures first and then try and make the music match. This must be resisted at all times. You just will not create a truly effective sequence where the music enhances the pictures. Lay down the selected section of music first for the exact duration to fit the slot in the programme. Listen to it, and then cut the pictures to fit.

You may have an idea of the exact pictures you want to start or perhaps to finish the sequence. Put those pictures in first and try and make the other pictures fit around those ones.

The other temptation is to choose your favourite piece of music and try and make it fit into the programme. By all means put one of your favourite pieces of music into the programme, but make sure it is appropriate. If not, change it for something that is.

Music in drama

Music is used extensively in feature films and action movies and good-quality television drama. Directors like to commission composers to write music especially for their production. Music does enhance the mood and emotional impact of a scene and can be a major ingredient in a movie. Think of John Williams's music in Spielberg films (*Jaws*) and you realize just what a big impact music can have on the viewing experience, particularly in the cinema.

Added music is much less effective in gritty, true-to-life dramas. It is best avoided in this kind of drama unless handled sensitively, or integrated into the action, such as in Dennis Potter's *Pennies from Heaven*.

In a drama, music is added after editing the dialogue. Think about what job the music is going to do in the scene and ask yourself does it really make the scene more distinctive. Keeping the music at the right levels, and fading it in and out of the dialogue involves complex track laying, and an experienced dubbing mixer.

The sound dub

The process of editing and mixing all the different elements of sound in a programme is called a sound dub (see Fig. 36.1). The word 'dub' comes from the film industry and means to copy. This is the last process in making a film or television programme.

Fig. 36.1 A sound-dubbing suite

The sound dub for a movie is a major undertaking and expense. There are many different types of sound as well as the speech and dialogue that need melding together to create the final dynamic surround-sound soundtrack.

For a factual television programme you will have at least three sources of sound. The sync. dialogue, the background atmosphere buzz track and the commentary. You will probably have music as well. This can be mixed on a desktop editing system with remarkably good results, as you are dealing with digital sound, so there is no loss of quality. A more complex programme might need to be tidied up in a professional sound suite.

A programme for broadcasting will have to have a professional sound dub at a suitable dubbing theatre. It is possible to do a good job on the sound at an online edit, but most programmes will need a final sound dub to make them transmittable.

Dubbing theatre

In the sound-dubbing theatre the dubbing mixer works from a time-coded copy of the pictures, and digitized copies of the sound tracks of the programme. The editor will have prepared these with overhangs at the beginning and end of each sound clip. This will give the mixer a chance to slide in each clip without it sounding bumped. Any extra sound needed is normally recorded first. This may be commentary or extra music or specially created sound effects (FX).

Spot FX

Specially created sound effects are known as spot FX. They can be anything from footsteps on a gravel path to the rustling sound of grass for a wildlife programme. These spot FX are created to simulate the actual sound, but are created by using an amazing assortment of bizarre objects.

The sound of a wild animal stalking its prey through the pampas grass is created by rubbing, between your hands, a bundle of quarter inch magnetic tape. Try it. Done in a soundproofed cubicle with a fixed mic. and matched to the pictures, it is very 'lifelike'.

If you visit Universal Studios in California you can enjoy a performance of adding spot sound FX onto film pictures, in what is known as a Foley sound studio. These are spot sound FX created in real time to match exactly the pictures. For instance, hitting a boxing glove gives just the right sound effect for a punch landing in an unfortunate cowboy's stomach. This is an interesting example of how they can make spot sound FX for movies.

In a modern dubbing theatre, special sound effects can be created and then stored digitally for instant replay, at the required position in the programme, or taken from an FX CD. A wide variety of sound FX can be found on CDs. The BBC produce a multi CD box of typical FX for use in television programmes. This ranges from a long track to put behind landscape shots with the gentle singing of birds and humming of bees known as 'countryside in summer' to the comedy wizzes and bangs made, apparently, by a piano being pulled backwards through a hedge!

Track laying sound

With non-linear editing, such as a desktop editing system, the sound is laid down in tracks that are visible on the computer screen. Most software allows several tracks to be viewed at the same time. Mixing them together can be done in stages but will take time and good speakers are needed to monitor the mixed sound.

Typically all the sound tracks are mixed onto two separate tracks – the sync. or dialogue onto one track, and the music and effects on the other. This is known as the M&E track.

The advantage of this system is that the sync. sound on track one can be replaced by, say, a foreign language version. The M&E on track two will not be affected. This can easily be mixed with track one to create a new version that sounds just like the original, but in the language the audience can under-stand.

Example of track laying for sound

For a short drama you will need at least four tracks.

- Track One: Dialogue A;
- Track Two: Dialogue B;
- Track Three: FX and background atmosphere;
- Track Four: music.

A scene has dialogue between two actors. The scene has been shot with single shots of each actor and a wide shot of both actors at the end. When the shots are cut together, the editor finds there is a small discrepancy in sound levels between the two actors, that the two-shot has some low-level background noise and also that the sound level for the two-shot is different from the single shots. To make the soundtrack of the scene smooth and continuous to the ear, the sound sources have first to be split up into tracks.

- Track One: Dialogue A – the clean dialogue from one actor.
- Track Two: Dialogue B – the clean sound from the other actor.

These are unsurprisingly known as the A and B tracks.

- Track Three: a buzz track recording of the low-level background noise of a hospital, recorded on location by the sound recordist.
- Track four: library music that will go under the dialogue.

Using the audio display on the monitor, and, most importantly, your ears, you are going to mix these four tracks down to two tracks. Then you can mix the two tracks to get a high-quality final sound mix to lay back onto the final programme tape.

- Balance the sound volume levels of the two actors on the A and B tracks.
- Adjust the equalization of treble and bass for each actor to get a naturalistic sound.
- Mix the A and B rolls to create a new mixed dialogue track; call it Track C if you like.
- Now you are going to mix the music and the FX track (in this case the atmosphere track of the hospital) to create a careful balance of music to hospital atmosphere.
- You now have two new tracks each with mixed and balanced sound.
- Mix the dialogue track C with the M&E track to give a consistent and balanced sound throughout the scene, with an appropriate stereo perspective.
- Check the final mixed sound for smoothness, clarity and for any 'holes' in the sound. Check the quality by listening to the mix on good-quality speakers in stereo with the volume quite high so that you can hear

every nuance of the dialogue. Then turn the volume down to the normal level for watching television. This will give you an idea of how the home viewer will hear the soundtrack of the scene.

♦ Record the final mixed sound on to a separate track, and label it *Final Mix*.

♦ Lay back the Final Mix onto the final programme tape and label it as the Final Version. Keep all tracks until you are sure you have finished the programme.

♦ Go out for a well-deserved pizza.

Titles and credits

Creating titles and credits is much easier on a desktop system than if you go down the off-line and then online route. Desktop systems normally have built-in software to generate graphics with many different font styles and colour effects.

Resist the urge to go mad and recreate the graphics for the *Rocky Horror Show*. It might shock your corporate client, and anyway fancy over-the-top graphics generally look out of place on television.

Titles

Go for clean, clear, stylish graphics for titles that reflect the mood and substance of your programme. By all means be creative with your opening sequence of titles and pictures. Be bold and dramatic but make sure the graphics are readable and make sense. Titles are an individual choice, but there are guidelines to avoid disasters. After all, the titles are normally the first visual element of a programme and have an important job to do. The titles have to inform the viewer about the name of the programme, as well as creating and stimulating the desire to watch the programme.

♦ *Font.* Choose a clear and easily read font – avoid italicized fonts or old-fashioned styles that tend to make the viewer feel the whole programme will be out of date.

♦ *Size.* Use a font size that is large enough for impact but does not swamp the subject. Too big and it can look like GODZILLA, too small and it suggests the content of your programme is of little significance.

♦ *Meaning.* Some people are good at inventing snappy titles for programmes. If you are not one of these blessed individuals, and most of us are not, then go for a title that says something about what the programme is about. One of my students made a very interesting documentary about the idiosyncratic differences between individual people from all walks of life. Bafflingly he called it *Sterotypes*, which was just what the programme was not about.

♦ *Wipes.* The title sequence is often seen as the ideal opportunity to try out all those wipe buttons on your editing software. Resist. Many of these wipes look like antediluvian television from the 1980s. The discrete use of the occasional or appropriate wipe can be dramatic and revelatory in a title sequence, but would a mix be better?

♦ *Digital effects.* Another temptation is to create clear, well-defined graphics and then twist them, flip them or distort them in some apparently exciting way. This is good for comedy programmes, but bad news for your average documentary and a total disaster for drama.

♦ *Music.* Try and match the graphics with the music you have selected for your title sequence.

♦ *Colour.* Be creative with colour but make sure the colour reads well against the background you have used. Red looks very dark against almost everything except white. White or yellow lettering works well against a blue background.

♦ *Check out expensive TV title sequences.* Look for inspiration at the title sequences of broadcast TV programmes. Broadcasters tend to spend a lot of money on creating invigorating graphics for their top shows. But remember: many titles sequences are made with high-end, digital episodic effects kit from firms like Quantel. They need skilled operators and are extremely expensive per hour. The first few seconds of your title sequence could run away with the budget for the whole show.

♦ *Fun.* Despite all that, title sequences can and should be fun to make. They can stretch your creativity and editing skills and give a real lift to the front of a show. Enjoy.

Bluescreen postproduction

A popular way of shooting interviews and pop videos is to use the bluescreen technique known as Chromakey. Adobe Premiere, and other desktop software, has a facility for doing bluescreen overlay.

This technique has been refined by the power of computing. There are computerized systems linked to the studio camera that create 'virtual sets' for actors and presenters to perform in. They can climb over virtual walls in the countryside, surf on virtual waves in Hawaii and walk up virtual steps at the Parthenon, all without leaving the studio.

For pop videos, the artist performs the song to a playback of the recording in front of a large bluescreen area in a studio that allows for dance and other movement. The blue areas are then replaced with a variety of striking images, often created on high-end digital postproduction kit.

Working with an editor

It can be a good idea to work with an editor, who can bring a fresh perspective to the production, and suggest alternative ways of editing a sequence or even the whole programme.

The editor can be objective about the rushes, and is usually more ruthless than the director in discarding marginal material. The director remembers the hassle and heartache in getting that amazingly difficult interview and will have all sorts of excuses about why the interview does not quite work. The director will only have to look at some scenes from his drama to be reminded of that very long day in pouring rain just to get two minutes of that crowd scene.

The editor will be able to tell straightaway that the scene just will not cut together with the dialogue. It is informing the director of this terrible piece of news that is difficult. A professional editor is a past master at subtle diplomacy who can gently persuade the production team and particularly the director that some things are better left 'on the cutting room floor'.

The editor is interested only in whether the scene works within the programme. This always makes for a better programme. An experienced editor has worked on a wide variety of different programmes and knows just what will stand up and what will not.

Filmmakers often work with the same editor, whom they know and who understand their way of working. The editor is an important member of the production team, who can offer new insights and make a real difference to the final programme, and is another pair of eyes to spot those tiny continuity errors and to offer a solution to that interview full of jump cuts.

An experienced editor will expect to have a detailed paper edit from which to make a first assembly, and will not expect hours and hours of rushes that the director is 'not sure about'. The editor will be as efficient as possible in digitizing only those rushes needed for the assembly. On a non-linear editing system it takes 'real time' to digitize. Only do those parts of interviews you actually need. You can always digitize more from your rushes, if necessary, at a later date.

On a desktop editing system the first assembly for a 10-minute programme should take only a few hours. Even for a half-hour factual programme the editor will be able to produce a long-version assembly within a day.

The next day you can work through this assembly and take out all the loose shots and dull material to make a rough cut. The structure should now be clear and the pictures and sound in the right order. The editor may have left the music sequence until later, when the shape of the programme has been finalized. The music may or may not fit. Now is the time to check and adjust for overall duration.

The rough cut will be too long, and this is where you really get the benefit of an experienced editor. Knowing what to take out without damaging the structure of the programme is really down to experience and feel, or plenty of time.

Desktop system

Working on your own desktop system does have advantages too. You can work at your own pace, when and how you want. You do not have to clear the disk drives of all digitized material just because another production is due in the editing suite. Best of all, you can take time out and go for a walk or a game of tennis. This can be very valuable thinking time. It allows you to stand back from the intense intricate work of editing and get a fresh momentum. It gives you breathing space to let your unconscious mind do some work on the programme.

Do not be afraid of showing your assembly or rough cut to a friend or other members of the production. Programme making is cooperative teamwork. Editing thrives on different views and new ways of looking at the material. Be flexible. Be humble. Explain your vision and see if the other members of the team can see it in the rough cut of the programme. If not, ask them how they would do it. They may not have a convincing answer.

Remember a good editor is a good diplomat.

The proliferation of hand-held cameras and the ease of non-linear digital editing have helped young programme-makers freshen up interview styles and change the way factual programmes are shot. This has led to rethinking many of the traditional ways of editing.

It is useful to know some of the rules that film editors work with, then you can break them for dramatic effect!

Editing drama

The wide shot

A scene may have been filmed with a wide shot containing all the action. This may end up being a very long and very wide shot of the action. When it comes to the editing stage, this wide shot may slow down the action.

Traditionally the wide master shot is used at the beginning as an establishing shot, and then possibly at the end of a scene to show that the action at that particular location has moved on. It is important that the director knows how the scene will be cut together before shooting begins. Good television comes from good teamwork and it is a very good idea to discuss the way the drama will be cut with the editor before principal shooting takes place. A detailed storyboard is a great help. The editor is often present on the set of a large drama shoot. There are usually changes of some sort that will affect the editing.

The over-the-shoulder two-shot

A scene between two actors may have been shot using cinematic two-shots. These shots have one character full face in the left of the screen, and screen right is the side of the head or shoulder of the other character. The shot is reversed for when the right-of-screen character speaks, or as a reaction shot.

These two-shots work well in widescreen and provide an alternative to cutting from one close-up to another. But do check the continuity of the two-shots that are being cut together. Also check the continuity of the wide shot that will probably be needed to make the scene work.

37 Copyright issues

This is one of those areas you might be tempted to skip. To save yourself a lot of problems later, read on.

What is copyright?

Copyright is an intellectual property right. It is a way of protecting the tangible result of creative work – such as music or writing – from being pirated and used by someone else. Throughout the world copyright exists. National laws cover different countries. The principles remain broadly the same, but there are differences between US and UK law. Always check before using copyright material.

Whenever you use music in a production from a CD, or when you copy music onto any format, tape, minidisk or MP3, you are involved in copyright issues. Writer Jonathan Swift got the first copyright Act passed in 1709 with published books protected for 21 years.

In the UK programme-makers need to know about the 1988 Copyright, Designs and Patents Act. The aim of this act is to protect the tangible result of creative work from unfair exploitation.

Can an idea be copyrighted?

Ideas cannot be copyrighted, but the expression of an idea in a tangible form can be copyrighted. This includes your own creative work. Copyright protects you from the piracy and copying of your original work. It could be a script, a film, a play or a TV programme format, or an original musical work such as a pop song.

This is a fiendishly complicated area and only specialist lawyers can fully understand copyright law. As a programme-maker you need to be aware of what material is likely to be covered by copyright, so that you do not unwittingly broadcast or copy this material.

It's also a feel good factor. When you start work in broadcasting, you will feel better if you know what is going on in the copyright area, and you will make a better impression on the people you are working for.

What is covered by the 1988 Copyright, Designs and Patents Act

Original literary, dramatic, and musical works

Not just books, plays, film scripts and magazines, but programme schedules, opinion polls, airline timetables and, bizarrely, TV signature tunes and 30-second radio ads are covered by the Act. Today literary, artistic, musical and dramatic works are protected for 70 years from 31 December of the year in which the author died.

Original artistic works

Paintings, drawings, maps, photographs and plans, as well as HMSO publications like *Hansard* that appear to be in the public domain and may not charge for use, are covered by the Act and protected for 70 years.

Be careful that you do not assume that, because the artist has been dead a long time, you can use the reproduction of a Botticelli masterpiece to illustrate your documentary on Florence. The colour photograph of the painting is almost certainly covered by copyright.

Sound recordings

Music

Music copyright is complicated because any or all of the people involved in producing a CD have rights – composer, lyricist, instrumentalists, singers, the record company, the arranger and the publisher of the music. This is fully explained under music.

The spoken word

This covers broadcasts such as *BBC News*, but also an interview. If you record an interview with a politician, the politician owns the copyright in the words, but you own the copyright in the tape. So you are both protected. You can use the tape in the way you have agreed, but the speaker has some defence against the words being used in a different context, or being deliberately distorted. Once an interview is given, the interviewee cannot change their mind. A refusal to be interviewed can be broadcast, as the Act cannot be used as a form of censorship of free speech.

Film clip alert
Using extracts from films without checking the copyright can be disastrously expensive. The channel you work for may have broadcast the film last month, but it does not mean you can use an extract from it in your daytime magazine programme. Each use is a fresh use.

Films
There is copyright on all films. Copyright is 70 years from the death of the last survivor out of the principal director, the screenplay author, author of the dialogue or the composer of the specially written music.

Film clips
Extracts released by the film distributor can usually only be broadcast in the week of release, but always check with the company. You may be lucky. But forget ever showing James Cameron's 1997 *Titanic* copyright free in your lifetime! But you could negotiate for a clip of Kate Winslet from the film if it is to be used in a programme about her rise to stardom.

As more digital TV channels spring up, the copyright of films may be renegotiated. The *Broadcasting Business* reported in summer 2000 that there could be 100,000 digital channels by 2004, many of them showing films. Copyright for movies broadcasting on the Internet and on digital channels may also require separate negotiations.

Copyright on the Internet
Contrary to what many people think, much of the original work on the Internet is copyright. This is usually stated on a web site. It is hard to enforce copyright on much Internet material, because some material may be 'borrowed'. It is best not to assume you can copy any creative material and broadcast it. Systems will evolve to police copyright on the Internet. Fortunately a lot of material on the Internet is deliberately copyright free.

Broadcasts
Copyright for broadcasts and computer-generated works lasts for 50 years from the end of the year of first transmission. Copyright for cable programmes lasts for 50 years from the end of the first year of transmission.

Published editions

Shakespeare's works may be out of copyright, but the published edition you use is almost certainly in copyright.

Still photos

The owner of the photo has copyright protection, and the subject in the photo may have privacy rights. You need permission to broadcast, or use in a video, from the owner and possibly the subject.

Archive film or sound recordings

These are protected by copyright and permission will need to be obtained to broadcast archive material.

What is not covered by copyright

Fortunately there are a few exceptions.

Works whose author died over 70 years ago are out of copyright, but you must check the edition. This means you can quote Hamlet's 'to be or not to be' speech, but you will have to pay copyright fees if you put on an amateur performance of Hamlet using a published edition.

There is no copyright in facts or in information

But what does this mean? The fact that an aeroplane crashed is not copyright, but the footage of video or film showing the crash will be owned by somebody – do not use without checking. The newspaper article describing the crash is copyright, so do not quote the exact words. But you may use the information in the article – check with another source to make sure it is correct.

Insubstantial parts

There is a very handy rule called 'insubstantial parts'– very short extracts from a copyright work can be used without consent. Quality as well as quantity counts, but it is very hard to establish what counts as insubstantial.

Quoting a paragraph of average length from an average length book is almost certainly acceptable. But for a shorter book, it could be just a few lines, depending on the context. Always check, or use less. A few lines from a long poem may come under the insubstantial parts clause, but one line from a shorter poem will almost certainly not be allowed. Ask permission from the publisher *first*.

Incidental use

Wherever you go you see copyright material in the form of logos, brand names, advertisements and names – nearly all are copyright. You may be filming in a street with some of these copyright visual images, so what do you do? It would be impossible to get copyright clearance on them all, so it is acceptable to use copyright material 'incidentally' in the programme. This means that the copyright material must not be featured, or be unduly prominent. It just happens to be in the shot incidentally, or 'naturally belonging' to the area.

It is almost certainly permitted to have a pizza restaurant shown in the background of a shot, or sequence, in a factual programme. But it is not all right to show a close-up of the name without permission. The rule is: always check. For a drama production you will definitely need to clear – or remove – any copyrighted images that may be in shot.

There is no copyright on ideas

This is a refrain often heard in television production offices. Many programme-makers worry that they could have their original programme idea stolen by a broadcasting company. This inhibits people from sending in ideas, but there is a way of protecting ideas to a certain extent. Ideas get protection under the Copyright Act only when they are realized in some material way, such as writing them down.

Proof of ownership

You should always write your name with the international sign for copyright © on every page of a script, or other document. This offers some proof that you are the author and rightful owner of the document. You can assert some rights on the copyright of that document.

For further proof of ownership post a sealed copy of the work to yourself, using recorded delivery or another service that will provide a date of posting. This will prove that the copyright work was in existence at a certain date.

Box 37.1 outlines how to protect your ideas.

Fair dealing

The CDP Act of 1988 allows for *fair dealing*, which allows for the use of copyright material for the purposes of reporting *news and current events*. In practice, this is usually pictures, audio material, sports footage and so on, and the use of short broadcast extracts with acknowledgement of the broadcaster, but not still photos. These fair dealing agreements are usually agreed in advance, so do not rely on there being an agreement with all broadcasters.

Box 37.1 How to protect your own ideas and works of genius

Copyright protects the expression of an idea and not the idea itself. Once ideas are recorded in writing they have some copyright protection.

- ◆ Write down your fabulous idea for a new programme, date it and give a copy to an agent or solicitor.
- ◆ Send a copy of your script to yourself in a registered, or special delivery, letter. Seal it with a date and signature in the presence of a witness who also signs it. It is not foolproof, but it will help establish you as the owner of the idea as written down by you.
- ◆ You can register your format, or well worked-out idea, with certain professional bodies such as PACT or the Writers' Guild. You would need to join and become a member. There may be a small fee.

These methods do not offer absolute copyright protection, but they help establish ownership.

Fair dealing is also allowed for review purposes. This means you can use a clip from a play or broadcast to review or criticize it, but you must give sufficient acknowledgement of the source of the material – for example, the theatre where the play is on. A small amount of selected copyright material of all types may be copied and reproduced for the purpose of reviewing the work within a critical context. The quotations used must be brief and relevant, and the sources fully acknowledged on the air. Publicity material generated by the copyright-owners comes into this category and can be used on news programmes and other productions. But do not expect to be allowed to use more than the tantalizing clip provided.

Fair dealing also allows you to use copyright material for research and private study.

Background music

Music used in the background of a shot in a documentary is not copyright if it is not at all recognizable. This is an exception open to interpretation, but many people think all background music is non-copyright. This is not true.

If you are filming in a club or restaurant where there is music playing, this will count as featured music as long as there is a recognizable tune, or the words of the song can be distinguished. It counts as background music only if it is entirely without any distinguishing features.

The rule of thumb is: could the composer recognize the music playing as being his or her music? If the answer is yes, then it is not background music. Generally, if you feature the band, artist or solo performer in any way, music details will have to be logged.

So what do you do about background music

In the long run it is best to ask the owner to turn off all music, and put on your own production music at the edit. Showing dancers in a club moving to a particular disc means that you will need to take down all the details of that disc. This is not background music and must be logged.

To be certain there are no copyright problems, it is best to select production music of the same style and dub that on later.

Music copyright

Working on a television or film production, you are bound to get involved with music clearance sooner or later. Using music can be expensive and fraught with problems, or it can be quite reasonable and stress free. It depends on the music. Make sure you have sufficient money in your budget to clear music and other copyright. Also leave enough time to pursue the ownership of source material. It can take forever!

All types of television productions can be enhanced with the use of music. Modern digital cameras can record sound in high-quality digital stereo. You can create music on your computer. You can download music on MP3 on your computer. The only snag is the thorny and devilishly complicated issue of copyright.

Think about it. You spend a long time composing a song. You get it recorded by an established artist and if you are very lucky it goes to No. I in the charts. Every time it is played on any broadcasting channel anywhere in the world you get a small amount of money.

But what about the composer whose music gets played only once or twice on a radio station and never reached more than No. 175 in the charts? That composer also gets a copyright fee that helps him or her to go on composing. It is not perfect, but it is a remarkably fair system, supported by just about everybody involved in all types of music. This system is run by music copyright protection societies, which collect the royalties on behalf of their members.

This system works only if everyone plays the game and fills in their music return sheets. The bottom line is that there are stringent laws to enforce this system and you fall foul of them at your peril.

There are three sources of music to consider for copyright purposes.

Commercial recordings

These can be from any source – CD, minidisc, old-fashioned vinyl, the Internet, cassette or your friend's personal library of recordings. They are all commercial recordings. Their use will need to be cleared for broadcast, and rights will need to be paid for. You will see written on commercial CDs a warning: unauthorized public performance, broadcasting and copying of this compact disc is prohibited.

Specially commissioned music

This is where you have asked a composer to record music *just* for your production. That is music that you have specially composed, performed and recorded exclusively for your production. This can be music recorded 'live', or created electronically on computer or a mix of both.

Production music

This is music that has been commissioned, composed, performed and recorded especially for television and audio productions such as advertise-ments, broadcast programmes, film and video productions. It is available from company libraries, which are very willing to send you copies of any CD you might be likely to use.

♦ There are now many small companies who record and offer production music of all types and styles. Look them up in The Knowledge on the web site: www.theknowledge.com

♦ MCPS (the Mechanical Copyright Protection Society) can supply a full list of over 60 specialist libraries: tel. 020 7306 4500; fax: 020 7306 4380.

♦ Larger companies such as Chappell or Bruton offer vast libraries of CDs, catalogued under helpful titles such as Christmas Crackers or Street Rock.

The value of production music is that there are no pre-clearance formalities. All you have to do is buy a licence from MCPS that covers all the rights required to include that work in your production. All the rights belonging to each recording have been 'bought out' by the company. This music can be cleared for world transmission, and paid for at a reasonable, set rate by obtaining a licence from MCPS.

What do you do to clear copyright on commercial music?

There are two basic sets of rights in commercial sound recordings.

♦ The rights to the Musical Work itself. This is known as 'the song'. The rights to the mechanical copying of the Musical Work are obtained from MCPS or the copyright-owner.

♦ The rights to the Sound Recording. The rights to the mechanical copying of the Sound Recording are most often obtained from the Record Company, or it could be one of the copyright societies – PPL or VPL or BPI.

You will need to log all music detail in order to clear both these rights. You will also need to make sure that the right to perform or broadcast your chosen commercial recording has been cleared through PRS or PPL.

Music details

If you want to record and broadcast a commercial recording, there are minimum details you must write down and keep. You should create a form, or copy the one shown in Box 37.2. Details can be found on the CD itself or on the inlay card; not every CD has all the details, but write down what is there and keep it safely. Box 37.3 shows an example of CD details.

Student work and educational use

For media students there is a special exemption on the copying of commercial discs. For projects where copyright discs are copied on a student video as part of an educational course, and used within an educational establishment, such as a college or university, no copyright payment or clearance is required. You should however log all music details on a form such as the one shown in Box 37.2.

Film festivals

This is good news. MCPS has introduced a Limited Availability Product Licence for copying of production music for film festivals and showings of student or amateur work outside educational establishments. This does not include commercial discs. Permission for the use of a commercial recording must always be obtained from the record company.

MCPS now has a flat fee, £17.63 in 2001, for the use of up to 30 minutes of production music in a film or video to be shown at a festival or to other non-paying audiences. This also covers up to 100 copies of the film or video.

Box 37.2 Music details

Production Company	Broadcaster
Your production title	Your name
CD title	CD no.
CD label/record company	
Track no.	Track title
Artist	
Composer	Author/lyricist
Arranger	Producer
Publisher	
Duration used	
Transmission time & channel	
Digital	Terrestrial
Cable/satellite	
Number of copies to be made	
UK Europe	World N. America

Box 37.3 CD details

CD Title	Spice Girls
No.	CDV2812
LABEL	Virgin
ARTIST	Spice Girls
TRACK	1. wannabe
WRITERS	Spice Girls/Stannard/Rowe
PRODUCER	Richard Stannard/Matt Rowe
PUBLISHER	Windswept Pacific Music Ltd/Sony ATV Music Publishing
DURATION	1'20"

So who are the copyright companies?

MCPS (the Mechanical Copyright Protection Society)

The Mechanical Copyright Protection Society
29–33 Berners Street
London W1P 4AA
tel. 020 7306 4500
fax 020 7306 4380

MCPS is the music rights society in the UK protecting copyright on behalf of songwriters, composers and music publishers. MCPS collects royalties from the recording or copying of music onto a big range of media including CDs, cassettes, minidiscs, TV programmes, adverts and non-broadcast material. MCPS run a very helpful and friendly licensing service offering advice on all music clearance issues.

PRS (Performing Rights Society)

PRS Performing Rights Society
29–33 Berners Street
London W1P 4AA
tel. 020 7580 5544
fax 020 7306 4050

PRS is the sister organization of MCPS. It is a non-profit-making membership organization that collects licence fees from music-users and distributes the money to its members – the writers and publishers of music.

PRS collects performance royalties due from the public performance and broadcast of music. If you go into a club or bar, you should be able to see in the window a PRS sticker. This shows the establishment is a member of PRS, and has paid for the right to play music or put on performances of musical items. There may be other royalties due as well.

PRS collects royalties from clubs, pubs, shops, concert venues. It collects royalties from TV and radio broadcasting companies and cable and satellite broadcasting companies. BBC and ITV have blanket licence agreements with PRS for the broadcasting of music.

Warning

It is the responsibility of the producer, or the production company, to obtain music clearance. This includes a licence obtained from PRS to broadcast music included in your video. If in doubt always check – they are very helpful on the phone.

The PRS hotline for information on obtaining a PRS licence: 08000 68 48 28.

PPL (Phonographic Performance Ltd)

PPL Phonographic Performance Ltd
1 Upper James Street
London W1R 1LB
tel.: 020 7534 1000
www.ppluk.com

PPL licenses the public performance and broadcasting of sound recordings. It represents over 2400 record companies. It issues licences and collects licence fees for the record companies, and performers, for the public performance of commercial records – this includes CDs, minidiscs and audiocassettes. Licences are applied for by broadcasting companies and other organizations that play commercial discs at a public performance. The licence fees, after deduction of running costs, are distributed to the record company members and to performers.

Who needs a licence?

PPL grants licences for the use of sound recordings in the UK to all broadcasters, including BBC television and BBC radio and ITV. It also grants licences to television production companies, commercial radio stations, cable and satellite television and radio channels.

PPL issues licences to anyone who wants to play sound recordings in public, such as in clubs, pubs, hotels, restaurants, shops and health/leisure centres. Individual users such as exercise or aerobics instructors and dance teachers can also obtain licences.

The licence is usually issued to the occupier of the premises. If you hire a music system, jukebox and/or sound recordings from an operator, the operator should obtain the licence on your behalf from PPL.

Television producers do not usually need to deal with PPL in terms of obtaining a licence, as the broadcaster will do this.

Video Performance Ltd (VPL)

1 Upper James Street
London W1R 1LB
tel. 020 7534 1400
fax 020 7534 1414

VPL is a sister organization to PPL and is at the same address. VPL collects licence fees for the cable, satellite and terrestrial broadcasting of music videos, or the playing of pop videos in public places such as pubs and clubs. Check with them that you can broadcast a music video created using a commercial sound recording.

VPL and PPL are very protective of their members' rights. Some television producers and TV companies have found it so difficult to clear the copyright on music videos, especially pop videos, that they have given up using them. But help is at hand. To try and help with the clearance of pop videos VPL has set up The Music Mall. This has a vast database of tens of thousands of music videos that are clearable. It is easily accessible through its web site www.musicmall.co.uk. This is a most useful web site to do with music videos and includes a video clip location and supply service.

For reference
♦ *Sound recordings.* The use of sound recordings in all forms of radio and television must be licensed by PPL, including terrestrial, satellite or cable, and Internet simulcasts of UK radio broadcasts.
♦ *Dubbing.* PPL also licenses the dubbing – rerecording – of sound recordings where it is associated with broadcasts.

- *Advertisements*. PPL does not license the use of sound recordings in advertisements, or where they are associated with brands or trade marks. Go to the record company direct.
- *Internet*. PPL does not license radio-type services that are dedicated to the Internet, nor any other use on the Internet beyond the simulcasts referred to above. Authorization for the use of sound recordings in advertisements and the Internet must be obtained directly from the record companies.
- *Broadcasting* enquiries to: Broadcasting.info@ppluk.com
- *Public performance* enquiries to: GLD.info@ppluk.com

Commercial recording alert
To use a commercial recording in your production you must contact the record company and get written permission.

Box 37.4 gives you a very quick guide to music copyright. And Box 37.5 is a quiz, so that you can test yourself.

Other useful web sites
BPI (British Phonographic Industry)
www.bpi.co.uk
The BPI represents the interests of British record companies and has 230 members, which together account for 90 per cent of recorded music output in the UK.

British Academy of Composers & Songwriters (incorporating the Association of Professional Composers, the Composers' Guild of Great Britain and the British Academy of Songwriters, Composers and Authors).
http://www.britishacademy.com
The Academy represents the interests of composers and songwriters across all genres, providing advice on professional and artistic matters.

IFPI (International Federation of the Phonographic Industry)
http://www.ifpi.org/home.html
The IFPI is the international trade association representing some 1300 record producers in over 70 countries.

Box 37.4 Music copyright checklist

If you want to use a commercial recording in a television programme that will be broadcast on television, you must clear it with the record company first.

Make a note of all copyright details about the recording – composer, writer, publisher, performer, record company, arranger, producer, and so on. Include the duration, and in what programme, and for what channel, you want to use it. For production music, get a licence for the use of the recording from MCPS to pay all royalties.

What to check

♦ A licence from PRS to collect public performance royalties for composers and publishers may already cover you. But you will need to submit details to them via your broadcasting company/production company, who should have a licence.

♦ You will almost certainly not need to get a licence from PPL to collect performance royalties for the record companies and performers. The broadcaster should have an agreement with PPL. Check to make sure, but you must fill in a music log.

♦ In certain circumstances copyright-holders may withhold rights to copy or broadcast. For example, it is well known that the Rolling Stones, and their record company, are very unlikely to allow the copying and use of any of their records in television programmes or videos.

The good news

♦ Normally the broadcaster and not you the producer will pay for these rights, but it is your job to clear these rights.

♦ If the music recording will not be used outside an educational establishment, then you need do nothing except list all details.

♦ Use production music and you need only get one licence from MCPS and it is not expensive.

♦ If you want to put your video in for film festivals, or make up to 100 copies, you can get a special Limited Availability Licence for Production Music from MCPS at a very reasonable cost.

Box 37.5 Copyright quiz

So you think you know all about copyright?
  Test yourself with these typical production situations.

Questions

1. You are working as a trainee assistant producer for a cable TV company. You recently recorded interviews with relatives of a flood disaster. One interviewee has subsequently written to you saying she now does not want the interview to be transmitted. What do you do first?
    ♦ Keep quiet and say nothing about the letter.
    ♦ Phone the interviewee and try to persuade her that it should be transmitted.
    ♦ Phone the producer/director and explain the situation.
    ♦ Check to see if you have a signed release form from this person then phone the producer/director.

2. An interviewee has phoned to say that she does not want you to use the still photo of her uncle that she allowed you to film. You are very keen to use this particular photo. What do you do?
    ♦ Ring the producer/director and explain.
    ♦ Check to see if you have a signed agreement to use this photo and then ring the producer/director to explain.
    ♦ Offer to pay the interviewee for the use of the photo.
    ♦ Panic and use it anyway.
    ♦ Tell the producer/director that the photo should not be used under any circumstances.
    ♦ None of these because . . .

3. You are making a documentary on the life of Elton John for a digital channel. You have discovered that he writes poetry as well as songs. You want to quote two lines from one of his longer poems. What are the copyright implications of doing this?
    ♦ This will cost an arm and a leg because Elton John is alive and still in copyright.
    ♦ No copyright payable or permission needed, as it is an insubstantial part of the poem.
    ♦ Log the source of the poem and the duration of the extract and seek permission from Elton John's agent.
    ♦ Ring Elton John and ask him if it is OK to use the extract.
    ♦ None of these because . . .

> **Box 37.5** *continued*
>
> 4. For the same documentary you would like to use extracts from many of Elton John's CDs. A colleague tells you it will be too expensive. What do you do?
>   - Log all details of the music to be used and give them to your producer.
>   - Log all details and check with PPL and PRS that you are able to broadcast these sound recordings.
>   - Log all details and check first with the record company(s) for permission to use the sound recordings in your programme.
>   - Forget it, and try and find production music that will fit.
>   - None of these because . . .
>
> 5. You are working on a programme about American female singers. You need to find archive film of Tina Turner. You have seen her singing 'The Acid Queen' in Ken Russell's film of the Who's rock opera *Tommy*. You think this would make an ideal clip. What do you do to clear the copyright?
>   - Ring VLP and ask them if you can take out a licence. You saw the film on video.
>   - Log all details from the video box label; pass them to the producer.
>   - Ring the film distributor and ask for permission to use the clip.
>   - Log all music details and the details of the clip, including any actors that are in the scene. Ring the distributor and negotiate a fee and permission to use the clip.
>   - None of these because . . .
>
> 6. You are working on a programme about protest movements. You want an opening sequence that shows a number of newspaper pictures of the Queen being splattered with paint. The soundtrack would be specially recorded electronic music based on a group of students singing a recognizable version of John Lennon's *Revolution*. What do you need to do regarding copyright?
>   - Use the pictures as they are from newspapers, and news is copyright free.
>   - Use the music copyright free because it is specially composed.
>   - Forget using the pictures as the copyright owners of the photos could sue under the moral right of integrity. Their pictures are being defaced.
>   - Log all details of the music, and seek permission from the publisher of John Lennon's song *Revolution*.
>   - None of these because . . .

Box 37.5 *continued*

7. You have written a script for a factual programme about a form of Indian dance found in the temples of Southern India. You take it to a production company, who seem very interested. When you telephone a month later, they say they have never heard of your proposal, but you learn they are going ahead with a programme on the same topic. What do you do?

   ♦ Go to a lawyer and expect to pay a lot of money to prove it was your idea.
   ♦ Pull out of your bottom drawer an unopened, dated and witnessed, registered envelope with your written proposal inside. Take the unopened envelope to a solicitor and ask him to write to the company asserting your right of paternity.
   ♦ Try to negotiate with the company.
   ♦ Make the film yourself on DV, and try and sell it to a broadcaster.
   ♦ Put a wet towel around your head and take an aspirin.
   ♦ None of these because . . .

8. I am working on short 'stings' for a magazine programme, and I want to use a few short extracts of music from three different Beatles' records. Each extract is about five seconds. Surely I do not need to log such short pieces?

   ♦ No, it is an insubstantial part.
   ♦ Yes, but just log them and forget about it.
   ♦ Yes, log all music details and make sure you have a licence.

9. I am working on a pop show. Record companies keep sending me free pop promo videos. Are these promo videos free to use without a licence?

   ♦ No need to do anything – fill up the show with free videos.
   ♦ Log everything.
   ♦ Log everything, but seek permission from the song publishers, even though the record company has given permission.
   ♦ Sorry, you cannot use any pop videos without contacting VPL.

10. I am working on a video/promo that I hope will sell in the shops, or by mail order. What is the royalties situation for the music in the video?

   ♦ No problem, as you just fill in a log sheet and send it off to MCPS.
   ♦ You have to negotiate with everyone individually from songwriter to arranger – very expensive.
   ♦ Fill in a log with all details; talk to MCPS Licensing Department and seek record company permission. Should be straightforward.

Box 37.5 *continued*

Answers

I have tried to say a little more about each situation to help with these typical production scenarios.

1. Check to see if you have a signed release form from this person, then phone the producer/director. If you have the signed release, you are in the clear, but the producer/director should still discuss the matter with the interviewee, and try for an agreement. Legally you may have done the right thing, but it is unwise to broadcast anything against someone's will, unless it is in the public interest.

2. Check to see if you have a signed agreement to use this photo and then ring the producer/director to explain what has happened. Even if you have a signed agreement with the owner and subject of the photo, it would still be unwise to broadcast a personal photograph without consent. The person in the photograph (the subject) might be able to invoke the right of privacy, and obtain an injunction against the broadcast. Best to try and use the photo in a way that is agreeable to the copyright owner and/or the subject.

3. No copyright payable or permission needed, as it is an 'insubstantial' part of the poem. This can only work for very short extracts.

4. Log all details as usual. Check first with the record company(s) for permission to use the sound recordings in your programme. Should be no problem.

5. Log all music details, and the details of the film clip, including any actors that are in the scene. Ring the distributor (in this case Columbia) and negotiate a fee, and permission to use the clip. You will need to explain exactly why you want to use the clip and in what context, and when it will be broadcast.

6. Log all details of the music, and seek permission from the publisher of John Lennon's song *Revolution*. Start by working through PRS. The pictures of the Queen could be in breach of the defamation law, and you will have to get permission from the newspapers. This item is unlikely to get through as it stands.

7. Pull out of your bottom drawer an unopened, dated and witnessed, recorded delivery envelope with your written proposal inside. Take the unopened envelope to a solicitor and ask him to write to the company asserting your right of paternity. Also write to the broadcaster who has taken on the idea. Broadcasters tend to be more sensitive to this issue. This could get expensive, so make sure the solicitor charges you only for writing the letters. Also you could make the film yourself on DV, but try and sell the idea to a broadcaster before you spend a lot of money.

> **Box 37.5** *continued*
>
> 8. Yes, log all music details and make sure you have a licence. The duration of each clip is in itself irrelevant. You need to log all details, and make sure the broadcaster has licences for all music in your production.
> 9. Log everything, but seek permission from the song publishers, even though the record company has given permission. The broadcaster will almost certainly have a PRS licence to cover music used for pop shows, but check for digital and other channels.
> 10. Fill in a log with all details; talk to MCPS Licensing Department and seek record company permission. This should be straightforward. On a retail video royalties are based on a standard MCPS rate of 8.5% (in 2000) pro rata of published dealer price. You will still need subsequent approval from other copyright owners.

IMF (International Managers' Forum)

http://www.imf-uk.org

The IMF was founded in 1992 and represents the interests of managers of popular music artists and record producers as well as providing training for its members to develop management skills and knowledge of the music industry.

Musicians' Union

http://www.musiciansunion.org.uk

The Musicians' Union has a membership of approximately 31,000 and represents musicians working in all areas of the profession and across all genres of music, including performers, instrumental music teachers and music writers.

PAMRA (Performing Artists' Media Rights Association)

http://www.pamra.org.uk

PAMRA distributes recorded performance remuneration on behalf of a wide range of artists for the public broadcast of recordings on which they have performed. PAMRA collects remuneration for its members both in the UK and overseas.

Moral rights – what are they?

The moral rights code introduced in the 1988 Copyright Act deals with more abstract concepts such as the reputation of an author and the integrity of his or her work. Moral rights are additional rights granted only to the author of copyright literary, dramatic, musical or artistic work and to the director of a copyright film. There are no moral rights for other kinds of copyright material such as broadcasts. Moral rights are vested in the author of a work during his or her lifetime.

There are four types of moral right.

♦ Paternity. The right to be identified as the author of the work. This is the right to have your name credited in public as the author of a literary, dramatic, musical or artistic work, or the director of a film. This right has to be asserted, and does not come automatically. In other words, you have to write to the producer or copyright-owner asserting your moral right to a credit.

♦ Integrity. The right to object to derogatory treatment of one's work. This is the right of a writer, film director or artist not to have his or her work altered or changed in a derogatory way that would adversely affect his or her reputation or professional career. This right exists automatically and does not have to be asserted. This is a very tricky area to enforce and prove. Unfortunately, it is unlikely that you can invoke the moral rights clause when an executive producer butchers your well-conceived and beautifully edited documentary.

♦ The right NOT to have a work falsely attributed to oneself. This can crop up when a screenwriter's original work has been rewritten in such a way as to make the original almost unrecognizable. The original writer has the right to demand that his or her name is struck off the credits.

♦ Privacy. The right to privacy of certain photographs and films. This has become an important right, often invoked by royalty or celebrities. It is the right to prevent the publication or broadcast of private photographs or videos without the owner's permission. There is no exception for news reporting.

38

Useful books

So, you are interested in getting into the television business, or the media industry. You want to know more, and what to do next.

In the UK there is Skillset, the National Training Organization for the TV, radio, film and interactive media industry. This is the voice of education and training in the industry. Skillset has produced an excellent and definitive guide to finding work in the world of media in the UK: *A Career Handbook for TV, Radio, Film, Video and Interactive Media*, by Shiona Llewellyn (London: Skillset, 2000). This is available from Skillset (103 Dean Street, London W1V 5RA, tel. 020 7534 5300, web site: www.skillset.org) and some bookshops. The book is aimed at anyone making choices about education, training, jobs or career progression opportunities in the media business. It really is a very useful and informative book. It has chapters on everything you need to know – for instance what sort of jobs are available in the industry and where they are; working freelance; working in the independent production sector and making a feature film. It includes lists of relevant magazines and web sites, and the addresses of all the relevant companies and organizations.

The best book about the technical side of television production is, in my opinion, *Television Production* by Gerald Millerson (13th edn; Oxford: Focal Press, 1999). This book covers everything from how television works to visual effects and the background to production, and is particularly comprehensive on television studio production.

If you are studying media or you want to keep up to date on new developments in the theory of media, the book to get is the *Dictionary of Media and Communication Studies*, by James Watson and Anne Hill (5th edn; London: Arnold; New York, Oxford University Press, 2000). It is extremely comprehensive and well written.

A book for anyone wanting to go into broadcast television as an independent programme-maker is *Guerrilla TV* by Ian Lewis (Oxford: Focal Press, 2000). It is particularly good on budgets for broadcast programmes.

For those who are interested in the writing of a TV script or movie screen-play, *The Screenwriter's Bible* by David Trottier (3rd edn; Los Angeles: Silman-James Press, 1998) is particularly useful.

Good luck. And above all, enjoy your work in programme making.

Index